W9-CBZ-640

Saint Peter's University Library
Withdrawn

NANCY MITFORD

A Memoir

A 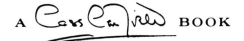 BOOK

NANCY MITFORD

A MEMOIR

HAROLD ACTON

1817

HARPER & ROW, PUBLISHERS
New York, Hagerstown, San Francisco, London

NANCY MITFORD: A MEMOIR. Copyright © 1975 by Sir Harold Acton. All rights reserved. Printed in the United States of America. No part of this book may be used or reproduced in any manner whatsoever without written permission except in the case of brief quotations embodied in critical articles and reviews. For information address Harper & Row, Publishers, Inc., 10 East 53rd Street, New York, N.Y. 10022.

FIRST U. S. EDITION

ISBN: 0-06-010018-4

LIBRARY OF CONGRESS CATALOG NUMBER: 75-345-80

76 77 78 79 80 10 9 8 7 6 5 4 3 2 1

To DIANA, DEBO AND PAM
with love and gratitude

CONTENTS

LIST OF ILLUSTRATIONS

ACKNOWLEDGEMENTS

ABOVE ALL I wish to express my profound gratitude to the Duchess of Devonshire, to the Hon. Lady Mosley and the Hon. Mrs. Derek Jackson, who have shown me every sort of generosity and helped me to sort out Nancy Mitford's letters preserved at Chatsworth. Without their bountiful co-operation this biographical memoir could not have been written.

My particular thanks are also due to Mr. Heywood and Lady Anne Hill: the former transcribed excerpts from Nancy Mitford's letters in his possession, lent me the manuscript of her *Tour de France* sketch, and both have supplied me with relevant anecdotes; to Mr. and Mrs. Handasyde Buchanan, who have also supplied me with letters and anecdotes of Nancy as a bookseller; to Mr. and Mrs. James Lees-Milne for putting a large selection of letters at my disposal and for allowing me to reprint a vivid recollection from Mr. Lees-Milne's *Another Self*; and to 'the Colonel' for his moral support.

I hope the many kind friends who provided me with letters and reminiscences, or both, will excuse me if I waive protocol and name them in alphabetical order, though some should be distinguished by stars, as in a Michelin guide, for taking so much trouble. Besides those above mentioned my warm thanks are due to Sir Cecil Beaton, M. Jacques Brousse, Mr. Donald Darling, Mme. Rita Essayan, Mme. Romain Gary (Lesley Blanch), Dr. Henry W. Gillespie, Mr Geoffrey Gilmour, Lord Gladwyn (for allowing me to quote from his *Memoirs*), and Lady Gladwyn, the Hon. Desmond Guinness (for the photographs of Nancy's wedding and William Acton's portrait), Mr. Hamish Hamilton, Lady Harrod, Sir Hugh Jackson, M. Philippe

Jullian, Lord Kinross. Mr. Valentine Lawford. Mr. Patrick Leigh Fermor, Prince and Princess Rupert Loewenstein, Mr. Roger Machell, Mr. Robin McDouall, Mr. Peter Mitchell, the Hon. Jessica Mitford (Mrs. R. Treuhaft) and Victor Gollancz Ltd. for permission to quote from her *Hons and Rebels*, Mr. Raymond Mortimer C.B.E., Sir Oswald Mosley (for permitting me to quote from *My Life*), Mr. Brian Pearce, Mr. Stuart Preston, Mr. David Pryce-Jones, Mr. Peter Quennell, Mrs. John Sutro, Mr. Christopher Sykes, Professor Hugh Thomas, and Mr. Mogens Tvede.

As I did not aim at a definitive biography I made no application to the Press, though this might have produced a richer harvest. In most instances Nancy Mitford's underlinings, capitalizations, gallicisms and punctuation have been respectfully retained.

I am also indebted to my good friend and publisher Hamish Hamilton and to his partner Roger Machell for their fraternal encouragement.

INTRODUCTION

WRITING ABOUT biographies to her mother (8 April, 1954), Nancy Mitford observed: 'Of course a family always expects nothing but praise, but lives of people must show all sides. Then imagine writing a biography and having to submit it to the family sewing in a lot of little anecdotes, etc, and altering the whole shape of the book! The result would never be any good . . . People who don't write, however intelligent they may be, simply do not understand the mechanics of a book—it never ceases to amaze me. Almost all depends on construction in the last resort. . . years of work and then frustration. A biographer must take a view, and that view is almost sure to offend a family. The whole problem is excessively thorny I do see, probably the answer is that no really good biography under such circumstances (living children in possession of the material) has ever or can ever be written.'

In this biographical memoir of a dear friend from whom even absence made the heart grow fonder—for my life in China, followed by the war and a return to my home in Florence, kept us apart for long periods—I was guided by a wish to celebrate the fragrance of her personality and its flowering in France. An Oriental proverb occurs to me now: to enjoy the benefits of Providence is wisdom; to make others enjoy them is virtue. Nancy possessed this virtue to a supreme degree.

I have attempted to show all sides of Nancy from her copious correspondence, and have not been afraid to sew in a lot of little anecdotes. Whether the result is any good I leave the reader to determine. I have only been limited by consideration for people who might be offended by remarks which, innocuous in talk, assume a more serious aspect in print. In a few cases this

xiii

has amounted to frustration but at least my conscience is clear.

In an age dominated by telephones Nancy Mitford was a voluminous letter writer and during her last years when she had not the strength or the desire to face friends for fear of harrowing them—the pain might get beyond her control—she wrote more and more letters as a temporary relief. Fortunately most of their recipients kept them, less on account of her fame than because they were intensely idiosyncratic. The average letter we receive nowadays betrays little of its writer's personality. Not so with Nancy's: even her spelling and punctuation, her capitalizations and underlinings were redolent of her speaking voice. If one loved her one could not part from those leaves, though they might not contain more than a date or a promise of meeting. At Chatsworth, where her papers are preserved, I marvelled at the cornucopia of her correspondence. Nothing had been thrown away. There is ample material for future biographers.

To her mother and sisters Nancy wrote frequently, and these letters were only a fraction of the total. To her friends Mrs. Hammersley, Mark Ogilvie-Grant, Alvilde and James Lees-Milne, Heywood Hill, Evelyn Waugh and Raymond Mortimer, she poured out her impressions and comments, her plans and ideas, with varying degrees of frequency. With the erudite Sir Hugh Jackson whom she never met personally, she corresponded as a faithful 'pen-pal' since 1956. To these and many others who have kindly allowed me to scrutinize their letters from Nancy I have paid tribute in a note of acknowledgement, but above all I am deeply indebted to Nancy's sisters: to Debo (the Duchess of Devonshire), Diana (the Hon. Lady Mosley), and Pam (the Hon. Mrs. Derek Jackson), without whose help in fishing them from big boxes crammed to the brim and sorting them out, I could not have produced this volume. Thanks to these generous ladies I have let Nancy tell her story in her own words wherever possible so that the reader may follow the progress of her career.

Except when she went to Russia, she never seems to have kept a diary. Usually she wrote in a reclining position, and her pen flowed over the paper on her lap as if she were talking with complete spontaneity. Of course many of her missives were concerned with practical matters, but even these had humorous touches and it is not always easy to extract the nuggets of ore. Apart from her published writings, her letters are the most poignant relics of her individuality. Innately modest but not self-effacing, she made no attempt to conceal her feminine nature, her love of life's little luxuries, of good but simple food, of genuine characters both simple and complex.

Inevitably some correspondents elicited a greater liveliness than others: foremost of these were Mrs. Hammersley and Mark Ogilvie-Grant. Victor Cunard, a resident of Venice and a malicious gossip with whom she corresponded for many years, might well have been added. She consulted him about her literary projects *inter alia*. When he fell ill she recounted all the incidents most likely to amuse him, week after week, and we may be sure that they would have amused us too. It was therefore a blow to Nancy—and to us—when his brother informed her that he had spent a whole afternoon tearing up her letters. They would have helped to replace a considerable portion of her unwritten diary.

Nancy's correspondence with Hamish Erskine, to whom she had been engaged before her marriage to Peter Rodd, might have yielded another harvest, but that was also destroyed. Her innumerable letters to Evelyn Waugh have been perused by his biographer Christopher Sykes and will probably be published. With so many others at my disposal I felt disinclined to trespass on Christopher's territory.

Some writers adapt themselves to their correspondents, even to the extent of changing their epistolary style. Nancy remained true to her colloquial self without frills or furbelows. In her letters to her family, however, we may detect variations of mood and attitude, a slightly more deferential tone to her mother, a more playful to her sisters, which were in her sprightliest vein. She was also prodigal of picture postcards both comic and sentimental. 'I hope you'll love this postcard as much as I do! You must look at every detail.'

As in the case of most writers Nancy Mitford's life was not externally eventful. Having evoked her years of childhood in *The Pursuit of Love*, she intended to write Memoirs of her life in Paris, which had become her second home after the war. Her migration to France was a clean break with her past—a past that had been none too happy though, owing to her cheerful disposition, she had made the best of it. Highly diverted by the difference of French and English social conventions, full of admiration for General de Gaulle, enchanted by the details and incidental episodes of the Parisian scene, she became ardently

Francophile, yet she remained English to the core. Most of the friends she continued to see were English. With one or two exceptions and the antiquated circle at Fontaines-les-Nonnes (to which she was introduced by Mrs. Hammersley) her French friends belonged to the international society which was equally at home in London, Rome and Paris. She loved the Cotswolds, where she had been brought up, and it is interesting to speculate on what books she might have written had she remained in England.

Her most memorable literary achievements were matured in France and when she grew tired of fiction French history provided her with characters to whom she could apply her psychological insight with profit and enjoyment. The same narrative skill was diverted to Mme. de Pompadour, Voltaire, and Louis XIV, hence plodding academic historians have sneered at her brilliant achievements in their field. Nancy was a votary of Macaulay, and Macaulay had written: 'The best portraits are perhaps those in which there is a slight mixture of caricature, and we are not certain, that the best histories are not those in which a little of the exaggeration of fictitious narrative is judiciously employed. Something is lost in accuracy, but much is gained in effect. The fainter lines are neglected; but the great characteristic features are imprinted on the mind for ever.'

In literature as in life laughter was the golden key to Nancy's heart. Nearly all her friendships began with a joke, and in her letters we seem to hear the jests as they sprang from her pretty lips. She will never appeal to readers without a sense of humour, but I fear that hers is so peculiarly English that it is almost untranslatable. Her humour seldom rollicked 'on high planes of fantasy or in depths of silliness', rather it rippled on betwixt and between them. I hope its ripples are reflected in the mosaic of this memoir. La Bruyère's famous maxim might also have been Nancy's: 'You must laugh before you are happy for fear of dying without having laughed.'

CHAPTER ONE

IN A LETTER dated 29th September, 1971, Nancy Mitford wrote to me: 'I'm going to write my memoirs beginning in '45 so as not to bore the world all over again with our childhood. Tell Vi (Trefusis) that, it will make her vaguely uneasy! But I must get well first – this vile pain has begun again in spite of my new dope. Not as bad as without the dope but nag nag nag, makes it impossible to concentrate.' Alas, the pain became implacable and one of the most potentially scintillating memoirs of our age was never written. Since 1945, when she decided to settle in Paris, Nancy enjoyed a physical and spiritual rejuvenation until she was stricken with an incurable illness. Her childhood had been evoked in the sprightly pages of her novel *The Pursuit of Love* as well as in her sister Jessica's *Hons and Rebels*, which reached an enormous public: *The Pursuit of Love* sold over one million copies.

As in a story by Hans Andersen, Nancy Mitford was the eldest of six comely sisters and a handsome brother, the progeny of impeccably English parents attached to family life in the country rather than in the town. Their home was their castle, closely guarded by a Cerberus whose bark was worse than his bite. Only their brother Tom was sent to school like other boys, and he brought back an exciting aroma of the outside world. The girls were consigned to the care of nurses and governesses, of whom Nanny Blor (whose real name was Dicks) had the predominant personality. The memorable Nanny in Nancy Mitford's novel *The Blessing* was based on the character of Blor and Nancy has also drawn an appreciative sketch of her in *The Water Beetle*: 'She had a wonderful capacity for taking things as they came and a very English talent for compromise. In two respects she was unlike the usual Nanny. We were never irritated by tales of paragons she had been with before us; and she always got on quite well with our governesses, upholding their authority as she did that of our parents. When we grew up she never interfered in our lives. If she disapproved of something one said or did, she would shrug her shoulders and make a little sound between a sniff and clearing her throat. She hardly ever spoke out—perhaps never—and on the whole our vagaries were accepted with no more stringent comment than "Hm"—sniff—"very *silly*, darling." '

Though she had the porcelain complexion and slender figure of a country-bred girl Nancy Mitford was born in London at 1, Graham Street, now Graham Terrace, on 28th November, 1904. She has admitted that she could remember almost nothing about her early childhood—'shrouded in a thick mist which seldom lifts except on the occasion of some public event'. For instance she retained a hazy impression of her parents at breakfast, both crying over newspapers with black edges: King Edward VII had just died. More clearly she could remember the dining-room wallpaper, 'white with a green wreath round the cornice.' Such seemingly trivial details are often etched on our memories like the flavour of Proust's *madeleine*, conjuring long submerged emotions. Psycho-analysts might read significant symbols into them: the green wreath might betoken a presentiment of future fame.

The sinking of the Titanic left a deeper impression, for it was accompanied by daydreams 'of a rather dreadful kind'. With disarming candour she related that she used to scan Blor's *Daily News* for an account of a shipwreck in which her parents (who sailed every other year to Canada in order to prospect for gold) might be 'among the regretted victims'. In spite of what psycho-analysts might infer, she loved her parents—with comprehensible reservations in the case of her father—but at the age of seven she nurtured an enterprising ambition to 'boss the others'. The brood, however, continued to increase, which she considered 'extremely unnecessary' at the time.

Her paternal grandfather Lord Redesdale was still alive, and she usually stayed under his roof in Kensington High Street while her sisters were born. Of the first Lord Redesdale, G.C.V.O., K.C.B., one derives a romantically gracious image, or series of images, from the two stout volumes of his *Memories* which had achieved a ninth edition in 1916, when Nancy was twelve years old. The photograph of the author reproduced as a frontispiece to the first volume portrays a dapper old Edwardian musketeer with a swirling white moustache. His gleaming top-hat is tilted at a rakish angle; spectacles hang from a button of his double-breasted overcoat and gloves are tucked under his left-hand sleeve. He confronts the future with dignified equanimity. His past had been crammed with episodes of historical interest, all enjoyed with such gusto that one cannot agree with his granddaughter Jessica's dismissal of his *Memories* as 'monstrously boring'. Indeed many of his youthful experiences in the diplomatic service were thrilling if not unique.

As second secretary of the Embassy at St. Petersburg during the winter of 1863–64 he was able to see the Russia of Czar Alexander II under favourable auspices. Even then the Ambassador Lord Napier warned him to send all his letters in the Foreign Office bag—'none by the Post Office, where all our letters are opened.' 'Surely,' he replied, 'they would not dream of opening the correspondence of so humble a person as myself.' 'Don't be too sure of that,' broke in Lady Napier. 'The other day my children's governess received two letters by the same post from different parts of England. Each contained a photograph. The two letters came in one envelope, the two photographs in the other!' His account of Court ceremonies and balls; of Prince Gortchakoff and Princess Kotchoubey's political salon; are as vivid as that of the fanatical piety of the people and of their saturnalia during the week before Lent in Admiralty Place, perpetuated in music by Stravinsky's *Petroushka*. His life in Peking during 1865–66 was described in greater detail in his delightful book *The Attaché at Peking*. His next post in Japan was the most exhilarating. 'Suddenly coming in full view of Mount Fuji, snow-capped, rearing its matchless cone heavenward in one gracefully curving slope from the sea level,' he was caught by the fever of intoxication which, as he wrote, 'will continue to burn in my veins to the end of my life.' Not only did he meet Prince Tokugawa Keiki, the last of the Shoguns, 'a great noble if ever there was one. The pity of it was that he was an anachronism'—he and the dynamic British Minister Sir Harry Parkes were the first foreigners to be presented to the sacrosanct Mikado and I am tempted to quote his entire account of the episode but will restrain this to a single paragraph:

'As we entered the room the Son of Heaven rose and acknow-ledged our bows. He was at that time a tall youth with a bright eye and clear complexion; his demeanour was very dignified, well becoming the heir of a dynasty many centuries older than any other sovereignty on the face of the globe. He was dressed in a white coat with long padded trousers of crimson silk trailing like a lady's court-train. His head-dress was the same as that of his courtiers, though as a rule it was surmounted by a long, stiff, flat plume of black gauze. I call it a plume for want of a better word, but there was nothing feathery about it. His eyebrows were shaved off and painted in high up on the forehead; his cheeks were rouged and his lips painted with red and gold. His teeth were blackened. It was no small feat to look dignified under such a travesty of nature; but the *sangre Azul* would not be denied. It was not long, I may add, before the young sovereign cast adrift all these worn-out fashions and trammels of past ages, together with much else that was out of date.'

With Sir Harry Parkes he narrowly escaped murder by reactionary samurai for his support of the reformers. His early book *Tales of Old Japan* (1871) has deservedly become a classic, and as a child I longed for more stories of the same kind, where blood was mingled with haunting poetry.

After fourteen varied and adventurous years in the diplomatic service he resigned in 1873. Meetings with Sir Richard Burton and Abd el Kader in Damascus, with Garibaldi in self-imposed exile at Caprera, with Brigham Young in Salt Lake City—the rest of his autobiography is sprinkled with dramatic encounters and anecdotes of historical personages. Disraeli appointed him Secretary to the Board of Works in 1874—ten days after he had purchased a black opal which a friend had prophesied would bring him luck precisely within that period. At the end of the same year he married Lady Clementine Ogilvy, a daughter of the seventh Earl of Airlie, and there is reason to believe that it was a happy marriage though he maintained that 'the veil of sanctity should mask the wedded life of even the humblest individual'.

During his twelve years with the Board of Works he was responsible for many improvements in Hyde Park, Hampton Court, Kew Gardens, and other neglected beauty spots. He then decided to turn country squire, which led to being 'mixed up with the horse world,' notably as judge and director of the International Horse Show at Olympia, and succumbed dutifully but reluctantly to membership of the House of Commons for three years. English to the core, he was yet a cosmopolitan polyglot in culture and his *Memories* reveal the multi-faceted type of *milordo inglese* now almost obsolete. 'Looking back,' he asserted, 'I claim the privilege of the sun-dial, and among the hours record only the serene.'

In 1906 he accompanied Prince Arthur of Connaught on a mission to invest the Mikado with the Order of the Garter in Japan—how transformed since his previous visit in 1868 when the juvenile Mikado, regarded as a demigod, 'had descended from the clouds to take his place among the children of men, and not only that, but he had actually allowed his sacred face to be seen by, and had held communion with, "The Beasts from Without".' Since capturing Port Arthur and annihilating the Russian fleet in 1904 Japan had become one of the great powers and there was a general imitation of everything European—to the detriment of many an indigenous art and craft. In lieu of their former elegance crude European dress was prescribed for officials. The rapid metamorphosis was prodigious even then, and Lord Redesdale had been lucky to witness the feudal *status quo*. 'Tell us how it was in the olden time,' the courtiers begged him, curious to hear of their bygone ceremonial from this venerable foreigner.

The second volume of his *Memories* ends with a rhapsody on Wagner: 'poetry and music are united in an indissoluble wedlock; the senses are enthralled, and the world bows before the great wizard.'

Lord Redesdale's grandchildren inherited many of his gifts, and in perusing his suave autobiography one is often reminded of this inheritance. Nancy's eyes resembled his, and a drawing of his profile at the age of twenty-eight by Samuel Lawrence resembled her brother Tom. In fact her generation appear to have had more in common with their grandfather than with their father and mother. One seems to hear Nancy's voice in his lighter anecdotes. She has related that when her fourth sister was born, on 8th August, 1914, just when war had been declared, 'she was christened Unity, after an actress my mother admired called Unity More (an early *Peter Pan*), and Valkyrie after the war maidens. [Unity herself always spelt it *Walküre*.] This was Grandfather Redesdale's idea; he said these maidens were not German but Scandinavian. He was a great friend of Siegfried Wagner's and must have known.' Eventually the actress and the war maiden were combined in Unity with tragic results.

Since the betrayal of Denmark in 1864, when the 'scrap of paper signed by Prussia in 1852, assuring the inviolability of Denmark, was torn up', Grandfather Redesdale had foreseen a calamitous general war, the outbreak of which was 'by far the most vivid' of Nancy's fitful recollections. 'When it appeared to be imminent,' she wrote, 'Blor told me to pray for peace. But I thought, if we had war, England might be invaded; then, like Robin Hood, one would take to the greenwood tree and somehow or another manage to kill a German. It was more than I could do to pray for peace. I prayed, as hard as I could, for war. I knew quite well how wicked this was: when my favourite uncle was killed I had terrible feelings of guilt.' Thus the ten-year-old innocent shared the private sentiments of many a grizzled soldier and politician.

Little Nancy's prayers were answered but 'the war turned out to be less exciting than I had hoped, though we did see the Zeppelin come down in flames at Potters Bar. I fell in love with Captain Platt in my father's regiment, an important General of the next war, and crocheted endless pairs of khaki mittens for him—I am not sure that they were inflicted on him. In any case, all this crocheting was the nearest I ever got to killing an enemy, a fact which I am still regretting.' She retained a lifelong interest in battles which I could not share, though I admired her perseverance in trying to follow the campaigns of Frederick the Great when she was already an invalid.

Another memory which made an indelible impression on Nancy at the age of seven, was of Captain Scott's tragic expedition to the South Pole. She devoured every book obtainable on the subject and would have won an examination on all its harrowing details *summa cum laude*. The hut under the active volcano of Mount Erebus where the Polar party were installed; Dr. Wilson's appalling winter journey sixty miles along the coast to Cape Crozier in utter darkness and a freezing temperature to find the egg of an Emperor Penguin; the ascent of the dreaded Beardmore glacier towards the Pole; Seaman Evans's death of frostbite and concussion; the suicide of Captain Oates who staggered into the blizzard with frostbitten feet 'to try and save his comrades, beset by hardship'; and the final discovery of 'Birdie' Bowers, Dr. Wilson and Scott, all dead in their sleeping bags—every circumstance engraved itself on Nancy's young imagination.

Captain Scott was to remain her hero of heroes, and the fact that he and his comrades 'really wanted to prove to themselves how much they could endure' haunted her till the end. The recollection of their sufferings often gave her courage to bear her own. Frequent references to Beardmore and Captain Oates cropped up in her letters, and she recounted their story in 1962, 'fifty years to the day that Scott died.' Paradoxically for a person with a frivolous façade, she admired sheer grit above other virtues. Most of her friends were epicurean but in a few instances she may have divined courage under the glossy surface, for it is a quality latent in the most unlikely people.

Of Blor's predecessors, the nannies who were employed to look after her during infancy, she tells us that the first one 'was quite untrained and knew nothing about babies; she laid the foundations of the low stamina which has always been such a handicap to me in life. I think she was also partly responsible for my great nastiness to the others.' No doubt she exaggerated this nastiness. Celestial harmony is rare in any crowded nursery, and close proximity to boisterous infants is bound to cause friction. Conscious of her seniority and precociously sophisticated, there must have been moments when, as her sister wrote in *Hons and Rebels*, her tongue became sharp and sarcastic. 'She might suddenly turn her penetrating emerald eyes in one's direction and say, "Run along up to the schoolroom: we've all had quite enough of you," or, if one had taken particular trouble to do one's hair in ringlets, she was apt to remark, "You look like the oldest and ugliest of the Brontë sisters today." ' Fundamentally she was devoted to her younger sisters, who were very blonde while she was comparatively dark.

Her attitude towards her irascible father was ambivalent. Thanks to her strong sense of humour she was able to laugh at his foibles with a secret admiration for the vigorous eccentricity of his character, the externals of which she borrowed for 'General Murgatroyd' in her early novel *Highland Fling*, and again for the unforgettable 'Uncle Matthew' in *The Pursuit of Love*: 'Much as we feared, much as we disapproved of, passionately as we sometimes hated Uncle Matthew, he still

7

remained for us a sort of criterion of English manhood; there seemed something not quite right about any man who greatly differed from him.' Uncle Matthew 'never altered his first opinion of people . . . his favourites could commit nameless crimes without doing wrong in his eyes . . . He always liked people who stood up to him.' An arrant chauvinist, he declared: 'I loathe abroad, nothing would induce me to live there, I'd rather live in the game keeper's hut in Hen's Grove, and, as for foreigners, they are all the same, and they make me sick . . .' His fits of temper were profitable to dentists as he invariably ground his false teeth. 'There was a legend in the family that he had already ground away four pairs in his rages.' Apparently his addiction to literature was limited; 'I have only read one book in my life, and that is *White Fang*. It's so frightfully good I've never bothered to read another.'

An endearing quality of Lord Redesdale was that far from being offended by this caricature, he was amused by it. Jessica Mitford's portrayal of him in *Hons and Rebels* is more severe. She regarded her family home at Swinbrook in the Cotswolds as a medieval fortress. 'From the point of view of the inmates it was self-contained in the sense that it was neither necessary nor, generally, possible to leave the premises for any of the normal human pursuits. Schoolroom with governess for education, riding stables and tennis court for exercise, seven of us children for mutual human companionship, the village church for spiritual consolation, our bedrooms for hospital wards even when operations were necessary—all were provided, either in the house itself or within easy walking distance. From the point of view of outsiders, entry, in the rather unlikely event that they might seek it, was an impossibility. According to my father, outsiders included not only Huns, Frogs, Americans, black and other foreigners, but also other people's children, the majority of my older sisters' acquaintances, almost all young men—in fact, the whole teeming population of the earth's surface, except for some, though not all, of our relations and a very few tweeded, red-faced country neighbours to whom my father had for some reason taken a liking.' This is more than an exaggeration due to bias, for as her sister Diana reminded me: 'We had guests every Saturday to Monday chosen by us. Farve didn't care for them but put up with it.'

In *Another Self*, James Lees-Milne's hilarious account of his juvenile vicissitudes, he relates that he had an Elysian impression of Nancy's home life at Asthall Manor, 'where this large and united family then lived.' Let us stress 'united', for the children were clannishly devoted to each other. For all their similarity in voice and feature their minds were not stamped in a single pattern: each personality had the advantage of free development.

Nancy's evocation of the Hon. Society of Alconleigh, huddled up in the disused linen cupboard at the top of the house, talking for hours about life and death, especially about childbirth, is one of the evergreen passages in *The Pursuit of Love*, and it rings absolutely true. One shares the bright children's excitement over their discoveries; one hears their giggles. The time for jokes never seemed to run out, and a good joke for Nancy was one of the highest forms of praise. She and her sisters revelled in private nicknames, some of which are baffling to an outsider. For instance Lord Redesdale, 'Farve', was also known as T.P.O.M. (The Poor Old Male) and Morgan; Lady Redesdale, 'Muv', as T.P.O.F. (The Poor Old Female) and Aunt Sydney or Syd. Diana had at least half a dozen alternative nicknames: Honks, Nard, Bodley, Cord, Dana, and Deerling. Pam was Woman, Wooms, and Woomling; Tom, Tuddemy or Tomford; Unity, Bobo, Birdie, and Bowd; Jessica, Decca, Hen, Henderson, Little D., Squalor, and Susan; Debo was Stubby, Stublow, Miss, and Nine (since even after marriage she was not supposed to have grown older—in ancient China nine was an auspicious number). Nancy was Koko to her parents and usually Naunce to her sisters. Such nicknames—all so English—create an atmosphere of youthful gaiety.

A school friend of Nancy's brother Tom, Jim Lees-Milne, describes Lord Redesdale with intuitive sympathy although he suffered from one of his alarming rages. He has kindly allowed me to quote the relevant passage, which would suffer from being summarized. Lady Redesdale 'presided, for that is the word, over her beautiful and eccentric brood with unruffled sweetness, amusement and no little bewilderment. Lord Redesdale was admittedly a dual personality. I cannot see that his children had in him much to complain about. Towards them he was Dr. Jekyll, indulgent and even docile. Although not a cultivated man he tolerated their intellectual pursuits and allowed them to say and do whatever they liked. He submitted

9

placidly to their ceaseless teasing, particularly Nancy's with its sharp little barb, barely concealed like the hook of an angler's fly beneath a riot of gay feathers. To Tom, whose straight-forward nature he understood better, he was touchingly devoted. The devotion was returned and they were like brothers, sharing each other's confidences.

'To outsiders, and particularly his children's friends, Lord Redesdale could be Mr. Hyde with a vengeance. But then he resented and hated outsiders for daring to intrude upon the family circle. He referred to one of their friends, a shy and diffident boy, as "that hog Watson" in front of his face, threatened another with a horsewhip for putting his feet on a sofa, and glowered at those who had done nothing wrong with such vehemence that they lost their nerve and usually broke things, thus provoking a more justifiable expression of his distaste. I was naturally terrified of him, but respected his uncertain temper. I made myself as inconspicuous as possible whenever he was in the room. The golden rule was to keep opinions to oneself in his presence, a difficult rule to observe in this household where the children spent their time arguing and discussing every subject under the sun from religion to sex.

'Unfortunately during dinner on the evening of my arrival I unwisely disregarded this rule, with distressing consequences. Lord Redesdale was in a sunny mood, chaffing and being chaffed by the children. Mouselike I ate in silence, smiled when I was spoken to and contributed nothing to the conversation. The cinema was being discussed which led to someone remarking that a film, called *Dawn*, about the shooting of Nurse Cavell was being shown in London. I had actually seen this film and was unduly proud of the fact. Casting discretion to the winds I raised my voice. "It is an anti-German film," I said. "It is high time that we put a stop to anti-German propaganda, now the war has been over for eight years. Instead, we ought to make friends with the Germans." These or similar words, tendentious but not altogether reprehensible, were what I uttered. The effect was electric. The smile on Lord Redesdale's face was switched off as though by a current. His proud and remarkably handsome features flushed scarlet. The scowl instantly appeared and threw a thunderous shadow across the table. "You damned young puppy!" he shouted, as he thumped the surface so that the plates and glasses clashed together like cymbals. "How dare

10

you? You don't know what the bloody Huns are like. They are worse than all the devils in hell. And you sit there, and have the damned impudence—" ... Lady Redesdale with a pained expression on her dear face put a hand on his arm, and just said in her plaintive, drawly voice, "David". He stopped, threw down his napkin, rose from the table and stalked out of the dining room. For a second or two there was a chilling silence, then a chorus of breath let out of girlish lungs. "Oh gosh!" I said, "what had I better do now?" The six sisters from Nancy, aged twenty-one, down to Debo, aged six, looked at one another and then chanted in unison:

> "We don't want to lose you,
> But we think you ought to go."

'Only Tom did not join in this rather callous couplet from the Great War music-hall song. He merely nodded assent. "What? Now?" I gasped, appalled, for it was already half-past nine, pouring with rain and getting dark. "We're afraid you simply must," they said. "Otherwise Farve really might kill you. And just think of the mess he would make." There was nothing else to be done. I sloped off into the night.'

Jim had propped his motor scooter under a tree while the weather was clear, but during the deluge water had got into the petrol and the machine refused to start. Drenched to the skin, he could only return to the house and a maid let him in by the back door. While she went to fetch Tom, Lord Redesdale appeared and took pity on his plight. 'To my amazement he put his arm round my shoulders, practically embraced me, and said that I was the most splendid boy he had ever known, that my courage and perseverance were exemplary ... Eventually I went upstairs to a hot bath and bed in the belief that Lord Redesdale was to be my lifelong friend and mentor. At breakfast next morning he was as cold and distant as ever. But I was allowed to remain at Asthall for a week.'

The second Lord Redesdale had mellowed, at any rate on the surface, when I met him in 1928. Privately he may have regarded me as a 'sewer', since he was reputed to abominate aesthetes, but in spite of an aggressive glare he spoke to me amiably in an agreeable voice. One could not help appreciating his supreme Englishness. To all his children except Jessica he was 'one of the funniest people who ever lived with a genius for making them laugh'. His periodical rages were the other side of the medal—thunderstorms to clear the air. Probably he chuckled at them in retrospect. He lacked his father's cosmopolitan sympathies. Old Lord Redesdale had been a friend of Whistler, who hated the Boer War, whereas he took pride in having fought and been thrice wounded in it. A pillar of convention, he was also a jingo—very unlike the English expatriates I had encountered in my native Florence.

Nancy's little acts of rebellion must have helped the mellowing process. Her sister Jessica relates that she 'dimly remembered the hushed pall that hung over the house, meals eaten day after day in tearful silence, when Nancy at the age of twenty had her hair shingled. Nancy using lipstick, Nancy playing the newly fashionable ukulele, Nancy wearing trousers, Nancy smoking a cigarette—she had broken ground for all of us, but only at terrific cost in violent scenes followed by silence and tears.' Even dimly I cannot remember Nancy doing any of these things. If she used make-up it was barely noticeable, and I never saw her smoking.

Her sisters were to benefit by Nancy's boldness, though her effort to break away from the exclusive family circle in order to study painting at the Slade ended in failure. Jessica, who has described the tension caused by Nancy's resolve, 'meals eaten in dead silence . . . the muffled thunder of my father's voice,' was 'terribly disappointed when she came home after a month.'

' "How *could* you! If I ever got away to a bed-sitter I'd never come back."

' "Oh, darling, but you should have seen it. After about a week it was knee-deep in underclothes. I literally had to wade through them. No one to put them away."

' "Well, I think you're very weak-minded. You wouldn't catch me knuckling under because of a little thing like underclothes." '

Jessica was made of tougher material, as she subsequently proved. Lord Redesdale won the first round with his eldest daughter. His aversion to society drew him inwards in a cocoon, remote from contemporary currents. While he and Lady Redesdale were satisfied with their healthy domestic life, their daughters were frustrated by their comparative segregation. In spite of the fun they enjoyed in each other's company, the girls had yearnings for greater freedom, like Chekhov's

Three Sisters who longed to go to Moscow. 'I ought to have gone to school,' Nancy wrote, 'it was the dream of my life—but there was never any question of that.' According to her, 'it was not so much education that he [Lord Redesdale] dreaded for his daughters, as the vulgarizing effect that a boarding school might have upon them.' Here Nancy's memory was defective, for she did attend the Frances Holland day school in London from about 1910 until 1914, when her family migrated to the country owing to the war.

CHAPTER TWO

A T T H E A G E of sixteen, Nancy went to a 'finishing school' at Hatherop Castle, where she made life-long friendships and whence, with other girls, she was shepherded for the first time to the Continent. Her mother religiously kept her letters from Paris, Florence and Venice. These are too long to quote in full, but a few excerpts convey her intense enjoyment, the freshness of her adolescent outlook.

From Paris (Grand Hôtel du Louvre, 8th April, 1922) she wrote: 'Darling Muv, Getting up early I had my bath, took a lift and progressed down stairs to pen this to you. We arrived here at 7, took a hasty but delicious meal and—went to bed? Not at all, we walked round the streets till 10.30, came home to iced lemon squash (we have been forbidden water) and to bed at 11. Brek is in a moment, at 9. It is so lovely here, there are telephones and hot and cold water in our bedrooms. I spend my time telephoning for baths, etc.

'All the shops look so heavenly and the Place de la Concorde when lighted up is too lovely . . . Why doesn't one always live in hotels? It is so lovely . . . We look out on to the Louvre.

'There are dozens of sweet little boys here (hall boys) perfect pets, I shall give them my chocs.

'Marjorie has such lovely clothes I feel like a rag bag . . . We don't want to leave Paris at all and I was so sick in the French train after an excellent Table d'Hôte lunch, I am sure I shall be terribly ill all the time. The hotel is so hot I slept in a thin nightie and only one blanket and then I lay half out of bed and was boiled. We had two huge French windows wide open too!

'. . . Jean is very nice and very Canadian. Both she and Marjorie powder their noses the whole time. I wish I could, I'm sure for travelling one ought to.

'There is one hall boy we call the Cherub. Miss S. wouldn't let us have an English brek (not that we wanted it, it is too hot to eat) and we had a very scrumptious "croissant" and coffee . . .

'We are going to lunch and dinner in restaurants today as Miss S. says only old fogeys eat at their hotel. Alas, I can't feel hungry and all the food is so delicious, especially lemon squash with straws . . . I find you have to tip everyone although Miss S. really does that, I do it too. I can't bear not to.

'Oh! such fun. I have never been so excited and Miss S. is so good. She quite understands that we want to do other things besides sight-seeing . . . I expect one of us must be run over. I escaped certain death by very little several times yesterday.

'How I loved the Louvre. One could spend weeks there and never get tired of it. We saw mostly Italian pictures, Titian, Giotto, Cimabue, and all of those to prepare us for Florence.

'We are all tired as we have walked *without stopping* since 10 this morning, but it was well worth it. I got postcards of all my favourite pictures. Mona Lisa is wonderful. Miss S. says men still fall in love with her—one man fell in love with her and stole her for several years.'

From Florence (12th April, 1922): 'I think I will pass over the journey in sad silence. I was only kept alive by a huge dose of brandy administered by Miss S. I was on the point of fainting (not an exag) as we were walking along for brek. Pisa was too heavenly. The 4 lovely buildings (Duomo, the Tower, Campo Santo and Baptistry). We spent half an hour with them—quite beyond description. *Too too too* heavenly.

'Being here is lovely too, although there is no building (except the Duomo) to touch Pisa. The buildings there are in a much better position, so white and in the middle of such green grass. Everything here is so brightly coloured, it must be the sun . . . I feel as though I have seen originals of every statue and picture I ever heard of . . .

'I am quite good at Italian already, as good as Miss S. and better than anyone else. I get along famously. I do all the bargaining for the others and always get things reduced. I talk as though I had been here a month and indeed I feel like it.

'As for the hotel the less said the better and I shall say nothing except we have used Keating's freely with but little effect (I have just caught one on my neck).

'Next day . . . Last night we went for a walk on the river and a man with a guitar and a girl with a heavenly voice serenaded us. I gave them two lira and they were overcome and went on for hours. It was too delicious . . . I found some lovely corals, small but down to my waist, 2 strings for £2. Most exciting bargaining is going on. They are really 180 lira and I am determined to have them for 160. In vain the woman weeps and wrings her hands, inexorable as fate I pursue my ends. Luckily she weeps in English as my limited Italian gives out now and then. I converse with the lift boy who corrects me with a cherubic smile. *Disgraziatamente* (unfortunately) our cameriera (chamber maid) speaks French, so we get no practice there. We always have brek in bed at 8.30. It is a meal not worth getting up for. The first morning we ordered toast and marmalade—absolute failure.'

More details about purchases follow: 'Do commission me to buy you some pictures, you will never have such a chance again! . . . I went to fetch my corals today, I had them strung differently. They reach down to my waist in 2 or to my knees in 1. When I was going to pay the woman she dragged me behind a screen and in a dramatic tone said that she saw a policeman and anyhow there are spies everywhere! I scented a bolshy plot at least, but on further explanation discovered that if I was seen to buy the corals I should have to pay 135 luxury tax! She told me to hide them till I got home, so away I crept feeling like a criminal! Nice of her. They are lovely, I must wear them all day under my clothes or they will be stolen, so I am told . . .'

She thought the Uffizi 'thousands of times nicer' than the Pitti, where the pictures were 'lovely but so badly arranged. About one beauty in each room, the rest—rubbish . . . I had no idea I was so fond of pictures before, especially Raphael, Botticelli and Lippo Lippi . . . If only I had a room of my own I would make it a regular picture gallery. I find to my horror that there are lovely pictures in London, Italian ones and lots of good ones. I have only ever been to the Tate Gallery. This must be remedied! I never knew that there were really lovely pictures in London. Marjorie knows the National Gallery by

1. Aged 2, with her mother and father

2a. Lord Redesdale,
1928

2b. Lady Redesdale, about 1958, at Inch Kenneth, Argyll

heart. I don't think it is too late to develop a taste in pictures at 17, do you? I really love them. As for the statues, I used to hate them, but when you have seen some of them here you can't help liking them . . . Only 3 more days here, how shall I tear myself away? Thank you *so* much for sending me, I am having a perfectly *heavenly* time, I have never been so happy in my life before, in spite of such minor incidents as fleas! If you knew what it is like here you would leave England for good and settle here at once.'

On Easter Sunday Nancy wrote an elaborate account with sketch, of the *Scoppio del Carro* (the explosion of the chariot) outside the Cathedral, of the afternoon races in the Cascine (one steeplechase and the rest flat races) 'most exciting and amusing', and of an old man in the hotel—'the others said he wasn't old but he is really, quite 45'—who was 'also an adorer of Ruskin. He seemed very surprised that I had read most of Ruskin's books and we talked for ages. Unfortunately (*disgraziatamente*) he went away this morning. I called him "my old man" ever since we came . . .' A film called *Dante* was 'most bloodthirsty and exciting. Eleven murders close to with details, a man's hands chopped off *very* close to and *full* of detail, and a man dying of starvation and eating another man *very very* close to and the death of Dante with great detail helped to add a mild excitement to a film full of battles (on land and sea) molten lead, a burning city and other little everyday matters. It lasted with two intervals from 9 to 12.15! I never saw anything like it before, it was enough to make you dream for nights. There was a seedy contingent with permanently waved hair wandering about in the desert, called the prophets of Peace, they stumbled on dead bodies at every step; a most realistic scene from hell, the devils reminded me of those drawn by Bobo [Unity]. Every time a person was murdered you saw him being taken down there with dire results. People died off so fast that only one character was left alive by 12.15 and it is a huge cast. That shows you! The one who did survive had just killed his wife, so one imagines he then goes mad.

'I am quite miserable at leaving here tomorrow. We get up at 6! . . . Do you think I shall ever come back here? I positively *must!*'

From Venice (Hotel Regina, 19 April) Nancy continued: 'I

like this in quite a different way to Florence. Here it is more the place that one likes, there it is the things, statues, pictures and buildings. Of course there are pictures here, but mostly Titian and Tintoretto. Secretly I hate Titian and loathe Tintoretto, but that, I fear, is my bad taste. I simply love the Florentine pictures, Raphael and Andrea del Sarto especially. Oh, and Botticelli I love! We saw the largest oil painting in the world in the Doge's palace by Tintoretto. It is *awful*, represents Paradise, and is merely a sea of faces.

'I would much rather have a villa in Florence than here because of the lovely scenery. Here of course there is none, no trees, no grass. However this is lovely too, quite heavenly.'

On 21st April Nancy confessed: 'I did a most rash thing yesterday, spent nearly all my worldly on a Spanish comb, knowing full well that you won't let me wear it, although Marjorie says all girls do. It is so nice, not carved, and looks rather like a shoe horn . . . Real shell of course. I *do* look so nice in it (ahem!) and wore it yesterday evening for dinner. It looks most habillé. Now I am absolutely broke, having just over 170 left, and still several presents to get . . .

'A dreadful thing happened last night. Turnip jumped very hard on Marigold's bed and burst her hot bottle. *Such* a mess! We "ragged in the dorm" violently after that and an old lady came along and said that she thought someone must be ill. That rather shut us up!

'. . . I hope you will let me wear that comb, it grows on me (this is not to be interpreted literally). I really look quite old in it, a femme du monde you know, especially when I wear a fur. I really am a femme du monde now. Living in an hotel is so *lovely*. Why does anyone live anywhere else. There is an atmosphere of excitement, of latent danger in an hotel which is not created by the home. Locking my door at night is a never-failing joy, as is going in the lift (I can work it myself now). Then the feeling that when you are out all your things may (according to Miss S. most probably will) be stolen causes pleasant thrills to frequent the marrow. One of the women here was walking today in a calle when a man snatched her bag. With true Anglo-Saxon doggedness she hung on to it, the man let go and ran away. And this might happen to one any day. How romantic! When I see anyone glance at my corals I give an invisible snarl and put them under my pillow at night.'

St. Mark's on St. Mark's Day: 'The golden altar completely unveiled, all the jewels sparkling in the candle light,' the gorgeous procession ('first choir boys, then priests, then 30 bishops, 20 archbishops and 15 cardinals, the bishops in Mitres (capital M) and priests with banners'), St. Luke's picture of the Madonna, the glowing mosaics, the Doge's palace, the Bridge of Sighs—Nancy described these enthusiastically to her mother as well as her various purchases: 'Corals for N.M. Comb for N.M. Frame and several pictures for N.M. A Leonardo print for Tom. Corals for Bobo. Crystals for Di. Crystals for Deb. Box for Nanny. Little bronze lizard for Pam. Photograph and countless p.c's for N.M. I haven't got Decca's [Jessica's] yet . . .'

As a child Nancy was a precocious reader who 'lived in books'. Even so it is surprising that she had read the works of Ruskin without visiting the National Gallery by the age of seventeen, though Ruskin's championship of Turner might account for her visit to the Tate. Apparently her spring tour with the girls of the finishing school was her first introduction to the figurative arts at close range. To Venice she returned frequently in later years, always with renewed enchantment.

Reading was tolerated but not encouraged by her father, who thought it a peculiar pastime. 'If you've got nothing to do,' he would say, finding Nancy with a book, 'run down to the village and tell Hooper . . .' Himself no reader, he had no objection to her browsing in the well-stocked library inherited from her grandfather, and she browsed to her heart's content. Her taste for literature was moulded there, and she retained a lifelong preference for biography, memoirs and letters. Carlyle and Macaulay made the deepest impression on her.

This passion for reading set her apart from her sisters though she shared their esoteric jokes and games. 'My vile behaviour to the others,' she confessed later, 'was partly, I suppose, the result of jealousy and partly of a longing to be grown-up and live with grown-up people. The others bored me, and I made them feel it . . . I expect I would have been much worse but for Blor.'

Lady Redesdale seems to have exerted a negative influence. According to Nancy she had 'always lived in a dream world of

19

her own'. Apropos of which she commented: 'I think that nothing in my life has changed more than the relationship between mothers and young children. In those days a distance was always kept. Even so she was perhaps abnormally detached. On one occasion Unity rushed into the drawing-room, where she was at her writing-table, saying: "Muv, Muv, Decca is standing on the roof—she says she's going to commit suicide!" "Oh, poor duck," said my mother, "I hope she won't do anything so terrible" and went on writing.'

This detachment may have been a subconscious defence against her explosive husband and boisterous children. Without knowing it Lady Redesdale was an incipient Taoist, for as Lao Tzŭ said, 'The weak overcomes the strong, the soft overcomes the hard . . . The softest things in the world override the hardest.' (Lao Tzŭ also said: 'Mighty is he who conquers himself,' which scarcely applied to Lord Redesdale.) Albeit no Christian Scientist, Lady Redesdale did not believe in illness, but she was prejudiced against certain foods and against pig in particular. Ham, sausages, fried bacon were all craved for by her children, as is usual with forbidden fruit. Lady Redesdale's brother, 'Uncle Geoff', seems to have swayed her ideas on health. He was an eccentric of a different kind who fancied that the fortunes of England depended on the use of natural manure in fertilizing the soil. He had violent objections to the pasteurization of milk, and his niece, Jessica, has left a funny description of his advocacy of the 'unsplit slowly smoked bloater' and other ingredients of wholesome diet, and she quotes a characteristic passage from a privately printed collection of his old letters to editors entitled *Writings of a Rebel* in her *Hons and Rebels* (required reading for all Mitford fans). Her mother, she tells us, added a few notions of her own to Uncle Geoff's. 'In defiance of the law, she refused to allow any of us to be vaccinated ("pumping disgusting dead germs into the Good Body!").' When Jessica in turn begged to be sent to a school, her mother sensibly remarked: 'If you went to school you'd probably hate it. The fact is children always want to do something different from what they are doing. Childhood is a very unhappy time of life; I know I was always miserable as a child. You'll be all right when you're eighteen.' One cannot visualize young Jessica submitting to school discipline. Though she might mock her Uncle Geoff she was one of nature's rebels. Unity went to two schools and was expelled from both. When one of her sisters said so, Lady Redesdale gently objected: 'Oh no, darling, not expelled, *asked to leave.*'

In a draft for a broadcast after *The Pursuit of Love* was published, Nancy wrote: 'I have described the early years of myself and my five sisters and one brother in my last book, with some alterations necessary to a work of fiction, but with no exaggeration. Indeed it would hardly be possible to exaggerate the eccentricity and restlessness of our upbringing. My father had two manias, for selling and for building. He would build a new house every time there was a boom, when labour was scarce and expensive. He would then live in it for a while, but as soon as there was a slump, as soon as labour became easy and cheap and values dropped, he would sell what he had built at a vast loss and we would all move on to the next house whose foundation stone would be laid on the first day of a new boom.

'Our first home was a large Elizabethan palace built by my grandfather in 1900. He had my father's mania to an even more marked degree, but concentrated it upon this one house. My father sold it as soon as he could, and thereafter we lived under the shadow, so to speak, of two hammers, the builder's and the auctioneer's, and fidgeted about from one house to another on different parts of my father's estate. Sometimes they were houses which already existed but which were then altered to suit the requirements of so large a family, sometimes they were built from scratch.

'The first room to be completed was always what my father called "the child-proof room" to which he would retire and snooze (for he never read or wrote) in peace after a day spent entirely in the open air. The child-proof room was invariably fitted with an immensely powerful mortice lock. However, we children usually managed to effect an escape . . .'

When they grew up Nancy and Tom were allowed to bring friends to stay. These included both athletes and aesthetes. According to Jessica, 'at week-ends they would swoop down from Oxford or London in merry hordes, to be greeted with solid disapproval by my mother and furious glares from my father.' My lamented friend Mark Ogilvie-Grant was among them. Even Lord Redesdale could not help warming to Mark,

21

SAINT PETER'S COLLEGE LIBRARY
JERSEY CITY, NEW JERSEY 07306

for he joined his shooting parties and appeared for breakfast punctually at eight o'clock, though brains turned his delicate stomach at that hour.

Of Nancy's contemporaries perhaps Mark exerted the most obvious influence on her taste, and it was even rumoured that he hoped to marry her. While adapting himself outwardly to social convention he was capable of exuberant flights of fantasy. He was a cousin of Nina, the shy young Countess of Seafield, for whom he acted as an impresario. Nina then resembled a juvenile Queen Victoria with red hair and a hesitant stammer. Having spent her infancy in New Zealand, she had inherited large estates in Scotland, including Cullen and Castle Grant where Nancy often visited her, surrounded by Mark's vivacious coterie, whose more serious members were determined not to seem so. Robert Byron exploited his pugnacity in a genial and unpredictable way. Oliver Messel, a skilful mimic, entertained the company with spicy monologues about tragi-comical White Russian refugee princesses, 'refained' governesses afflicted with wind, and wriggling débutantes whose conversational gambit was limited to 'Have you been to *No, no Nanette?*' Mark had a vast repertoire of absurdly sentimental Victorian ballads which he trilled and warbled with a gusto only rivalled by Robert Byron's booming vociferation.

Nobody could have dreamt of the future developments of these young bloods fresh from Oxford whose talent and intelligence were often veiled by flippancy. They parodied the pursuits of bucolic neighbours and their peculiar dialect. Nancy's first novel reflected their behaviour, the invasion of Presbyterian Scotland, as it were, by Evelyn Waugh's Bright Young Things. Her protagonist Albert Gates, for instance, was suggested by Robert's cult of Victoriana to which most of us subscribed in a playful spirit. ('My name,' said Albert with some asperity, 'is Albert Memorial Gates. I took Memorial in addition to my baptismal Albert at my confirmation out of admiration for the Albert Memorial, a very great work of art which may be seen in a London suburb called Kensington.') A far cry from Robert's subsequent Byzantinism! Mark was to reappear as the 'Wonderful Old Songster of Kew Green' in Nancy's *Pigeon Pie*. Short, spare, clean-shaven, he remained one of her closest confidants.

I never visited Asthall or Swinbrook, but while I was at Oxford I was regaled with lyrical accounts of Nancy's precocious wit and intelligence—'a delicious creature, quite pyrotechnical my dear, and sometimes even profound, and would you believe it, she's hidden among the cabbages of the Cotswolds'—from an improbable source, my former Eton crony, Brian Howard. He was so scornful of feminine intellect among contemporaries that I felt it was more than a special compliment. I still wonder how Brian and Lord Redesdale coped with each other, if they were allowed to meet. The contrast between them evoked extreme burlesque, and Brian's posturings and paradoxes must have helped to stimulate the composition of Nancy's first novel.

As a débutante Nancy enjoyed a conventional succession of seasons during that hectic period immortalized by Evelyn Waugh, when Noël Coward represented the younger generation of gatecrashers and jazz was in the air, though it was the genteel jazz of Jack Hylton and Ambrose, less frenzied but more suave than its Afro-American precursors. Nancy attended the coming-out balls as regularly as her coevals but with a colder, more critical eye as time went on. She was too clever to enjoy the platitudes of her callow dancing partners who were a source of disillusion to her, as to Sophia in her novel *Pigeon Pie*. Like Sophia, 'she was not shy and she had high spirits, but she was never a romper and therefore never attained much popularity with the very young.'

During the winter she rode hard to hounds, stayed with friends, and invited them to her parents' house. A nostalgic passage in *Pigeon Pie* betrays her love of hunting: 'The first meet she ever went to, early in the morning with her father's agent. She often remembered this, and it had become a composite picture of all the cub-hunting she had ever done, the autumn woods and the smell of bonfires, dead leaves and hot horses. Riding home from the last meet of a season, late in the afternoon of a spring day, there would be primroses and violets under the hedges, far far away the sound of a horn, and later an owl.'

Until Nancy was twenty-three her parents lived at Asthall in Oxfordshire, about half the size of the 10,000 acres Lord Redesdale had inherited at Batsford Park in Gloucestershire, which he sold in 1919. In 1927 he also sold Asthall and moved to Swinbrook, where he built a house on the site of one of his farms called South Lawn, a name he wished to dispense with. None of his children liked Swinbrook House, described by Jessica as 'a large rectangular structure of three stories . . . neither "modern" nor "traditional" nor simulated antique . . . It could be a small barracks, a girls' boarding school, a private lunatic asylum, or, in America, a country club.' To tease her father Nancy used to address her letters: 'Builder Redesdale, The Buildings, South Lawn, Burford.' A compensation for Swinbrook was that he bought 26 Rutland Gate, so that the girls could enjoy more time in London.

CHAPTER THREE

U NFORTUNATELY LORD REDESDALE had little flair for finance and his father had been extravagant, like so many denizens of the horse world. Gradually he felt obliged to part with valuable possessions, usually at a loss. His houses were often let, especially the London residence, whereupon his family were squeezed into the Mews behind it, or into Lady Redesdale's cosy cottage at High Wycombe. It was economy rather than a resolve to keep Nancy at home that prevented her from moving into a private flat. Nowadays she would have looked for a job, but such an idea would not have occurred to Lord Redesdale: it was not even discussed. Whatever Nancy could earn from her writings was added to her meagre dress allowance. She chafed under the tedium of rustic life though this impelled her to read voraciously and, eventually, to write her first novel.

Jessica has related the circumstances with *brio*: 'For months Nancy had sat giggling helplessly by the drawing-room fire, her curiously triangular green eyes flashing with amusement, while her thin pen flew along the lines of a child's exercise book. Sometimes she read bits aloud to us. "You *can't* publish that under your own name," my mother insisted, scandalized, for not only did thinly disguised aunts, uncles and family friends people the pages of *Highland Fling*, but there, larger than life-size, felicitously named "General Murgatroyd", was Farve. But Nancy did publish it under her own name, and the Burford Lending Library even arranged a special display in their window, with a hand-lettered sign: "Nancy Mitford, Local Authoress" . . . In spite of the brief row that flared when Nancy insisted on publishing *Highland Fling* under her own name, it became evident that my parents, and even the uncles and aunts, were actually quite proud of having an author in the family . . . '

In fact it was no novelty to have 'an author in the family' since both Nancy's grandfathers had published several books. Her maternal grandfather, Thomas Gibson Bowles, was the founder of the sensational Victorian journal *Vanity Fair*, whose coloured cartoons of celebrities line the walls of smart London clubs but whose controversial contents were to antagonize many of his fellow members of Parliament. Nancy inherited his sharp and acid wit. Lewis Carroll (the Rev. C. L. Dodgson) was one of his friends and it is curious in these days to read that he wanted *Vanity Fair* to promote 'a daily fly-sheet (which might be called "Where shall we go?" or the "Vanity Fair Play-bill") with a list of all amusements to which ladies might safely be taken, and a warning against objectionable plays'. James Tissot and Carlo Pellegrini ('Ape') were two of *Vanity Fair*'s leading cartoonists, and Bowles was joined by Tissot when he went to Paris as a war correspondent in September 1870 before the Prussian siege. His despatches to the *Morning Post* during that period were extremely graphic and amusing. Apart from his political and journalistic activities he had a passion for yachting and became a notable authority on naval matters.

After her eighteen-year-old sister Diana's marriage to Bryan Guinness (now Lord Moyne) in January 1929 Nancy often stayed in their Buckingham Street house (now Buckingham Place), a delightful trysting place of the generations, where past and future consorted merrily with the present. Diana and Bryan attracted a galaxy of literary and artistic friends who might have been considered 'sewers' by Lord Redesdale. Bloomsbury was represented by Lytton Strachey and his doting Carrington; the Sitwells by Sir Osbert, Sacheverell and Georgia. Evelyn Waugh, Robert Byron, Henry Yorke, Brian Howard, John Sutro, Hamish Erskine, Henry and Pansy Lamb, Mark Ogilvie-Grant, with a bevy of fashionable beauties—many of Bryan's and Tom Mitford's Oxford cronies, my brother and I included, enjoyed their exhilarating hospitality. Nancy's wit blossomed freely in this uninhibited atmosphere, which tended to make her more impatient of parental authority. At the age of twenty-four it seemed high time to leave the nest.

26

Two of her closest girl friends were Lady Pansy Pakenham and the Hon. Evelyn Gardner, both aspiring writers who had shared lodgings before their marriages, the former to Henry Lamb and the latter to Evelyn Waugh. (Henry Lamb was to paint the best likeness of the male Evelyn at this time.) The newly wedded Waughs found a modest flat in Canonbury Square, Islington, to which they lent a personal charm as remote from the modish as it was from Bloomsbury and Mayfair. They looked like a juvenile brother and sister. The male Evelyn's first novel had been acclaimed with salvoes of judicious applause. But one swallow makes not a spring, and Evelyn's second novel proved even more successful than his first, though its gestation had been interrupted by his wife's illness. After her convalescence he needed a spell of solitude to finish his book, so he decided to work in the country during the week and join his wife in London for weekends.

At this juncture a temporary solution was found for Nancy's yearning for independence. The Waughs offered her a room in their flat and she accepted it with alacrity. Evelyn's wife gained an enchanting companion during his absence and Nancy, in creative mood, sparkled in this unconventional environment. *Highland Fling* was about to be published and she was producing topical articles for *Vogue*, embellished by Mark Ogilvie-Grant's illustrations.

Everything here seemed favourable to a budding novelist of slender means. She enjoyed the simple life spiced with jokes and spontaneous fantasy: it seemed idyllic. But it was too good to last. In July a thunderbolt fell. Mrs. Waugh confessed to Nancy that she had only married Evelyn to escape from her stifling family. In the meantime she had fallen in love with John Heygate, the ebullient author of *Decent Fellows,* a naughty novel about Eton. While Nancy could sympathize with her motives she could not approve of her method. Apart from her admiration for Evelyn's brilliance, she appreciated his human qualities. He inspired affection in his intimate friends, who readily forgave his peccadilloes. He was too young and too fond to tolerate infidelity and it was not in his nature to laugh it off like those contemporaries he satirized in *Vile Bodies.* The shock of disappointment had lasting repercussions. Only his conversion to Catholicism could heal the wound, whose traces are distinct in *A Handful of Dust.* Nancy packed her bags and

27

departed from Canonbury Square. Her sympathies were with the he-Evelyn and they remained lifelong friends.

Nancy had written *Highland Fling* to amuse herself before amusing others. It was a frolicsome performance of which later she became unreasonably ashamed, but in a Christmas cracker way it was effective. If, as she maintained, she wished to emulate P. G. Wodehouse, she had chosen the wrong model and Evelyn Waugh's influence was not yet apparent. Family pride in the sprightly relation who startled her uncles and aunts with her all-too-recognizable caricatures must have gratified and encouraged her to stick to her guns. To her friend James Lees-Milne, who had expressed his enjoyment, she replied: 'such letters are far more encouraging than reviews in newspapers. The book is going fairly well, it went into a second impression three days after it came out but won't I fear be a best-seller or anything like that. The publishers however are pleased and surprised at the amount sold . . . By the same post as yours I had a letter from an aged friend of mama's saying that the silliness of my young people is only equalled by their vulgarity and that if by writing this I intend to *devastate* and lay *waste* to such society I am undoubtedly performing a service to mankind. And a great deal more. I fear now that I shall never be mentioned in her will . . .'

Already a faint whiff of the professional author may be detected.

In the meantime I set forth on my wanderings and eventually settled in Peking, so there is a considerable blank in my vision of Nancy, a gap of nearly nine years. On the last few occasions I saw her before sailing from Europe she was invariably escorted by Hamish Erskine, an elegant and amiable young social butterfly who was also a 'Hon', and for a long time it was rumoured that they were about to marry. In fact they were blithe companions floating on a frivolous tide, playing a charade of Pierrot and Columbine and sharing endless jokes to compensate for lack of lucre. Mutual friends who enjoyed them separately became as exasperated as Nancy's parents by this indefinite flirtation. Hamish, who could seldom face crude reality before midday, was to distinguish himself for his courage in Italy during the war. Maybe Nancy had divined the pluck which was one of his attractions.

The infatuation was stronger on Nancy's side for Hamish was

an overt narcissist, and he must have been flattered by her *béguin* for him. Nancy's letters to Hamish have been destroyed but through her intimate correspondence with Mark Ogilvie-Grant we may follow the wavering graph of her emotions. Mark was in Cairo at the time and Hamish was still up at Oxford. While in London he dragged her to the night-clubs and parties frequented by Evelyn Waugh's characters, leading her a dance in which she was a far from happy partner, though she exaggerated her woes as many of us do in youth. For a girl of twenty-five her letters are touchingly ingenuous.

From Redesdale Cottage, Otterburn, she wrote on 30th December, 1929: 'Here I am as you see banished from Hamish for three weeks. I thought I should die but am bearing up nicely partly because I adore this place and partly because my grandmother is such an angel. Also I am working really hard . . . [Recently in London] went to the Café de Paris, having borrowed £2 from Evie. Well then we found (when we'd got there) that after paying the bill we had 7½d between us. We were panicking rather when the sallow and disapproving countenance of old Mit [her brother Tom] was observed. He cut Hamish but lent me £1 and we went to the Bat. As we never pay there now we are treated as poor relations and put behind the band where we can neither see nor hear and we have the buttered eggs that the Mountbattens have spat into and left. All so homey and nice don't you think. Still I feel we lend a certain *ton* to the place. Hamish has been an angel lately, not drinking a thing. I really think that bar all the good old jokes which no one enjoys more than I do, that he has literally the nicest nature of anyone I know. He gets nicer every day too.

'My grandmother is divine about him although she knows and hates all his relations and forbears. A propos of his religion [he was a Catholic] she said, "so long as a person is devout it doesn't the least matter what his religion is, only I (no doubt wrongly) would never feel quite the same about a very devout Hindu or Buddhist. And of course Low Church people are very holy but they do so treat God like their first cousin."

'I must go to bed. It is dark here all day and I keep looking out for the midday moon, haven't seen it yet . . . Have had to alter the book (*Highland Fling*) quite a lot as it is so like Evelyn's in little ways, *such* a bore.'

From Redesdale Cottage again on 8th January, 1930: 'I've

been here nearly a fortnight, and apart from missing Hamish dreadfully have enjoyed every minute of it, such beautiful country—I've been desperately trying to finish the book, which has improved a lot since you heard parts of it . . . The sweet angel [Hamish] is always so sensible about everybody but himself isn't he. Poor Hamish was in a fearful state when his brother-in-law died suddenly because it was the third sudden death in his family this year which I must say is dreadful for them.' . . .

Later: 'I've got a job offered me to write a weekly article for £3 a week and I keep putting off and putting off but can't start this evening as I've just spent the day in Oxford with you know who and that always stops me working. He's going to Canada in March for ever, and we're both so unhappy about it, specially me. Isn't life perfect hell, that beastly old Harry has found a job for him at £100 a year with a rise of £10 every six months which looks as though he'll be able to support me and our 5 children jolly soon doesn't it. However, he's being such an *angel* about it that one simply must not put him off and it may be the making of him yet I suppose . . . You won't know Hamish again, he's a reformed character, gets up at 9.30 every morning and has quite given up drink and intends to work like a slave in Canada. I love him much more than ever.'

From Old Mill Cottage, High Wycombe, 1st February, 1930: 'The children [her sisters] have a hen called Mongrel Child, but when they are feeling pleased with it Golden Eagle. They also have one called Double She because it lays double yolked eggs. I fear these farmyard details are likely to bore.

'Lunched with Hamish on Thursday and arriving at one o'clock found him in pyjamas having breakfast so I hounded him into his bedroom and finished up his grapefruit and coffee. He has no money until the end of the term and daren't run into debt again. I must say he's being an angel about it and we gnaw chicken bones for lunch now instead of oysters . . . Hamish is going to ride in a grind on Saturday, simply awful for me but I'm behaving like a mem sahib about it and pretend to be pleased . . .'

19th February, 1930: 'Thank Heaven Canada is off for the moment. I really think it would have killed me . . . Will Hamish ever grow out of liking all these painted dolls I wonder, and will our house overflow with them always? I've just finished Maurois' *Byron*, very readable. Byron is so like Hamish in character, the other day Hamish said to me in tones of deepest satisfaction, 'You haven't known a single happy moment since we met have you.' Very true as a matter of fact, what he would really like would be for me to die and a few others and then he'd be able to say "I bring death on all who love me". It's so sad, when you're away there's nobody I can laugh about Hamish with and he *is* such a joke isn't he?

'. . . Did I tell you I have got a job of writing weekly articles for *The Lady* at about £250 a year (they haven't quite settled my wages yet). It is rather fun to do but a bit of a strain every week to think of subjects. My book has gone to the agents whose verdict I await in a state of palpitation. I'm afraid it won't be accepted. Everyone thinks it very bad, specially Hamish.'

10th March, 1930: 'Oh dear *how* unhappy Hamish does make me sometimes nobody knows except I think you do because you know us both so well. I'm so exactly the wrong person for him really that I simply can't imagine how it all happened. It's all most peculiar. But sometimes I really wish I were dead, which is odd for me as I have a cheerful disposition by nature. I'm sorry to grumble like this. I really do honestly think everything would be all right if we were married, it's partly living down here that makes me so depressed and miserable.

'My book has been accepted by the agents which is a cheering thought. I don't know how much that means but I suppose they don't take something that's absolutely unmarketable . . . What do you really think of *Vile Bodies*? I was frankly very much disappointed in it I must say but some people think it quite marvellous.

'I met M. Boulestin the other day such a little dear and he says he's going to start a restaurant in Oxford. So I told John [Sutro] and John was furious and I couldn't make out why and at last he said "Oh to think there was nothing like that when I was at Oxford!" Poor sweet I so understand that point of view. He and Christopher [Sykes] are so *silly* together I couldn't stop laughing. P.S. That awful grumble doesn't mean anything except that I'm in a very bad temper so don't take the smallest notice of it *please*.'

From 4 Rutland Gate Mews, 30th March, 1930: 'I'm making such a lot of money with articles—£22 since Christmas and more owing to me so I'm saving it up to be married but Evelyn [Waugh] says don't save it, dress better and catch a better man.

Evelyn is always so full of sound common sense. The family have read *Vile Bodies* and I'm not allowed to know him, so right I think . . .'

From Old Mill Cottage, 31st March: 'How can one ever tell with Hamish? I think he is really devoted to me, anyhow as much as he ever was but I don't believe it's in his nature to be passionately in love with anybody . . . Tomorrow we go to London for two months. As a list of those forbidden the house now includes all my best friends I foresee more tiring rows with the family . . . However I am now making £4.4. a week by writing articles and hope I may soon become self-supporting. I regard financial independence as almost the sum of human happiness don't you?'

From 26 Rutland Gate, 11th April: 'Here I am in London again feeling much more cheerful and happy about everything. *The Lady* people have now definitely taken me on at £5.5. a week to write a sort of running commentary of current events, starting with the all England croquet championship at Brighton. They are sending me to everything free, the Opera, the Shakespeare festival at Stratford, etc. I think I shall get lots of fun out of it all don't you.

'So to celebrate this I went out today and bought myself a divine coral tiara—the family think I've gone mad. I do love spending much more than I can afford on *myself* don't you—something quite useless too.

'Hamish is in the country which is sad as I'm not allowed down there . . . Henry [Yorke] says Robert [Byron] will go through London like a flail putting everything to rights again . . .'

17th April: 'Once more you must assume the ungrateful role of confidante for which I can only hope that your reward will be a heavenly crown because I fail to see how any earthly benefit can be your share.

'More to-do's of course need I say in the Hamish affair. Oh Mark, talk about getting to know each other or knowing one's own mind—if I had been married to Hamish for five painful years and borne him six male children I couldn't know him better and the curious thing is that I'm quite certain that I shall never never be so fond of anyone again. All this as I am on the point of losing him for I don't see how he can fail to break off our engagement after what I've done . . .

'I had a perfectly heartbroken letter from Lady Rosslyn [Hamish's mother] . . . saying Hamish is going to the bad as fast as he can, can't you advise me what can be done? So in a white heat I took my pen and said "The bottom of all this is Oxford. Hamish at Oxford doesn't lead one single day of ordinary normal life—these parties which are incessant will ruin him, etc, etc, can't he be taken away now and given some job—if this were done I would give my word not to marry him" and so on . . . However I can't and won't plot with Hamish's parents behind his back so wrote at once and told him all. Mark he'll *never* forgive me if this results in his leaving Oxford . . .

'Then by this evening's post a screed from Hamish saying everybody nags him the whole time and that Farve has written again to Lord Rosslyn complaining we see each other too much. Oh my life is difficult trying to manage Hamish *and* the family. And what will he say when he hears this I can't bear to think of it—and rightly because what business is it of mine to find fault with his character, much more for him to complain of mine really considering our relationship. But if anybody was ever worth a struggle it is Hamish because you know underneath that ghastly exterior of Rosslyn charm etc he is pure gold at least I think so, in fact I'd bank everything on it but what chance has he [with such ineffective parents] . . . Sometimes I think it is too much for me or anybody else. Only I believe that I'm something quite solid in his life, which is the only comforting reflection.'

From Old Mill Cottage, 17th November: 'My life recently has been one huge whirl of gaiety and I've had no time even to think let alone write letters. But next week promises to be quieter and I'll write you my usual five volumes then . . . a ball at Blenheim the other night . . . it was grand fun. I motored from London in an open Rolls in my ball dress, the misery of it. Edward James motored me back in his car which becomes a bed at will . . .'

From 4 Rutland Gate Mews, 10th December: '. . . awful the way everyone treats me as Hamish's nanny isn't it? I believe he's been sent down from Oxford, at least everyone I see tells me so but perhaps it is only a merry joke. Personally I shan't mind if he is, I find Oxford very dull now.

'I've got out of going to Switzerland thank heavens, it is a blessed relief to feel that I've escaped those snow-capped peaks. Like my hairdresser, when I said why do you hate Switzerland,

"Ah les montagnes", was all he could say in a sort of groan. I so agree don't you—I think natural scenery is THE END.'

27th December: 'Hamish and I . . . have had a complete reconciliation, everything is now as merry as a marriage bell. He has left Oxford and is looking for a job, to my relief as I hated his beastly little room there.'

4th February, 1931: 'Hamish's family, behaving with their usual caddery, have taken him away for ever to America. I've broken off the engagement. So there you have the situation in a nutshell.

'I tried to commit suicide by gas, it is a lovely sensation just like taking anaesthetic so I shan't be sorry any more for school-mistresses who are found dead in that way, but just in the middle I thought that Romie [Drury-Lowe] who I was staying with might have a miscarriage which would be disappointing for her so I got back to bed and was sick. Then next day I thought it would be silly because we love each other so much everything will probably be all right in the end . . .

'I've made friends with a sweet and divine old tart called Madame de P.—she rang a young man up the other day at 11 a.m. and said, "What a dull night it's being let's do something." She *is* nice and has lovely parties and adores Hamish who confides in her and then she tells it all to me which is lucky because it is things I like hearing. But I am really very unhappy because there is no one to tell the funny things that happen to one and that is half the fun in life don't you agree . . . I'm in the state in which I can't be alone but the moment I'm with other people I want to get away from them . . . How can I possibly write a funny book in the next six months which my publisher says I *must* do. How *can* I when I've got practically a pain from being miserable and cry in buses quite continually? I'm sorry to inflict this dreary letter on you, as a matter of fact everyone here thinks I don't mind at all—rather a strain but I think the only attitude don't you agree.'

From 34 Great Cumberland Place, 28th February: 'It is too awful for me because Hamish, instead of staying a few months in America as he was to have done is returning next week. It will be ghastly seeing him everywhere. Also I think he'll try and make it up again which I'm determined not to do at present. So everything is very complicated. I had a long letter from him written before he got mine breaking it off, he seems to be enjoying himself . . . *Highland Fling* comes out on the 12th . . .'

From Old Mill Cottage, 15th March: 'Hamish has come back and it is all too frightful, we met at a party and of course it all began over again. Heaven knows what will happen in the end, he seems at present to be busy drinking himself to death saying "my bulwarks (that's me) have gone". We aren't seeing each other at all. I suppose it will have to be the gas oven in the end, one can't bear more than a certain amount of unhappiness.

'The book is doing well I'm glad to say, has had very good notices already . . . Everyone thinks your cover *too* good, a dreadful man said to me, "I must buy your book, it has such an amusing cover." . . . I've just spilt a mass of ink on Muv's favourite carpet and am sitting with my foot on the place hoping she won't notice. She will soon of course. Oh dear.

'They have been simply too odious lately, and had a fearful row the other day ending up by accusing me of drinking. I must say I do go to awful sorts of parties so I'm not surprised they are in a state, but if one can't be happy one must be amused don't you agree. Besides I always have John [Sutro] to chaperone me. I must go and take the dogs for a walk. P.S. The gas story is quite true, it makes Robert [Byron] laugh so much.'

28th March, 1931: 'If I can pass the tests etc I have been engaged to act in a film in Kashmir, leaving London for three months at the end of May . . . I expect I shall be longing to see a human face by then, as my co-actors, the ones I've seen are hardly exciting to say the least of it. But it will take me away from London for three months and that's all I care about—obviously I shall either die of some unsavoury disease or be raped away into Mr A's harem—preferably of course the latter. For this I get £150 the day I sail, 1st class return tickets and a share in the profits if any of the film, besides a good chance of becoming the English Garbo. Anyway material for at least three novels. All this of course depends on whether I can pass the necessary tests which I try for at Elstree after Easter. Oh I do hope I shall.

'I'm through with Hamish for good, he has the grace to appear thoroughly miserable and depressed and sits at parties (I'm told) gazing sadly into space. I meanwhile have settled down into sound spinsterhood. It is sad as we were so completely suited to each other. *Highland Fling* went into a second impression last week and sells a steady 30 a day which I'm told is definitely good for a first novel . . .

'I can't tell you how much I long to go but alas am very doubtful about the tests. I've never done any acting at all you see. It will be quite an exciting part, riding about over rocky passes etc. Diana holds out small hopes of me ever returning alive and I think she may be right. Robert's [Byron's] parting present is to be a small phial of poison for when I'm about to be tortured by enraged Tibetans, and John's [Sutro's] of course, a pot of caviar. The family, which seems odd, don't mind at all and are rather intrigued by the idea, as for me I can hardly sit still for excitement but oh the tests are a fearful snag. It is to be in sound *and* colour and opens with Tibetan music whatever that may be.'

From 105 Gloucester Place, 15th May, 1931: 'I'm having a perfectly divine time, it is certainly more fun not being engaged . . . Also I'm so rich from all my writings that I can have some really divine clothes at last. Hamish is being a very good boy and really looking for a job and seriously intends to work so everything is honey. It drives me nearly insane when he gets these bouts of drinking etc but I really do believe he's settling down at last the angel . . .

'I've just got £30.30. from Harpers for a tiny short story, isn't it heaven. I'm so rich I go 1st class everywhere and take taxis, and even refused £10 a week to write gossip for *The Tatler*. London is heaven just now, the Ritz before lunch is a party where you see everybody you've ever known and there are no deb dances because people are too poor to give them. In fact a perfect season. I'm very comfy here with two rooms and a latch key and meals when I want them for all of which I pay £2.10. a week. The family are safely at Swinbrook and unable in any way to make a nuisance of themselves. In fact I haven't been in such spirits for years. . .'

28th May: 'What a summer! Pouring rain varied only by occasional thunderstorms . . . Meanwhile I have broken all records (for me) by having been up really late every night for three weeks, and here I am now, in bed with a poached egg and a long sleep at least I hope so.

'I was photographed by Cecil Beaton this afternoon, a fantastic experience. "How do you manage to be so skinny with such ruddy cheeks?" Too easy I might have replied, one has only to be crossed in love and adept at make-up . . .

'Dined with Maurice [Bowra] to meet Yeats on Tuesday, it

36

was very interesting. I have made friends with some heavenly Americans at Oxford, they give cocktail parties almost daily at which one drinks champagne in brandy glasses, they are quite divine.'

4th December: 'Hamish has got his job but finds there isn't nearly enough for him to do poor darling which makes him quite miserable as he longs for some real work. He talks of going to Canada after all, I almost hope he will . . . Hamish and I saw a particularly grisly murder by the Adelphi arches which gave us plenty of cocktail conversation, except that Hamish invented and embroidered till no veresimularity was left and now no one believes we saw it at all . . . I had all my hair cut off like a baby's and 100 little curls put in which took two hours and cost a mint, looks deevy.

'My new book is jolly good, all about Hamish at Eton. "All father's sisters married well thank God," is his opening remark. Betjeman is co-hero . . . Well deary bed bed bed. I'm so tired for no reason except this endless climate which is wearing me down. I may have to go to bed for a fortnight because of being too thin, but the children say it's only worms. P.S. The poor old Duke of Connaught (who is obviously dying of cold) made a speech on the wireless extolling the climatic glories of Devon. Every word came with a sneeze, cough or audible shudder as accompaniment.'

From Biddesden House, Andover, 5th January, 1932: 'Everyone here has gone to Bath but I'm still feeling quite moribund after the Chelsea Arts ball last week where I ran about screaming for about six hours with the result that I lost my voice and caught the cold of a lifetime . . . I am wedded to culture ha ha . . . There is an aeroplane looping the loop just outside, too beautiful.'

Another young man proposed to Nancy at this time but in spite of his worldly advantages she preferred the unworldly and capricious Hamish. On 22nd January she told Mark: 'X. laid his gingerbread mansion at my feet last Monday, and incapable as ever of giving a plain answer to a plain question I said I couldn't hear of it anyhow until my book is finished. So now I get letters by every post saying hurry up with the book, it is rather awful. I didn't do it from the usual genuine motive of liking rides in his car etc but believe me from sheer weakness. However, it's all right, I shall wriggle out somehow and anyway the book can't be finished for months. Meanwhile he intends to go into Parliament, little knowing how much I abominate politicians and all their works. But it is awful how easily one could be entrapped into matrimony with someone like that because it *would* be nice to be rich. I'm not surprised girls do that sort of thing. Besides the old boy is really awfully nice and kind in his own way. But think of having blond and stupid children. But then one could be so jolly well dressed and take lovers . . . But it is better to retain one's self-respect in decent poverty isn't it? My life is a bore, I would so much rather be dead . . . Hamish gave me a ring from Cartier which has been a consolation to me in these hard times.

'I don't think it's caddish telling you about X. because of you being so far away and also you don't know him do you or do you? Which makes it all right I think. Besides you know all the details of my cheerless existence.'

From Swinbrook, 19th February, 1932: 'It's *all* right it's all *right*, I've burned my boats so isn't that a relief. At least I never considered it only I was so bored down here and Muv went on at me about it and said you'll die an old maid and I hadn't seen Hamish for months and months so I toyed with the idea for five minutes during which time I suppose I wrote to you.

'But I shall never marry anybody except Hamish really you know and it's just as well because I should be too awful to anyone else. I mean you've no idea how awful I can be if I try. But he would get the being awful in first which would be much better for my character. I've just had three heavenly weeks seeing him every day and every week-end . . . And now I've come home for ten days to recouperate financially and physically because nothing is so expensive or so tiring as going about with the old boy . . .'

From Redesdale Arms, Otterburn, 10th April: 'I am up here in attendance on a very ill grandmother. It is more than depressing in every way . . . However, it gives me a chance to finish my book . . .

'Hamish is in Ireland, in acute money difficulties owing to having wagered £50 on some losing horse, of course £20 of my hard-earned savings have been despatched by wire with promises of more . . . What is rather galling is that he always grumbles at me being so inexpensively dressed and £50 would have been quite a little help when ordering the summer ermine cape from Nurse Furrier . . . However I intend to make him promise never to bet again except in cash as long as he lives don't you agree.

'I had another proposal from X. in great style, orchids, etc, at the Café de Paris with Hamish giggling at the next table and I gave him the final raspberry. He was very cross and said I should be left on the shelf (impertinence) so I went off with Hamish to the Slipspin (new and horrible night club) which made him still crosser. Lousy young man, I don't answer any of his letters now even.

'The book [*Christmas Pudding*] is rather good you know if only I can ever finish it.'

From Castle Grant, Strathspey, 27th May: 'Hamish came last week, he has been so beastly to me over bridge that I really can't bear much more, it seems such a silly and unimportant thing whether one leads a club or a heart but to him it is sufficiently vital to make him forget all the elements of good manners and decency. Really sometimes I could kill him . . . Hamish may get a job in Shell at £600 a year, wouldn't it be lovely. It means three years in India but even so it is a wonderful opening . . . Hamish is really being very sweet, only I am furious with him at the moment if you understand what I mean. He is sulking in his bedroom at present.'

From 31 Tite Street, S.W.3, 20th June: 'Hamish is going to America on the 2nd to seek our fortunes. This is in the well known Mitford wail. I am frightfully unhappy but slightly hopeful at the same time. After all, better that than this awful waiting about in England. Hamish's character is so much improved, we travelled from Scotland in a 3rd class sleeper with two commercial travellers overhead and he never murmured once! He is a sweet angel isn't he? . . . P.S. Poor Muv always says "never write in a letter what you wouldn't like read out in a Court of Law".' On the top of the envelope Nancy had written: 'From the paralyzed wives of noblemen's association,' and at the back, with a sketch of a woman in a wheel chair, 'under royal patronage . . . these poor good old women, too often with nowhere to go . . .'

27th June: 'Hamish is not now going to America . . . Comforting, only he poor duck is disappointed . . . My book has to be finished by the end of August. After that I shall be free to contemplate life on the ocean wave with you. It is a rotten book and needs at least six weeks of very hard work to make it remotely readable . . . Randolph [Churchill] has announced that he intends to install me as his maitresse en titre. Thank you . . . I have just written a piece of my mind to Hamish so I suppose we are having a row. But if I don't lecture him sometimes nobody else will. Oh dear, I wish it was all over one way or the other, it's such a tiring struggle.'

10th July: 'John [Sutro] the angel, is sending Hamish to Munich to learn all about films, it sounds very much the old boy's cup of tea don't you think. So perhaps he'll end up as a film producer of the most opulent type which would be nice.'

From Swinbrook, 11th November: 'I've got a new idea for a book, a sort of half sham memoir called Childhood and Girlhood, pretending I was born about 1870 of rich and noble parents, and with lots of bogus photographs, all of Bobo [Unity] dressed up and called My Mother, My Uncle Charles, Grandpapa, etc. But I have bagged being beautiful Sister Effie who died young and Bobo is so cross she has gone to bed, hence this letter. Life here is hellishly boring.'

When the news of Nancy's marriage in November 1933 to a very different person reached me I was less surprised than if she had married Hamish. Even so it seemed a gamble. Peter, the second son of the highly cultivated ambassador, Lord Rennell, was a young man of boundless promise, and one could visualize him as a future cabinet minister, a law lord, or a prominent editor. He had abundant qualifications for success in any profession he deigned to choose. So far he had chosen none. His intellectual range and his knowledge of languages had been impressive as an undergraduate at Balliol. With his devil-may-care manner and handsome features, the more handsome by contrast with a bohemian unkemptness, he had an alluring panache, and his self-assurance was superficially convincing.

Nancy craved adventure and Peter invested his slightest activities with an aura of risk. His background was cosmopolitan-romantic. His father, Sir Rennell Rodd, later Lord Rennell, had been so popular as ambassador in Rome during the First World War that he had been presented with a fine property near Naples by the Italian government. While at Oxford, where he had been a friend of Oscar Wilde, he had also won the Newdigate Prize, and in 1882 Wilde wrote an 'envoi' to Rodd's book of poems

Rose Leaf and Apple Leaf, for which he had suggested the title.*
Having arranged for its publication, Wilde had brazenly inserted
a dedication to himself as 'heart's brother' which embarrassed
Rennell Rodd at the time, and even more during his diplomatic
career. Peter was said to have hunted for rare copies of this
volume and sold them profitably to his parent. This was quite in
character, for Peter was the model for Evelyn Waugh's Basil Seal.

I never encountered Nancy and Peter together but I imagine
they provided plenty of amusement for each other during the
early years of their marriage. That Nancy had fallen in love with
Peter more seriously than with Hamish, who seems to have
prolonged her adolescence, is apparent from her letters to Mark
Ogilvie-Grant. On 14th August, 1933, she wrote: 'Oh goodness
gracious I am happy. You *must* get married darling, everybody
should this minute if they want a recipe for absolute bliss. Of
course I know there aren't many Peters going about but still I
s'pose everybody has its Peter (if only Watson). So find yours
dear the sooner the better. And remember true love can't be
bought. If I really thought it could I'd willingly send you £3
tomorrow. What I want to know is why nobody told me about
Peter before—I mean if I'd known I'd have gone off to Berlin
after him or anywhere else. However, I've got him now which
is the chief thing . . . We are going to be married early in
October and then live at Strand on the Green . . . We're going
to be damned poor you see.' And later: 'I have no news, the
happiness is unabated at present and shows no immediate signs
of abating either . . . I don't expect we shall be married much
before November which gives you plenty of time to save up for
a deevy presey . . . We think of living in a house called Glencoe
at Chiswick.'

Of her honeymoon in Rome where the Rennells had a house
on Via Giulia, Nancy wrote to her sister Unity, 8th December,
1933: 'Why do people say they don't enjoy honeymoons? I am
adoring mine.' A week later, however, she was writing to Mark,
on a postcard of the garish Victor Emmanuel monument: 'This
of course is *much* the prettiest thing in Rome. I go and look at it
every day. I am having a really dreadful time, dragging a badly
sprained ankle round major and minor basilicas and suffering
hideous indigestion from eating goats' cheese. However, I
manage to keep up my spirits somehow.'

*See *The Letters of Oscar Wilde,* edited by Rupert Hart-Davis. New York:
Harcourt, 1962.

Back in England, she wrote from Rose Cottage, Strand on the Green, Chiswick: 'I am awfully busy learning to be a rather wonderful old housewife. My marriage, contracted to the amazement of all so late in life, is providing me with a variety of interests, new but not distasteful, and besides, a feeling of shelter and security hitherto untasted by me. Why not follow my example and find some nonagenarian bride to skip to the altar with. Remember 'tis better to be an old girl's sweetheart than a young girl's slave . . .'

If ever Nancy woke up to the fact that Peter could become a bore, she was far too loyal to admit it. Yet she must have had Peter in mind when she described a first-class bore as one who 'had a habit of choosing a subject, and then droning round and round it like an inaccurate bomb-aimer round his target, unable to hit: he knew vast quantities of utterly dreary facts, of which he did not hesitate to inform his companions, at great length and in great detail, whether they appeared to be interested or not.'

Peter was a compulsive lecturer who enjoyed bombarding one with a miscellaneous jumble of facts: he belonged to the tribe of doctrinaires and he was seldom, as Evelyn Waugh expressed it, 'disinclined to be instructive'. While he was beaming with youth and enthusiasm these monologues about the Senussi and the Tuaregs and the locality of Atlantis might dazzle and amaze one, but one surmised that Nancy might be surfeited with such volleys of abstruse information. During the war I suspected that many were inventions, as if to prove that he knew more than the rest of us. He sounded plausible: a very superior con man.

When I returned to England from China with dire forebodings in the summer of 1939 I heard much of Peter's activities in Perpignan among the refugees from the Spanish Civil War. Nancy had joined him there in May, and Chapter XV of *The Pursuit of Love* is based on her experiences at this time. Christian is a thinly disguised version of Peter: 'He did not ask how she was or whether she had had a good journey—Christian always assumed that people were all right unless they told him to the contrary, when, except in the case of destitute, coloured, oppressed, leprous, or otherwise unattractive strangers he would take absolutely no notice. He was really only interested in mass wretchedness, and never much cared for individual cases, however genuine their misery, while the idea that it is possible to have three square meals a day and a roof and yet be unhappy or unwell, seemed to him intolerable nonsense.'

Peter was as much in his element at Perpignan as Basil Seal at the Ministry of Modernization in Azania. He was too concerned with the problems of refugees to pay much attention to Nancy, who for all her kindness of heart was absurdly miscast in the role of social worker. Like Linda in the novel she 'went to the camps every day, and they filled her soul with despair. As she could not help very much in the office owing to her lack of Spanish, nor with the children, since she knew nothing about calories, she was employed as a driver, and was always on the road in a Ford van full of supplies, or of refugees, or just taking messages to and from the camps. Often she had to sit and wait for hours on end while a certain man was found and his case dealt with . . . the sight of these thousands of human beings, young and healthy, herded behind wire away from their womenfolk, with nothing on earth to do day after dismal day, was a recurring torture to Linda. She began to think that Uncle Matthew had been right—that abroad, where such things could happen, was indeed unutterably bloody, and that foreigners, who could inflict them upon each other, must be fiends.'

From Perpignan Nancy wrote to her mother (16th May, 1939): 'I never saw anybody work the way these people do [Peter and his associates], I haven't had a single word with Peter although I've been here two days. They are getting a boat off to Mexico next week with 600 families on board and you can suppose this is a job, reuniting these families.

'The men are in camps, the women are living in a sort of gymnasium in the town, and the children scattered all over France. Peter said yesterday one woman was really too greedy, she already has four children and she wants three more. I thought of you! These people will all meet on the quayside for the first time since the retreat. Peter sees to everything . . . I believe he will be here for life, refugees are still pouring out of Spain where it seems the situation is impossible for ex-Government supporters and their families. Over 100 a day come out.

'There is the original General Murgatroyd here, oh goodness he is funny. He has been sent by the Government to help with the embarkation, speaks no French or Spanish but bursts into fluent Hindustani at the sight of a foreigner and wastes poor Peter's time in every possible way. All the same he is a nice old fellow and very pro-refugee. Indeed no one who sees them could fail to be that, they are simply so wonderful. I haven't yet been to one of the awful camps, just the women's one in the town and to a hostel which Peter started at Narbonne, where people who are got out of camps can be cleaned up and rested before they go off to their destination. There are about 70 there and it is very nice indeed, with a garden which they have planted with vegetables. It is run by an English girl entirely on her own there, most of the present occupants are going in this ship to Mexico.

'Peter has two helpers, one called Donald Darling is a young man who owned a travel agency in Barcelona and is now of course ruined. He only thinks of the refugees although his own future is in as much of a mess as theirs. The other is Humphrey Hare, a writer who lives in the South of France, came over to see the camps and stayed on. They both, like Pete, work 14 hours a day for no pay and all three look absolutely done up. It is a most curious situation, apparently the préfet here said, "supposing there were refugee camps for Norwegians in England and three young Frenchmen went over and began telling the English how they should be run"—Actually however they have got the French quite fairly docile I can't imagine how . . . "

And on 25th May Nancy continued: 'If you could have a look, as I have, at some of the less agreeable results of fascism in a country I think you would be less anxious for the swastika to become a flag on which the sun never sets. And, whatever may be the *good* produced by that régime, that the first result is always a horde of unhappy refugees cannot be denied. Personally I would join hands with the devil himself to stop any further extension of the disease. As for encirclement, if a person goes mad he is encircled, *not out of any hatred for the person*, but for the safety of his neighbours, and the same applies to countries. Furthermore, I consider that if the Russian alliance does not go through we shall be at war in a fortnight, and as I have a husband of fighting age I am not particularly anxious for that eventuality. You began the argument so don't be cross if I say what I think!

'Well, we got our ship off. There was a fearful hurricane and she couldn't get into Port Vendres, so all the arrangements had to be altered and she was sent to Sète (150 miles from Port

Vendres) and at three hours' notice special trains had to be changed, etc, etc, the result was Peter was up for two whole nights, never went to bed at all. However he is none the worse. I was up all yesterday night as the embarkation went on until 6 a.m. and the people on the quay had to be fed and the babies given their bottles. There were 200 babies under two and 12 women are to have babies on board. One poor shell-shocked man went mad and had to be given an anaesthetic and taken off, but apart from that all went smoothly if slowly. The women were on the quayside first and then the men arrived. None of them had seen each other since the retreat and I believe thought really that they wouldn't find each other then, and when they did you never saw such scenes of hugging. The boat sailed at twelve yesterday, the pathetic little band on board played first God Save the King, for us, then the Marseillaise and the Spanish National Anthem. Then the poor things gave three Vivas for España which they will never see again. I don't think there was a single person not crying—I have never cried so much in my life. They had all learnt to say Goodbye and thank you, and they crowded round us so that we could hardly get off the ship. Many of them are great friends of Peter, and I know a lot of them too by now as some have been working in our office, and it was really sad to see them go—to what? If all Mexicans are as great horrors as the delegate here, they will have a thin time I am afraid. Franco's radio has announced that the ship will not be allowed to reach her destination and we all feel anxious until she has safely left Madeira.

'And now there still remain over 300,000 poor things to be dealt with, 500,000 counting the women, and more arriving all the time. The Red Cross are not much help, they issue shorts which Spaniards abominate, having a sense of dignity, and refuse to help with special diet for the many cases of colitis in the camps . . . I expect I shall come home soon as we can't really afford for me to be here and keep [the house in] Blomfield Road going.'

Mr. Donald Darling, who appears as 'Robert Parker' in *The Pursuit of Love*, has kindly corroborated that 'Linda's' experiences at Perpignan were those of Nancy at the time. 'When she arrived,' he told me, 'there was not much she could do apart from chauffeuring and odd jobs. However, she cheered me up immensely by her humour and off-beat manner of describing people and events. I remember she used to wear a sort of Chinese hat, of straw and conical, which looked odd but was practical. One day she announced that Unity too, might arrive to help and this caused havoc among the Quakers and leftish do-gooders who had collected in that part of France. But Unity thought better of it and the scare was over . . . Nancy carried out many acts of kindness to individuals, which I saw myself. She also made some funny remarks about "how to be a refugee —wear a false rubber arm to take all the injections people will give you and carry a life-like baby doll in your arms", etc . . .

'Nancy was a great help to us in getting off the boatload of refugees . . . There were a lot of expectant mothers and also a cadre of Communists who had a portable printing press, with which to bore their fellow passengers during the journey. The ship was due to leave from Port Vendres but a few hours before sailing time the wretched wind came up and made it impossible for her to dock there. We had to transfer all the passengers, the expectant mothers and the Communist printing press to Sète by road, quite a long distance. Nancy drove loads of mothers, slowly round the curves of the Corniche near Port Vendres, and got one load safely there . . . I always found Nancy the "soul of kindness" and conscious of the troubles of others . . .

'I should have mentioned the WIND, which is the curse of Perpignan, all the time, and which Nancy and I once decided we could stand no longer. We set out on a Sunday to get up into the Pyrenees, whence it came, and discovered a valley where there was hardly a breeze. Fleeing from the wind became important to us, in that it raised the dust and almost took off the roof of our makeshift office in the Avenue de la Gare and also put out the gas jet in the water heater. I remember one night going with Nancy and Prod* to a café in Port Vendres which had dancing outside. But the wind was so strong that the music could not be heard on the floor and only behind the building. I also recall they played a recording of "Violette" eternally and we became almost hysterical over it. We eventually left . . .

'Prod at Perpignan was very practical though his language and approach to French dignitaries horrified some of the Quakers and the Duchess of Atholl in particular. I remember one Sunday at Colliours when Prod, who had been carousing until the dawn, appeared at breakfast with a draft of a rude letter to

* Nancy's nickname for P. Rodd.

46

the local Prefect, which he had just written. He then dived into the sea and went for a long swim.'

In whatever lurid or quixotic light Peter appeared to others Nancy was determined to see him as a hero. Reverting to her obsessive Captain Scott of the Antarctic in a letter to James Lees-Milne who knew Lady Kennet, Scott's widow, Nancy wrote to him (5th March, 1942): 'I think she is hard on Cherry [Cherry Garrard, who wrote *The Worst Journey in the World*, a moving account of Scott's expedition], it's not likely he could have lived nine months in such close proximity with the owner [of The Hut] and never spoken to him. Besides Dr. Bill [Wilson] chose him for that winter journey and spoke very well of his behaviour. And I don't think Cherry pretended to know Scott at all well. Perhaps she feels bitter he didn't go on and find them and perhaps a real hero (her Peter or my Peter) would have done so and now I come to think of it of course they would. Well I die to meet her. Personally I am glad to be a decadent as they get far the most fun out of life but I like to study and admire the others so long as they are real and not just low brow toughs. My Peter is the same up to a point but he would never do a thing without knowing exactly why and he has a great instinct for self-preservation. Also he minds discomfort so little that he has no need to arm himself against it.

'The Duke of Aosta was almost exactly like Scott—slept always on the floor without a mattress and if he cut himself would scrub it with a nailbrush and ammonia to teach himself to endure pain.'

Having admired Peter's handling of the Spanish refugees at Perpignan, Nancy half-humorously regarded herself as a hedonist in comparison. Her heroes had to have brains as well as guts. Those of us who were less familiar with Peter thought him irresponsible: his pendulum might swing in unforeseen directions. In politics he and Nancy considered themselves Socialists.

CHAPTER FOUR

A
s soon as the Second World War broke out Peter
dashed off to do his bit and Nancy found herself alone
in 12 Blomfield Road, W.9, whose patch of garden was
her greatest solace. 'Peter looks very pretty in his uniform
and is spoiling to be off but doesn't even leave London for
another week,' she wrote on 9th October, 1939. Early in
September: 'I am driving an ARP car every night from 8–8.
So far have only had one go of it and feel more or less OK
(it is mostly waiting about of course). Soon I hope they will
have more drivers. There is only one other woman and she
and the men in my lot (about 30) have had no sleep for four
nights, and have to work in the day, they are all in and all
going on again tonight.

'When I went to fetch my car from the garage which is
lending it I immediately and in full view of the owners crashed
into another car, wasn't it awful. It is a large Ford. However,
I have it under control now but driving in the dark is too
devilish. All the other people are charming, they think I'm
rather a joke, so obviously incompetent. I have signed on for
a year . . .'

Before Christmas 1939 she had finished writing *Pigeon Pie*,
an ingenious fantasy of the phoney war period. To Mark
Ogilvie-Grant she described it (13th November, 1939): 'Must
tell you how the book is developing. Well you are called Mr.
Ivor King the King of Song and your wigless head horribly
battered is found on the Pagoda (headless wig, favourite, on
Green) so you are presumed dead and there is a Catholic,
because you are one, memorial service at which Yvonne appears
as a French widow. Well as you were about to open a great

48

3. Nancy in 1931

4. Nancy in 1933

world campaign of Song Propaganda for the BBC sabotage is suspected—UNTIL

your dreadful old voice is heard in Germany doing anti-British propaganda and singing songs like

"Land of Dope you're Gory".

Well both the English speaking and Catholic worlds are appalled and your wife the Papal Duchess, the only woman to be buried inside the Vatican grounds is quickly dug up and removed to the Via della Propaganda. Pope diplomatically explains this by saying that owing to petrol shortage some of the younger Cardinals are learning to bicycle and, unseemly for them, to continually fall over the Papal Duchess's grave.

'Well of course in the end you have been a gallant old spy all along and you are made an English Bart and Papal Duke and covered with praise from all . . . Think up some wonderful old songs for me.'

Peter might have suggested the plot, and we glimpse him in the role of Rudolph Jocelyn who 'had a shock of tow-coloured hair, spoke indistinctly, dressed badly, and was always in a great hurry'. The songster of Kew Green was, as I have said, suggested by Mark Ogilvie-Grant, who had a charming house there. Nancy herself 'had a happy character and was amused by life; if she was slightly disillusioned she was by no means unhappy in her marriage'. The First Aid Post and many of the details are realistic, and she aired her prejudices as in her later novels—against the wireless for instance. 'When she turned it on, she thought of the women all over England in lonely little houses with their husbands gone to the war, sick with anxiety for the future. She saw them putting their children to bed, their hearts broken by the loneliness of the evening hours, and then, for company, turning on the wireless. What is the inspiration which flows to them from this, the fountainhead, as it must seem to them, of the Empire? London, with all its resources of genius, talent, wit, how does London help them through these difficult times? How are they made to feel that England is not only worth dying for but being poor for, being lonely and unhappy for? With great music, stirring words and sound common sense? With the glorious literature nobly spoken, of our ancestors? Not at all. With facetiousness and Jazz.' Otherwise the tone of *Pigeon Pie* is jubilant, and it should have been popular for its entertainment value when it was published on 6th May, 1940, but as Nancy stated in the second edition of 1952, 'it was an early and unimportant casualty of the real war which was then beginning.' Perhaps the reading public was indifferent to such light fiction with Bellona in the background. Nancy bore her disappointment with smiling fatalism.

After her experience as an ARP driver she was working 'five hours a day but not on end, with evacuees—most of them are going to Canada soon—they need more settlers overseas and some will probably stay and the others come back very tough and healthy. I'm all for it.' (Did Evelyn Waugh also borrow some of the characteristics of Nancy's refugees for *Put out more Flags*?) Peter was still near London: 'his regiment was in the end much less cut up than at first feared—about half lost at Boulogne and less than half in Flanders, where they were holding the rear guard all the time and did magnificently. The casualties in Flanders seem to have been amazingly small—the soldiers who are here never lost a man all through and keep saying what *fun* it all was.'

On 12th September, 1940, she wrote her mother from Blomfield Road: 'We are catching it here all right as they are gunning for Paddington. On Tuesday Pete appeared with two babies of one of his soldiers (5 and 3) who had been blown up in Brixton and whose mother is dying of a miscarriage. We put them to bed in the kitchen—at 2 p.m. the house next door got an incendiary and caught fire so I (in my night dress) put the children into an eiderdown, got a taxi and put them to bed at Zella's [her former governess]. Came back here, having been nearly blown out of the cab when Fitzjohns Avenue went, and shot at by the home guard on the way for not stopping. Then we had a rare pasting here—five houses in Portsdown Road just vanished into smoke, two bombs in Warwick Avenue, one in Blomfield and three in the Harrow Road. Next morning at 9 I got a very sporting taximan who took the babies, Gladys [her maid], Milly [her pug], my fur coat and all my linen to Diana Worthington. I have gone to live with Zella for the present as I can't very well be here quite alone at night. I don't at all advise you to come to London, it is not very agreeable I assure you.'

On 30th September she wrote: 'The nights are noisier than ever but I should say fewer bombs—two more of my best friends have lost their houses . . . It is obviously only a matter of time before we all do. Peter spent a night at Blomfield and had an incendiary, if he hadn't been there to put it out that would have gone.'

Buoyantly Nancy returned to Blomfield Road with her stalwart maid Gladys and Milly the pug. Her little garden where she grew vegetables and kept hens, remained a pleasant diversion. 'Words long forgotten like creosote and bran mash are never off my tongue,' she wrote, 'not to speak of droppings board and nest box.' She took her gardening seriously and fed her old hens punctually. Gladys was compulsively addicted to the wireless and even listened to the news in Norwegian.

Nancy's war work was interrupted by a difficult and delicate uterine operation in the University College Hospital which she could ill afford at the time. Characteristically she made light of it in a letter to James Lees-Milne (24th November, 1941): 'I am not quite so wonderfully well as I was, running a little temperature. I suppose I am full of sponges and things like all the jokes about operations . . . I am reading *Mémoires d'Outre Tombe* and was madly enjoying it until a French person came to see me and said "Chateaubriand—assommant", after which I began to wonder if it was. But it isn't you know, actually, at all!'

*

A fresh chapter of Nancy's life opened in March 1942 when she began to work for modest wages—but every penny counted—in Heywood Hill's remarkable bookshop in Curzon Street. Nancy had always cherished books and there was a growing hunger for them during the war, when paper became scarce and there were few intellectual distractions. Heywood Hill's was a shop with a relaxed individual flavour. Besides recent publications, rare first editions and old folios with handsome bindings, Heywood specialized in pretty early Victorian toys and automata, embroidered pictures and unusual prints, almanacs and children's books of the Kate Greenaway period in mint condition. He had a flair for the decorative Victoriana which Robert Byron and I had collected at Oxford. The shop was graced by attractive feminine assistants, including his wife Lady Anne (until she expected a baby) and, for a short while, the languidly lovely Lady Bridget Parsons, who made

51

customers shift for themselves (she told the King of Greece to climb a ladder to find a book on the top shelf) and Mrs. Frieze-Greene who was to marry Handasyde Buchanan, Heywood's future partner. Heywood himself was called up for military service later in the year.

Evelyn Waugh described the shop at this time as 'a centre for all that was left of fashionable and intellectual London". Nancy infused the atmosphere with impromptu comedy. All agree that she was delightful to work with: 'she never let one down.' She memorized the names of publishers and recent books and quoted the comments of prominent reviewers, and during the darkest years of the war her gaiety was contagious. A former shop assistant of Heywood Hill's wrote to him after Nancy's death: 'Mrs. Rodd was such a lively person and didn't deserve to suffer as she did. During the war she asked what I would do when my age group was called. I said I thought I would be a "Clippie" on a bus. Some weeks later a twangy pure cockney voice bawled through the shop "ALL FARES PLEASE—PASS ALONG THERE". Mrs. Buchanan and myself were in fits of laughter at her. There was never a dull moment. She was so gay.' A peculiar shop idiom was evolved: 'a couch' signified a pile of books on the floor waiting to be picked up by someone or put on the tables or in shelves, and 'to couch' meant to add things to piles and forget about them. 'Govs' usually referred to Americans, since they could be 'rather like governesses'. Little did the casual customer suspect that he might be a target of mockery.

When Nancy was bored a glassy stare confronted the offender and her manner became frosty or vague. Publishers' travellers and customers who appeared to be quick on the uptake were welcomed with radiant smiles and 'dull ones had hell'. While she attracted many new customers she frightened some of the older ones away. One who was waiting to be served while Nancy was absorbed in a long telephone talk, remarked testily: 'A little less "darling" and a little more attention please!'

Many used the pretext of seeking a book for the pleasure of seeing Nancy. A brief chat with her would brighten the rest of the day for them. Among the habitués were Evelyn Waugh, Lord Berners, Sir Osbert Sitwell and Raymond Mortimer, and the very books seemed to join in the laughter during their exchange of gossip. Nancy's laughter rose above theirs in a carillon that was almost operatic, a specimen of coloratura. This must have reached the ears of the gallant Free French who began to frequent the shop, beguiled by Nancy and Mollie, the Merry Wives of Curzon Street. At that time Nancy's French was of the *est-ce-que* variety with an unmistakably English pronunciation and just as we enjoy English spoken with a French accent, the French are titillated by the sound of their language with a languid English drawl. The effervescence of the Free French suited her temperament. At last she could dance with partners whose chatter amused her. P——, the most distinguished and high-spirited of these, was always spoken of as 'the Colonel', the faithful right-hand man of General de Gaulle. Then and there he conquered her heart and her imagination. He was to exert an immense influence on her future, and in the meantime he heightened her zest for life.

Nancy's amiability with the French differed from her cavalier treatment of the American soldiers who ambled in from their hostel next door. To them the shop was known as 'The Ministry of Fear'.

Whatever the weather or state of emergency Nancy's punctuality was exemplary. Nearly always she walked to and from the shop, many miles from her dwelling in Blomfield Road, regardless of blackouts, air raids and encounters with drunken soldiers. She walked briskly, for the sake of the exercise *faute de mieux*, even after a tiring day's work or a night's rest broken by air raids. Taxis were sporadic luxuries, and Lady Anne Hill remembers waiting with her for hours in pouring rain while at least sixteen packed buses rumbled tantalizingly down Park Lane. During week-days they would lunch at a neighbouring canteen or at a British Restaurant where a vile three-course meal cost one shilling and ninepence. Perhaps Nancy was reminded of the seal flesh and pemmican which were the staple diet of her heroes in the Antarctic.

Fortunately she could often spend her Saturdays to Mondays at Faringdon with Lord Berners, a composer, painter and writer of whimsical originality who was also an epicure. In spite of the prevalent austerities he managed to conjure succulent meals for his guests. His sense of humour was akin to Nancy's and they shared many an extravagant joke. He had a special talent for parody and pastiche: one recalls his 'Red Roses and Red Noses'. Nancy was to introduce him as 'Lord Merlin' into *The Pursuit of Love* and I suspect she regarded him as her mentor, consulting him about her writings. His influence counterbalanced that of Evelyn Waugh. He made startling remarks in a quiet matter-of-fact tone, and this tone pervades his fanciful novels. His witty *Valses Bourgeoises* should be revived in piano concerts; it would be more difficult to revive the Berners-Diaghilev ballet of 1926, *The Triumph of Neptune*. The epitaph he composed for himself ran:

> Here lies Lord Berners,
> One of the learners.
> His great love of learning
> May earn him a burning
> But, praise to the Lord,
> He seldom was bored.

Likewise Nancy seldom was bored—except when she had to add up accounts in the shop. Lady Anne Hill remembers that 'she used to look quite ill and peaked from the boredom of this'. When she felt overwhelmed she would delegate the chore to her mother who, she maintained, enjoyed the meticulous process of addition.

Fire-watching was another duty she failed to relish for it entailed spending part of the night in a camp-bed at Crewe House. On these occasions she would don old trousers and a tin hat, and sally forth into the blackout armed with a stirrup pump. Once she and Mollie extinguished some fire bombs in Hill Street off Berkeley Square, Nancy carrying the pump and Mollie two buckets of water, laughing all the way. 'She *made* my war,' said Mrs. Buchanan. When the flying bombs descended Nancy would plead in her cooing voice: 'Come and look at the V.1s. They are so pretty. Do admit.' Survivors staggering out of the rubble they left behind them were less prone to admire their prettiness. But when her grocer was bombed out of his house she invited him to hers with his wife and children and they stayed for several days. 'He was not an attractive or interesting grocer,' added a friend who was one of his customers.

To her mother she wrote (26th February, 1944): 'You never saw anything like the burning. I pack a suitcase every night and always dress which I *never* did before, but the raids are very short, exactly one hour, so that's no great hardship only chilly. Also we have a very good fire party here so I have great hopes that we could get anything under control.' And later in July: 'Nobody minds the bombs any more (I never did) but they are doing a fearful amount of damage to houses. One going over here knocked panes of glass out of my neighbours' top window simply from the vibration of the engine, which is unbelievable unless you have heard the thing . . . But how can the Germans be so stupid as to get everybody into a temper now, just as they must see they have lost, it is really too idiotic of them and seriously I think minimizes the chance of a decent peace . . . I do dread losing the house because oh *where* would one live?'

When so many mooched about with long faces Nancy's resolute cheerfulness was a tonic. Hers was a peculiarly English type of beauty and it did not belong entirely to this age. Her clear smooth skin and clear quizzical eyes under a high forehead with chestnut hair like a wavy turban above it would have been portrayed to perfection by Sir Joshua Reynolds. She appeared much younger than her age and her humour had the gaiety of girlhood. In spite of her intellectual bent she could not be described as an intellectual, nor could she be described as sensual or worldly. She had natural good taste, not only in the clothes she wore. In those days she could not afford to indulge her love of elegance yet in the neat black velvet jacket and black wool skirt she usually wore in the shop she looked better dressed than many a more prosperous friend: her husband contributed nothing to her few amenities, if he ever wasted a thought on them.

In March 1944 Peter was 'living near the ruin of our villa (the Rennell villa near Naples) and using our servants and burning my ma-in-law's frightful furniture for firewood, isn't it strange. He goes to the beach head every day—says it is hell on earth.' He was back in London before Easter. 'Peter is to and fro and one never knows which until he appears and he doesn't know from one minute to the next. I think he is getting a very important job and he goes on being a colonel, which people generally don't when they come home and which makes a huge difference in money.' No huge difference to Nancy, however. Usually he was to be found at the Savile Club, and he would ask me not to tell Nancy that he was in London. Soon after finishing *The Pursuit of Love* in May 1945, Nancy informed her mother: 'Peter has rushed off to Transport House to see about a constituency, egged on by me, as candidates get 90 coupons. I fear it will be no good though, married to a Mitford!'

Although she felt 'a pudding of tiredness' she hoped to go to Paris in August. As a result of this fatigue she wrote from Heywood Hill's: 'What *do* you think I did? I decided not to come here Saturday morning as I was really tired, and forgot to lock the door on Friday so the shop was full of wandering people trying to buy books from each other. Wasn't it a nightmare? By the mercy of Providence Heywood was passing through London and happened to look in. He wasn't best pleased and I don't blame him. The fact is I'm too tired but it's no excuse for such dottiness.' In the meantime Peter was 'skipping about canvassing for Mason Macfarlane. Isn't it typical, the Christian names of our candidates are Mason, Brendan, Clifford and Wegg. Why aren't politicians ever called Tom, Dick or Harry?'

Despite her feminine volubility, Nancy was too proud to speak of her troubles, yet they were only too real. It was far from pleasant to think of her sister Diana (Lady Mosley) in prison, and of another sister Unity still suffering from the trauma of near suicide, her mind confused by divided loyalties. And when Diana was released from captivity Nancy had to cope with a siege of inquisitive journalists. The shop rang continually with their telephone calls which she and Mollie took turns to answer. Fortunately the beautiful Diana had an overflowing share of the Mitford *esprit de corps*. As her husband relates in his autobiography:* 'After telling me one day about the treatment of the women in the early days by one or two old harpies in a company of wardresses . . . she remarked that she yet felt she had an advantage over them: "It was still lovely to wake up in the morning and feel one was lovely *one*"—it went straight into one of Nancy Mitford's books.' The sisters were reunited with screams of delight. But the death of their brave and handsome brother Tom, who was killed in Burma, was a deep and lasting sorrow, though Nancy tried to console herself with the thought that he had thoroughly enjoyed his

*Sir Oswald Mosley: *My Life*. London: Nelson, 1968.

life. All his friends had basked in the radiance of his intensely musical personality.

Peter's escapades had become painfully embarrassing. He spent whatever money they scraped together (or rather what Nancy scraped) and he was notoriously unfaithful. After one of his nocturnal rackets he would peal the bell of their little house in Blomfield Road at 5 a.m. in a state of maudlin intoxication and undress, without money to defray an exorbitant taxi fare. Nancy either kept such incidents to herself or laughed them off. She was far too reserved to admit her essential loneliness with Peter. She could forget it in Heywood Hill's shop which had become a rallying point of her friends in uniform or mufti who happened to be in London. And in the meantime the Free French had fired her imagination with a growing love of France. I suspect she was already looking forward to pastures new when she embarked on her semi-autobiographical novel, *The Pursuit of Love*. This begins in the bosom of her family and ends with a glowing Parisian romance. Fabrice, duc de Sauveterre, is an embodiment of the gallant Free Frenchman who had captivated her mind and coloured her future outlook. Fabrice, the hero of the Resistance, was caught by the Gestapo and shot but Nancy revived him in her future novels and historical biographies. She remained on friendly terms with Peter Rodd, but her annoyance was noticeable on the rare occasions he invaded the bookshop.

That Peter could show a chivalrous side to other women has been confirmed by a lady who had a happy affair with him. According to her, he could be passionately romantic, even poetical, and he wrote the most beautiful love-letters. She still remembers him with tenderness. Unfortunately his attitude to Nancy was one of cynical and selfish exploitation, or so it seemed to her friends. In his case the jokes which Nancy so keenly enjoyed with others went too far. Probably he was a natural philanderer who could not endure the marriage tie. Though Nancy had longed for children she never complained of 'Prod'. But she had given up any pretence of enthusiasm for his eccentricities, which had left no warm after-glow.

On 22nd July, 1945 she wrote to Heywood Hill: 'I have been given £5,000 to start a business with, would you like to have me as a partner. I can't work full time any more . . . I want to concentrate on the import and export side which I shall know more about when I have been to Paris . . . I have a personal letter from Oliver Lyttelton imploring me to trade in books, and another from the F.O. recommending me for an exit permit . . .'

To me, still seconded to S.H.A.E.F. in Paris, she wrote breathlessly: 'I am planning to put some money into the shop and be a partner and my dream is to be fixed up with some Paris shop and do delicious swops so that I can be the purveyor of high brow frog books here and vice versa. Anyhow I can find all that out when I arrive—meanwhile I am planning to enjoy myself and to become deliciously baked (it is snowing here, need I say) . . . There is a new man in the shop, a pro:, taking my place as after this week I am only going part time. He thinks I am perfectly raving mad and keeps saying under his breath "This is a *most* extraordinary establishment". His favourite writer (because a best seller, I don't think he reads) is Mazo de la Roche and he wants to order hundreds of his (her?) forthcoming book and fill the window with it. I have gone quietly, so to speak, into the Maquis and am using underground methods of sabotage with complete success.

'Tomorrow the Rothermere party for the election. We are asked from 12.30–3.30, fork luncheon. Evelyn [Waugh] says, "I intend to arrive at 12.30 and stay to 3.30 using my fork all the time." It is rumoured there are to be 150 people and only 6 lobsters so one must hope for a miracle.

'I'll tell you as soon as I know when I arrive—don't know where I shall stay . . . Oh! I am excited like a child.'

On 4th August she wrote again: 'Advised upon all sides I have settled now to go in September, it seems more sensible, and P. writes that he may be in America if I go in August which would be a pity as I shall need all the support I can have. I do hope you won't have gone for good by then it would be disappointing . . . Our new young man is a menace . . . I struggle away, you can imagine! but dread to think what the shop will be like in my absence. The thing is he is awfully NICE and one doesn't want to wound him in any way.

'I've been correcting my proofs, always enjoyable I think— it reads better than I had expected really.'

Those were the proofs of *The Pursuit of Love*, which was to enjoy a success surpassing Nancy's wildest expectations.

The slim blue volume of 195 closely printed pages on poor paper 'in conformity with the authorized economy standards' was published later in the year at what might correctly be called the psychological moment. The general climate was one of war weariness and disillusion after the elation of victory. Churchill's government had fallen to a Socialist majority under Mr. Attlee. The verdict of the General Election had forced our colossus to tender his resignation, and the verdict was shocking for its base ingratitude. Amid the ensuing gloom, with mediocrity vengeful and triumphant, *The Pursuit of Love* was like a gloom dispersing rocket. Evelyn Waugh's *Brideshead Revisited* had paved the way for it and Nancy submitted the manuscript to his scrutiny before sending it to Hamish Hamilton, her enterprising publisher.

A master of the craft of fiction as well as a staunch friend, Evelyn offered several suggestions including the title, for which Nancy always gave him credit. But the feline humour and lightness of touch were entirely Nancy's, and the style is more finished than in her previous novels. There are hints of Evelyn in the 'entrenching tool, with which, in 1915, Uncle Matthew had whacked to death eight Germans one by one as they crawled out of a dug-out', but I cannot detect 'the inspired silliness of Ronald Firbank' which L. P. Hartley noted. Though free from intellectual pretension it will be consulted by historians as an authentic record of a phase of English civilization and of country-house society when more consciously sociological novels will be mouldering in dusty shelves. The characters may be caricatures but they have the vitality of a Rowlandson at his best. The sheer fun of existence at Alconleigh sets the pace. Uncle Matthew and all the Radletts are drawn with the assurance of intimate knowledge. Unwittingly she started a hare that is still running, to judge by recent letters in *The Spectator*. Uncle Matthew's pronouncements on correct English usage had the honour of being quoted by Professor Alan Ross of Birmingham University in an article on 'Upper Class English Usage' which was printed in a learned Finnish journal, the *Bulletin of the Neo-philological Society of Helsinki* (1954). This had a hilarious sequel which was solemnly swallowed by those who accused Nancy of snobbishness. In fact she was teasing the snobs but she kept a poker face while doing so. But I must not anticipate. The sequel, inspired by Professor Ross, appeared ten years after *The Pursuit of Love*, and some people still think twice before mentioning words classified as non-U.

In spite of, perhaps even because of, the accusations of snobbishness, *The Pursuit of Love* appealed to an enormous public, and Nancy found herself more secure from financial stress. Unfortunately, having been posted to Germany, I missed Nancy in Paris, and I was at home in Florence when she wrote to me on 28th December: 'I'm not enjoying the party much at present, I so hate being back in London, was so completely *blissful* in Paris. Perhaps darling John [Sutro] will film my book and make millions for me and then I could live where I like. I am sending it to you by the way and hope you will be able to read it . . . The shop is doing brilliantly and I am a partner now.'

Nancy was so encouraged by the success of *The Pursuit of Love* that she retired from Heywood Hill's shop in March 1946 to devote herself to writing. But she corresponded frequently with Heywood and his partner Handasyde Buchanan and, having bought shares in the shop, considered herself a 'sleeping partner'.

CHAPTER FIVE

For the next twenty years, the happiest in her life, Nancy settled in Paris. Even before settling there she had put these words into the mouth of her hero Fabrice: 'One's emotions are intensified in Paris—one can be more happy and also more unhappy here than in any other place. But it is always a positive source of joy to live here, and there is nobody so miserable as a Parisian in exile from his town. The rest of the world seems unbearably cold and bleak to us, hardly worth living in . . . '

Paris, when she arrived there, in September 1945, was still suffering from the after-effects of German occupation. Many essential commodities were scarce and expensive; the black market was still flourishing. But the aesthetic and intellectual compensations were overwhelming. The recovery of the fine arts seemed to have been stimulated by the recent Liberation. The theatre, the ballet, film production, were being revived with Gallic energy and refinement of taste. And the beauty of the city remained inviolate. Always a strenuous walker, Nancy was able to familiarize herself with the intimate old Paris behind the boulevards and the Hôtel de Ville, the quays and narrower streets with high-roofed buildings, with the venerable Place des Vosges and the classical mansions on the left bank of the Seine so long inhabited by French nobility whose names had inspired Balzac and Proust. Balzac's Madame de Sauve might even have suggested Nancy's Sauveterre. The British Embassy was full of her friends. Our Ambassador Duff Cooper and the glamorous Lady Diana made it sparkle as never before with poets, painters and musicians. Nancy was avidly receiving and assimilating new impressions.

'I must come and live here as soon as I can,' she told her mother in September 1945. 'I feel a totally different person as if I had come out of a coal mine into daylight . . . It seems silly when I struggled for a year to get here not to stay as long as possible.' Her friend Betty Chetwynd lent her a flat in 20 rue Bonaparte. 'The angelic concierge (how helpful the French are) got into the Métro at rush hour for me, went all the way to Montmartre, and returned with the prettiest femme de ménage you ever saw, all like magic. Imagine a London porter, all grumbles and groans and puttings off and certainly no lovely girl at the end of it! Oh my passion for the French I see all through rose-coloured spectacles! There was a tremendous row in the street this afternoon, two men roaring at each other and ending up *et vous*—*et vous*—and this refrain was taken up by a hundred heads out of windows, chanting *et vous*—*et vous*. It was like a scene in a film . . . It is such a holiday—getting up when I like (shamefully late), sleeping all the afternoon or reading a book in the boiling sun by the river and *above all* having enough to eat . . .

'Peter . . . loves the idea of a peaceful life but when it comes to the point he never can get away from his club and so on!

'I'm doing a lot of business of various kinds—getting my book translated I think, giving an interview to a French paper and so on besides book business. All great fun. I am as happy as can be . . .

'On Sunday to the Fould Springers at Royaumont—perhaps the most beautiful house I've ever seen . . . At luncheon somebody said, and what are your politics? at which a clenched fist flew over the table. It has never been forgotten. P. enchanted. "La famille Mitford fait ma joie" . . .

'I'm doing business in a rather desultory way—writing one or two articles for French papers which pay frightfully well, selling and buying books etc, but really I'm having an absolute rest and the result is I feel so wonderful I don't know it's me. Enough to eat twice a day, always a glass of wine and staying in bed most of the morning have made a new woman of me . . . Oh the food. Every meal is a recurring pleasure. I don't know how I shall be able to drag myself back to starving London. (The joke is the French think we've got everything in the world and simply don't believe me when I try to tell the truth!) And always a verre de vin, so good for one.' There is a hint of teasing here.

Her friend Alvilde Lees-Milne has given me a bleaker account of material conditions when she was living outside Paris at Jouy-en-Josas: 'In the winter of 1945 when we were both back in France, Nancy making do in cold hotels, I struggling in an unheated house with no help and precious little food, she would come and stay and all the horrors turned into jokes. The smoking damp wood, the staple diet of carrots and potatoes peeled and washed in a bidet and cooked on a primus in the bathroom (the kitchen was unusable), the long walks to Versailles and villages to cajole various black market people we had been told of to sell us some eggs or butter, and the endless blackouts through constant electricity cuts and so on, were turned into fun and there was a laugh to be got out of the gloomiest situation.'

After two months when her permit had expired, Nancy could hardly bear to return to 'Blighty', as she called it.

*

In London she was comforted by the success of her *Pursuit of Love* and by the return of her faithful crony Mark Ogilvie-Grant, who had been a prisoner of war in Italy. 'You will be glad to hear that Mark is back,' she had written her mother in the previous April. 'He looks like a horror-photograph, his knees are enormous lumps and his arms like sticks, but alive and well and immensely cheerful. He says in prison they dreamed of nothing but food and *his* dream was—do you remember that layer-cake with jam you used to have?—well that! Isn't it too funny, I'd quite forgotten it but of course it used to be a feature in our lives. He has been in 13 prisons . . .'

When Nancy's house in Blomfield Road was let she often stayed with Mark at Kew Green. He made no mystery of his 'special tastes' and she often chaffed him about them. Since Oxford days when he dressed up as a comical cockney charlady at the Hypocrites Club I had not been privileged to see him in one of the wigs Nancy introduced into her *Pigeon Pie*, which was dedicated to Mark. The wig theme recurred in her letters to him even when he was a prisoner of war: 'Thought you'd just like to know I take your wigs out and shake them every Sunday, the moths have been terrible this year and I don't want you to come back to a bald (or patchy) wig.' Mark's nonsense just happened to suit her nonsense, which is reflected, often abstrusely, in their correspondence. Robert Byron, another bosom friend with a sense of humour on the same wave-length, had been drowned by enemy action in 1941—a grievous loss to all who knew him, though Evelyn Waugh mis-trusted the violence of his opinions. Robert jeered at Evelyn's Catholicism; Evelyn sneered at Robert's mosques and minarets.

While in London Nancy wrote to Mark (8th February, 1946): 'I got a postcard to send you of some thoughtful sheep in deevey Perthshire scenery but suppose I must answer your letter now. Glad you liked the book, it is doing well. I've already made £1,250 here and £100 in America so I have suddenly become la tante à l'héritage and lazy Daze [a nephew] has been most deferential of late. I'm hoping for big things in the States and film folk are nibbling.

'The talk is all of the BALL. Michael Duff's—it was heaven on earth. I hitched an old white satin shirt (oyster with dirt) on to my best night dress—it was a wow and I've never enjoyed an evening more. *All* the old buddies—and a ghostly voice was heard in "She wore a wreath of roses", it was very moving. Annie had to spend £200 in order to wear her jewels on account of the wave of crime, Daphne fell down, Daisy Fellowes arrived with her own magnum of champagne and Chips [Channon] said to Emerald [Cunard], "*This* is what we have been fighting for." (We!) Emerald, very cross as she is at parties, replied, "Oh why dear, are they all Poles?"

'I spent yesterday at Brighton buying jet jewellery and postcards and once more the voice was heard, while an antique yellow wig could almost be seen whisking round the next corner. (By the way I really can't dedicate *all* my books to you, you know.) I'm off to Paris again I hope in about a month.

'Darling Prince Peter of Greece has been here, he asked us (typical of foreign royalty) to dinner in a kind of Chinese ping pong room and there were some Chinks who luckily knew Harold my dear and some terrible little Greek insect women, one called Alice something ducky and one called Sitwell. I told Osbert and he said, "oh yes the jigga jigga Sitwells."

'It was a funny evening I must say but it went on too long and I was dead by the end of it . . .

'Prod went to see his mother and she began telling him about the allowances she gives the others . . . (she gives us 0). So Prod, goaded, at last said, "Well what about me?" "Oh *you always* manage to keep alive somehow." Isn't she bliss. She said "Sir Stafford Cripps likes Nancy's book but he doesn't like the *subject* and I don't like the *subject* either." Did it remind you of Swinbrook days? Brains.'

Until she could find a permanent foothold in Paris Nancy stayed in various cheap hotels and borrowed flats. Early in June 1946 she wrote to her mother from the Hôtel de Bourgogne: 'I generally get an hour or so sunbathing on the roof. I lie in the nude with my head flopping over into the Place du Palais Bourbon, watching the arrival of the Députés and with a view of all Paris up to Montmartre, it is heaven.' And to Mark: 'I am blissful here as usual and making plans to live here and let Blomfield Road . . . Love here is on a high plane. The 35-year-old husband of an 85-year-old Princess madly in love with the 7-stone husband of a 14-stone Princess (weight). Both Princesses furious—both husbands in tears but also in the throes of such unrestrainable love that their tears don't avail much.

'I have so far cashed in £4,500 on the *Pursuit of Love* (a little more actually) and that's before it comes out in America. So you see the pen is mightier than the sword, whatever that may mean.

'I've got a friend here called Mogens [Mogens Tvede, husband of Princess Dolly Radziwill], pronounced Moans. I keep saying why not Grogens, but nobody laughs . . .'

In a note entitled *Smells* she compared the French with the English to the latter's disadvantage: 'French smells: garlic, hot drains, hot sweat on poor people, bad petrol. Compensations: Perpetual whiffs of scent, chestnut flowers, wonderful cooking smells, flowers and fruit smell twice as strong. English smells: cold sweat, cold mutton, dirty hair, uncleaned woollen clothes. *All this among the well-to-do.* Nobody seems to use any scent at all.

'The rich French smell delicious always and all use scent and lotions. Admittedly all smells are stronger here, good and bad, but one never wants to retch, as in England, now.'

'I am in full house-hunting campaign,' she told Mark, 'and trudge the streets following up clues sometimes with terrifying results as this morning when I had to go and see a lunatic and

65

ask if he would unbrick a room of a prospective flat (what can he keep there—Prod thinks a nun). I had to go alone as all was said to depend on charm and an English accent which he is said to love. However he took one look at me and said he didn't want any *tapage*. I said, hissing my SSes like l' Honorable Mrs. Pemberton in *Lakmé* that I wasn't a *tapeuse*. He softened rather and may consider me——! But it's always the same and always leads nowhere, so discouraging!

'Huge Gaullist meeting of 40,000 people the other day. I went, feeling awfully like my sisters. It was a wild success.'

Peter, 'full of the most nefarious plans for black marketing of all descriptions,' had been offered a lucrative job in Abyssinia for four or five months, and Nancy wrote: 'I now find I can deny myself nothing and of course that is an expensive frame of mind to be in.' But 'if I'm not careful I shall be turned into a train-meeter, money-lender *and* British restaurant.'

In May 1947: 'Awful Peter [back from Ethiopia] went and lost £50 worth of francs (stolen), it's his fault and not my lack of foresight . . . Meanwhile I've got a job here as English adviser and translation supervisor to a new publisher—£400 a year and (even more precious because it means I can't be forced back into the tunnel) a carte d'identité de travailleur. Now I must find a flat . . .

'Very funny letter from Evelyn [Waugh] back from Hollywood where he seems to have spent the whole time in the cemetery. It's called South Lawn, organ music peals from the flower beds and the loved ones (as they call the corpses) are frozen and kept in drawers. The children's section is called Slumber Land. The keeper of it said to Evelyn, "We have *great* trouble keeping pince-nez on the loved ones' noses." '

To Mark she wrote in July: 'The season here has become giddy, people are doing all sorts of things they will regret later. Someone we all know at a party the other night took off his collar and tie and revealed on his bronzed neck a collar of rubies, three rows, with a ruby and emerald tassel hanging down HIS back. His protector who was present remarked drily, "X is a very good chap but he can't expect to live on his charm for ever" (X having said, on showing the rubies, "not bad for a working girl"). Are you jealous?

'I've found and practically got the most divine flat you ever saw—oh how I pray it comes off. I'd far sooner have it than the Moulin—bathed in sunlight . . . I shall be here all August—come and stay. Only August is so dull, every cat leaves the town. I like it . . . Any flying saucepans at Kew?'

Evidently due to currency restrictions she wrote in September: 'Utter parsimony is now the note and I live on teeny bits of cat when not asked out. I've given up baths, coffee and wine, buses and even the métro and find one can exist (in this very cheap hotel) for £1 a day in all, which amazes me I must say. But I don't know that one could keep it up for long in the winter.' At the same time she was considering a flat 'rejected as too expensive by Doris Duke, in which I am planning to camp out. It is three vast frescoed state rooms— *aucun confort* (i.e. no loo).'

Nancy's open-air English charm was appreciated by the Anglophile denizens of the Faubourg St. Germain and she was quick to realize that this was a theatre whose comedies and tragedies could afford her perennial entertainment as well as literary pabulum. Through her closest confidante, Mrs. Hammersley, she was all but adopted by the old Comtesse Costa de Beauregard, who lived in eighteenth-century style at Fontaines les Nonnes par Puisieux. Fontaines was to provide the emotional resources of a French family background. In a remarkably short time she discovered, like George Moore, 'the delicate delight of owning *un pays ami*— a country where you may go when you are weary to madness of the routine of life, sure of finding there all the sensations of home, plus those of irresponsible caprice.'

Violet Hammersley, to whom Nancy was indebted for her introduction to Fontaines les Nonnes ('my treat of the whole year'), had an extremely subtle and original fascination. Her husband had been a prosperous banker and she had been accustomed to a life of generous affluence surrounded by a court of writers and artists. Wilson Steer painted a masterly portrait of her in her heyday when she was compared to a Siamese princess, seated in a billowy gown under flickering leaves. Duncan Grant had also depicted her in later years. Slight and dark with an olive complexion, she had cavernous black eyes over high cheekbones and an expression of sad resignation illumined by Mona Lisa smiles. Her colouring and intensity evoked an El Greco. Somerset Maugham jestingly described her as Philip IV's mistress, and Osbert Sitwell

67

caricatured her as a germ-carrier in his story '. . . That Flesh is Heir to . . .'

Her wealth had evaporated and this blow darkened her outlook: she became a prey to neurotic anxieties and fears. Her voice was a musical sigh when it was not a gentle moan and she dwelt more and more on life's miseries as she grew older, not without a soupçon of relish. Since the loss of her fortune she lived quietly at Totland Bay on the Isle of Wight, but she paid frequent visits to the mainland and stayed periodically with her half-sister Comtesse Costa at Fontaines, where she was cherished as well as dreaded, for she could be very exacting and had a tendency to dramatize domestic situations. Invariably dressed in black, wrapped in shawls and veils, she glided about like a mournful spectre, observing everything with an ironic sense of humour.

Though genuinely fond of her Nancy teased her unmercifully. Her letters to 'Mrs. Ham', alias 'the Wid', who called her 'Child', were often signed 'Fiend' and 'Horror comic'. 'Cystitis indeed!' she wrote, '*I* heard of you, arriving at the island with a 20 lb. salmon in that black net which sometimes drapes the hats taken from my cupboard. *Salmonitis*, you can tell Dr. Broadbent with my compliments.

'Oh if I could draw, I would write an illustrated Life of You. The nets, the veils, the shawls, the scarves, the crepe, the cape, the wildly waving weeds, the unvarying get-up of cliff and turf and cresson and rue de la Paix. Who could do justice to it?

'I'm having a day in bed which I love more than anything on earth, and do about once a month. "She's been in bed 17 years." "Oh Mrs. Ham how lucky!" '

'I so love Fontaines when you are there to tease and torture,' she exclaimed. 'I see you are better. The ink is a darker blue, not grey on grey as when you were ill.' 'Whenever one thinks you really ill it always turns out you are on a spree somewhere . . . I really think you ought to stay quiet for a bit, but of course you've got so many lovers that your life is a perpetual balancing trick. You should settle down with a Totland Totterer—what about a Lesbian affair with Lady Tottenham? It's all the go now, and I hear X has left Y and their 7 children for a woman.'

Mrs. Ham was sensitive on the subject of her reduced

circumstances, so Nancy would tease her about her 'unearned income': 'I'm not a Wealthy Widow but a Working Woman.' When Mrs. Ham hoped to supplement her income by translating Madame de Sévigné's letters she was exposed to more teasing. 'How the text of Sévigné seems to have been altered in the 19th century. Somebody said yesterday, "I hope your friend has left in all the naughty bits." I said, "you can be sure she hasn't." ' And when the translation was published: 'How mercenary you are. Book Society recommendation (*I* am always *Choice*) does not bring money, only a modified laurel wreath, which surely you prefer? It is the enormous sales which will pour unlimited gold into your lap—perhaps. I shall expect *un cadeau important*, a jewel at least . . .' (since Nancy was to contribute the introduction).

Nancy offered various suggestions for other translations. No Scott-Moncrieff had turned Saint-Simon into an English classic, 'so I hope the publishers will be knocking at your door. I rather foresee that you'll live to be 100 so there's heaps of time. When I'm 75 shall I still be Child?' Evidently Mrs. Ham had considered Mlle. de Lespinasse for Nancy objected: 'Lespinasse is the Queen of Bores. Why not blissful du Deffand? But if you do letters in your highly personal style, they'll read like more Sévigné.' Later, 'if La Tour du Pin has been done, how about Boigne? In some ways more amusing, she's so much nastier.'

Nancy's letters to Mrs. Ham, who belonged to her mother's generation, were among her sprightliest for Mrs. Ham remained resilient in spite of her misfortunes. Perhaps Nancy's secret intention was to cheer her solitude. Telling her that she had seen several advertisements in *The New Statesman* of people wanting 'help' in interesting households, she suggested: 'You should advertise. Draft for advert. Really interesting fairly progr. widow, godmother of John Lehmann, requires help in bungalow stuffed with Camden School works and valuable bibelots. Mine of inf. on progr. subjects ancient and modern. Rendezvous of Huxleys and Priestleys. A. J. P. Taylor drops in. Days off for Aldermaston. (Think better not mention the word Mitford).

'I think you ought to dress like Mme de Maintenon from the age of fifty, in dark brown and white with a cross of enormous diamonds the only ornament. Well you do practically, only no cross.'

In a way Mrs. Ham supplanted her mother, always somewhat distant, in her affections. She had an all-round cosmopolitan culture and a consuming curiosity even if, as Nancy wrote to her: 'Your letters are always full of mysterious informants who, hooded I imagine, like Spanish penitents, lean over you whispering woe...' Above all she shared Nancy's devotion to France and the French, whom she understood instinctively since she had grown up in Paris. In England she seemed faintly exotic.

On one of her fleeting visits to England Nancy wrote (to James Lees-Milne, 27th February, 1947): 'I felt like darling Captain Oates, leaving Paris, but find London isn't *nearly* as Beardmore as I was led to suppose—I'm quite disappointed by the warmth the luxury the gaiety and the enormous masses of food which seems to abound (not to speak of blazing lights— I thought we were down to whale blubber).' The saga of Captain Scott and his comrades was still part and parcel of Mitford imagery.

Her gossipy letters to me—(I would have received more of them had I not been in Mexico at the time)—showed that she was vastly enjoying her new life while searching for a suitable apartment. 'Oh the *potins*,' as she exclaimed. 'Too long to describe.' However, she described a good many, and though some of the protagonists are dead and gone they evoke Parisian smart society at that period and the background of her future writings.

From 19 Quai Malaquais she wrote to me in November 1947: 'I've got this lovely flat, lent me by Audrey Bouverie, jusqu'à nouvel ordre—anyhow I think until February—which is really most lucky for me.

'There was an article in *Samedi Soir* a few weeks ago, *made* for you. It was called *Les Nouveaux Pompadours* and it began about how immediately after the war parachutists were all the go and then a long thing about two brothers who pretended to be parachutists and what has become of *them*. Then it told about that man who looks like a tie pin, X., and the flat Lopez has bought for him and how une jeune comtesse tried to buy him from Lopez with Louis XV's microscope but Mrs. Lopez said "he's not worth it, I advise against——" ...

'I'm writing a novel [*Love in a Cold Climate*] but it's so dull I'm in despair. One thing, masses of people must like dull novels that's very sure.

'I saw Dolly Radziwill just now and she told me the following story.

'Her *vendeuse* at Balmain had a new client, a M. Lecomte, who chose about six dresses and said, "My wife is not well, will you bring them round for her to see." So round she goes— luxury flat, exquisite creature appears with a curtain of gold hair, darling little waist, long elegant legs and so on and they begin trying on the dresses. Suddenly the *vendeuse* becomes aware that the pretty little bosoms are *not quite real*—looks again at the face—horrors! M. Lecomte himself!! He sees that she is very much put out and says, "Jusqu'à présent je me suis habillé chez Jacques Fath, vous n'avez qu'à lui télé-phoner pour des renseignements sur moi." So as soon as she gets back Balmain himself gets through to Fath who says, "Vous êtes vraiment veinard, c'est un client comme il n'y en a peu, doux, gentil et riche à milliards." The end of it is he has ordered several dresses including a shell pink ball-dress——!! The hair was a wonderful WIG. Do admit——!!'

Before the end of 1947 she had the good fortune to discover an ideal apartment, the ground floor of an old mansion between courtyard and garden in the Rue Monsieur, which she referred to henceforth as 'Mr. Street'. 'I've got a perfectly blissful and more or less permanent flat,' she informed me in December 1947. 'Untouched I should think for 60 years. I spent my first evening removing the 25 lace mats with objects on them mostly from Far Japan (dainty). The furniture is qualité de musée—such wonderful pieces, now you can see them.' Her individual taste was most evident in the arrangement of this luminous residence. One cannot imagine it without her, so intensely did it reflect her personality. I remember it as a serene emanation of the *entente cordiale*, French in its sophisti-cated simplicity yet English in a certain cosiness and feeling for privacy. As Lady Gladwyn wrote, Nancy 'eliminated all that was unnecessary in her rooms, retaining only objects of intrinsic merit . . . From the large square grey salon, pink-curtained on the crosslights, one could glimpse the white muslin on her bed and there, in that small bedroom in an arm-chair by the window, her books were written.' She was attended

71

by a devoted elderly *bonne*, Marie, who guarded her against unwelcome intruders. To her mother Nancy wrote: 'I've never liked any house I've lived in as much as this one or ever known even among your servants such a treasure as Marie. She simply literally never thinks of herself at all, never wants any time—let alone a whole day—off. She is an excellent and reliable without being wonderful cook . . .'

Later, when an English interviewer asked Nancy her reasons for living in France, 'My maid Marie is at least half of it,' she explained. 'She's the sort of person you find only in France. Maids are so much more important than men.' The interviewer, who had expected revelations about 'the bliss of love in France', was slightly disappointed.

Some of Nancy's furniture was sent from England. It arrived, she told Mark, 'rather thin and wan as if it had been in a concentration camp. But the clever French are at work, mending and rubbing, and it will soon be all right again. I was pleased to see the well-known old faces after so many years.' These included 'my Sheraton writing table and Farve's lovely Chinese screens and they all fit in very well. *La politique du tapissier* is in full swing, all great fun. Also a great deal (12 pairs) of Muv's linen which is worth its weight in gold now, and my Dresden china clock. Yes, the verre de Nevers is my treasure, a great find, for nearly nothing too. I happened to know about it since I haunt the arts décoratifs at the Louvre.' Later she 'bought various pictures, notably a Longhi said by Francis Watson to be quite first class'. To Mrs. Hammersley she confided: 'With infinite cunning I have made it impossible to have anybody to stay at Mr. because the only way now into the bathroom is through my bedroom. Perhaps I could have you however—I'm arranging a little summer bedroom the other side of the bathroom.' And to her mother: 'We bought a hen to eat, live, and now of course it has become our best friend and no doubt will live in the garden until death (natural) us do part.'

Her rooms in 'Mr. Street' were to become a cultural annexe to the British Embassy, a congenial rendezvous of French and English letters. At last, very cautiously, she was able to indulge her flair for clothes and replenish her wardrobe. 'Went yesterday to order a suit at Dior. £120. Evening dresses start at £342. Impossible to get inside the building.

I had to use INFLUENCE to be allowed to order. Why is everybody so rolling—they can't all have written *Pursuit of Love*.' (19th February, 1947 to Heywood Hill.)

Our friend Gillian Sutro reminds me that Nancy was 'the first Englishwoman to catch on to Dior, and she bought clothes from him at the beginning when no one had heard of him in London. With her long lean frame she was a perfect clothes horse, like a Balenciaga model.' Though the war had ended clothes rationing was still on in England, and Gillian remembers how stunning she appeared on a visit from Paris, 'in a black wool Dior suit, with the new long skirt no one had seen before.'

A year later Nancy was writing: 'I am now always torn between clothes and antiques but with me clothes are almost a matter of health, you know . . .' They had become 'a matter of health' since settling in Paris where, for the time being, 'I am seeing nobody but the Grand Old French—they make my joy and I long to write a book about them—but how to translate the jokes? I don't see how it can be done. "Depuis 40 ans je suis membre du Jockey et jamais je n'y ai entendu prononcé le nom d'un couturier—voilà que tout à coup on n'y parle que de Dior." They think I'm awfully eccentric because I YELL with laughter every time they speak, but they don't really seem to mind and go on asking me . . .'

CHAPTER SIX

ARISTOCRATICALLY ENGLISH TO the French, Nancy
began to seem rather Frenchified to her English
friends, but she never acquired the chameleon quality
of a Violet Trefusis whose performance of the idiom reminded
one of Max Beerbohm's essay 'On Speaking French'. In
Violet's virtuosity there was a supercilious ostentation com-
mensurable with her linguistic advantage. Having lived in
Paris before the war, she fancied herself a Paul Morand
character, whether from *Ouvert la Nuit* or *Fermé la Nuit* one
could not make out. She had published fiction both in French
and English, wore the ribbon of the Légion d' Honneur night
and day, and owing to her prolonged intimacy with Princess
Edmond de Polignac she could claim familiarity with the
painters, poets and musicians of the avant-garde as well as
with prominent politicians. In her heart she resented Nancy
as a poacher on her preserves. The resentment swelled with
the growing popularity of Nancy's Francophile novels and
burst when she turned to historical biography. Superficially
they were on amicable terms. Nancy was glad to see friends
but she withdrew from them when she wanted to write. Violet,
who posed as a professional *femme de lettres*, preferred to be
surrounded at all times; her writing was no more than an
exhibitionistic exercise. Unlike Nancy she had a fat independent
income.

Since Violet also had a villa in Florence I often heard her
attribute Nancy's knowledge of French society to her own
guidance and intervention while she poured ridicule on her
general attitude and accent. But the society they both frequented was narrow enough for them to collide with comic

results. Nancy used to say, 'Never tell me anything in confidence,' as it made her want to pass it on immediately. Violet passed on everything she heard with rococo embellishments of her own. Many of her traits contributed to the character of Lady Montdore in Nancy's next novel, *Love in a Cold Climate*. One can almost hear Violet remarking, like Lady Montdore, 'I think I may say we put India on the map. Hardly any of one's friends in England had ever even heard of India before we went there, you know.'

Love in a Cold Climate is far from dull—Nancy was exaggerating her modesty. Raymond Mortimer considers it the best of her novels. The conquest of tough Lady Montdore by Cedric Hampton, 'a terrible creature from Sodom, from Gomorrah, from Paris,' was what reviewers used to call audacious, but many dowagers whose names I could mention found youthful companions like Cedric who subjected them to a course of rejuvenation. Nancy herself was drawn to the ornamental type of homosexual, whose preoccupations were feminine apart from sex. She described Brian Howard as 'blissikins' and in Paris there were many others who brought grist to her comedic mill. ('I had 12 people yesterday in before dinner and afterwards I thought I was the only normal one,' she told Alvilde. 'It *is* rather strange one must admit. Nature's form of birth control in an overcrowded world I daresay.')

The scene with Uncle Matthew when Cedric bought *Vogue* on the platform of Oxford station and was shaken like a rat; the alarm of hearty Jock who expected Cedric to pounce on him in the train when they were 'quite alone together after Reading' and maintained that he had been hypnotized into moving Cedric's heavy suitcase off the rack—such incidents were based on real happenings. The narrative ripples along in the brisk and colloquial style Nancy had made her own.

Love in a Cold Climate was selected by the Book Society, the *Daily Mail*, and the *Evening Standard* as book of the month for July. Gay, clever, witty, startling, brilliant, enchanting, extravagant, adroit, spirited, joyous, pungent, piquant, frisky, post-Waugh, were among the adjectives applied to it by reviewers, though a few complained of its lack of moral indignation. To certain Americans it appealed as a portrayal of aristocratic England in full decadence and of pedigreed poodles in a corrupt menagerie. Nancy was described as 'the prettiest novelist in Burke's Peerage'.

The novel was most original, perhaps, in depicting the dragonfly Cedric as a beneficent rather than as a pernicious influence: here for a change was a harmless fairy wand. Since then some of the social stigma attached to Cedric's type has faded and Nancy's witty tolerance might have helped the fading process. At the time, however, Cedric was generally considered an affront to normality by the English novel-reading public, less sophisticated than the French. The atmosphere of prosperity was faintly overshadowed by a sense of doom and there is more than a hint of nostalgia—a tear for the passing of incorrigible individualists, however ludicrous. Choleric Uncle Matthew reappeared with a fresh superstition. If you wrote a bugbear's name on a scrap of paper, the creature would expire within a year.

Evelyn Waugh wrote laconically on a postcard from Piers Court: 'I have finished the book. The last half is not as good as the first but there is more construction than I remembered. The climax is very bad, so is the unnecessary scene of Lady Montdore dining in North Oxford, but her transformation is plausible and excellently written and Cedric is genuinely funny all through. Of course whenever the Radletts appear, all is splendidly well. They are *genial*. E.'

To Mark Nancy wrote from the Château de Montredan, Marseille, 30th July, 1949: 'Dear old Hyde, I'm so glad you liked it—the American reviews so terrible I am flattered, "no message or meaning" they rightly say. But the English are for it and I'd rather it was that way round on account of ONE's friends not gloating over these cruel words.

'I am in perfect happiness here with Dolly Radziwill, been here a month with a week off on the Mosley yacht at Cannes, and go back to them next week, back here and so on, but I shall be in Paris waiting with open arms in September. I long for ye . . . The bliss of Marseille it is made for you in both capacities (Jekyll and Hyde).' And again, on 21st August: 'Having lived here for most of my days, it seems, I am off in about a week to Paris, dreading the cold rather, as my blood (oh that word, forget it) must be rather thin after these weeks of torridity.

'My book is a great best seller so are you impressed? Even

in America, where the reviews are positively insulting, it is on the best seller list. I have a secret feeling that the other novels on the market can't be very fascinating at present, but this may be my native modesty. Anyhow I shall never write about normal love again as I see there is a far larger and more enthusiastic public for the *other sort*.'

'America is taking exception to Cedric the sweet pansy,' she told her friend Billa [Lady Harrod], who had suggested 'the Waynflete Professor of Moral Theology' and perhaps his future as Ambassador. 'It seems in America you can have pederasts in books so long as they are fearfully gloomy and end by committing suicide. A cheerful one who goes from strength to strength like Cedric horrifies them. They say "Cedric is too revolting for any enjoyment of the book". So I write back "how can you hate Cedric when he is such a *love?*" '

If not exactly a love, one must agree with Evelyn Waugh that Cedric was genuinely funny. While studying the type Nancy for once was prejudiced in favour of her compatriots. 'The pansies here,' she informed Billa, 'are all so pompous in comparison with our darling English ones. Brian [Howard] came here with a terrible creature called S— I thought I would hurt myself with laughing. Brian must have been a gov. in a former life.' With regard to readers who tried to recognize her models she confessed: 'It is the worst of taking bits of houses, circumstances, and so on, that people then begin to see other resemblances, and yet I don't know how it is to be avoided by somebody who must write about what she knows like me . . . I thought Alfred un-Roy [Sir Roy Harrod] might go to Paris in some capacity—Ambassador even (Franks) but this is all pretty nebulous in my mind and will take years to work out. I must go on with Fanny. I work much more easily like that—I started this book without an I, but couldn't get along at all.' Here we have the germ of Nancy's last novel *Don't tell Alfred*.

Personally I prefer *The Blessing*, but before this was published in 1951 Nancy began to experiment with translation. She tackled *La Princesse de Clèves*, that pioneer of modern psychological fiction which was her favourite, perhaps because it is so limpidly French, though it is profoundly sad and disillusioned. Nothing could seem farther from Nancy's temperament, yet the dignity and refinement of the heroine's emotions

77

must have appealed to hidden depths in her own character. Under her smiling mask there was undoubtedly a vein of repressed melancholy.

Her family loyalty was too intense to be hidden, and strong political dissent could not weaken her devotion. When her sister Unity eventually died of her head wound in 1948 she wrote to James Lees-Milne (8th June): 'We are all dreadfully sad and cast down. Lately she had been so very much better and had become quite thin and pretty again, and seemed to enjoy her life again. But her real happiness in life was over— she was a victim of the war as much as anybody wasn't she.

'Mabel said "I sent for the Church Worker of our district and I said is Miss Unity with Mr. Tom *now* and she said yes she thought so." Wasn't it touching—as though the Church Worker kept an ABC of trains to Heaven.

'I must tell of X's behaviour, Not one word of sympathy but when I arrived here *from the funeral* a telegram saying will you dine on Wednesday followed by a spate of furious telephone calls when I said I wouldn't. "But I've asked the Hamish Hamiltons *specially* to meet you." Can you beat it!'

Having wholeheartedly identified herself with the Nazi movement before she was twenty, Unity had barely survived near suicide when her ideals were shattered by war. Nancy had made fun of her in her novel *Wigs on the Green* (1935) but she always spoke of her with special tenderness and denied the popular assumption that she wanted to marry Hitler. Her letters to Unity, whom she called 'Head of Bone' and 'Heart of Stone', are puzzling in their blend of mockery and affection, for instance (29th June, 1935):

'Darling Stonyheart, We were all very interested to see that you were the Queen of the May this year at Hesselberg.

Call me early, Goering dear,

For I'm to be Queen of the May!

Good gracious, that interview you sent us, fantasia, fantasia.'

No doubt fantasy had played a preponderant role in her short and ultimately tragic life. Twenty years later Nancy told Christopher Sykes: 'About dying, I have always found that one minds terribly when they are the ones of whom everybody else says for the best. I minded when Bobo [Unity] died much more than when Tom did who had had a happy life and little sorrow . . .'

Translation from the French served as a creative stopgap between writing novels and, sporadically, when applied to the theatre and films, it promised lucrative possibilities. Nancy's talent for dialogue became sharpened and polished in the process. It seemed a curious coincidence that Nancy, always haunted by The Hut of Captain Scott's Antarctic expedition, should have won her single success in the theatre with a version of André Roussin's frivolous farce *The Little Hut*, then still running in Paris after 1,000 performances.

Would it run in London? She described it to her mother as 'a terribly funny play about husband, lover and wife on a desert island—lover gets very low all alone in the little hut while the husband and wife sleep in the big one, insists on taking turns. Husband not absolutely delighted but sees the logic, that they have shared her for six years and might as well go on doing so. Then a handsome young negro appears, ties up husband and lover by a trick and indicates that he will only let them go if Susan will go into the hut with him, which she's only too pleased to do as he is very good looking. "Disgusting," I hear you say. And so on—you see the form. It is terribly funny, *I* think, but I never counted on it much as everybody said the Lord Chamberlain wouldn't pass it. Here it has run over three years, a wild success. I've skated over the worst indecencies, in fact the reason I was asked to do it was that I'm supposed to be good at making outrageous situations seem all right. Roussin the author, an utter love, doesn't know a word of English so I've got away with altering it a great deal . . .'

The theme was frothy enough; the situation what used to be called risqué. Owing to a felicitous blend of talents and Nancy's tactful treatment of the dialogue, it was saved from crudity, but its three rollicking acts struck me personally as overblown. Bedroom farces even when transferred to the tropics have their hackneyed limitations.

At first it was exciting to make her début in the theatrical world which was new to her. But being a very private person in spite of the publicity she had given her family in *The Pursuit of Love*, she did not take kindly to actors. Their narcissism and blinkered absorption in their profession bored her. Theatrical gossip was the only gossip she could not endure. After dining with the influential manager Binkie Beaumont, whose party included 'Noël Coward, who kisses me now, Gladys Cooper, Robert Morley, Athene Seyler and the Kaufmans and a lot of stage hangers-on', she exclaimed: 'It's dreadful how dull they all are but don't say I said. Also Communists I note . . .'

From Edinburgh she wrote (25th July, 1950): 'After a day of terrible nerves and disastrous dress rehearsals the play was an absolute whizz and even the old *Scotsman* is on its side. Oh what a relief. Oliver Messel had privately informed me that he was deeply shocked by it and quite expected the audience to get up and demonstrate, and I must say when I saw the dress rehearsal I quite agreed and very nearly didn't go to the theatre at all I was so terrified. But the fact is nothing shocks anybody nowadays—they screamed with laughter throughout and clapped and cheered for ten minutes at the end. Now there is a lot of work to be done on it . . . What we do is this. Certain bits fall very flat. I sit, with script, and note which ones, and next day I rewrite them. Then see how that goes. And so on. I doubt if it will be à point by next week, very much. It is a *most* laborious, and I see *most* necessary process . . . The actors are dreams of funniness and egocentricity, so exaggerated you can hardly believe it.' A woman in the audience was heard saying: 'It's all quite mad but of course Mitfords are.'

To Mark she wrote in trepidation from 'Caledonia (stern and wild)', before the first performance: 'I am so ground down by physical miseries I can think of 0 else. Tired (went from the train at 8 to rehearsal till past 2) and hungry. Then some brute in human form opened my door saying *8 o'clock* this morning, after which I never got off again. Do spend your holidays in Britain. Then after two meals in the train of a sort of sub spam I thought anyway Scotch breakfast—well I won't go on, such a bore. Then I'm low about the play. The girl is simply awful. I thought so when I came for the rehearsal but they all said she'd wake up, which in my view she hasn't. However she's quite lovely looking which is a help. Morley is blissful. But I rather dread tonight.

'Edinburgh is beautiful in its black way. Freezing cold. Every man woman and child I've spoken to says awfully close, so think what it must be like as a rule! Poor poor poor Marie Stuart, I feel for her . . .'

From Glasgow: 'Yes well the Glasgow papers say "this

5. Nancy's marriage to Peter Rodd, 1933

6. Peter Rodd
(*from a painting by Mary Rennell*)

play may be screamingly witty in Paris and if so poor Miss Mitford hasn't quite seen the point." Leading lady ill and off for a week so we are all rather lowered. Vive l'Ecosse. Money rather tight . . . I'm overtired from rewriting scene after scene and watching rehearsals *and* the play every night. However, I've seldom been so fascinated in my life . . . You don't know how famous I am, people come to my bedroom with *Pursuit* (Penguin) for me to sign do be impressed. Mobbed at the stage door too.'

After the preliminary tour of the provinces she wrote (28th July, 1950): 'Well, it was touch and go, and the second night not good, last night better again, but really ACTORS!!!! "Sorry, you know, but I can't say that line." "Then, what about MY EXIT?" and the girl talks for two hours about what she calls her "hair-do".' From Newcastle, however, she wrote (11th August): 'Wonderful reception of the play here so we are all happy again . . .'

While in London she proposed to stay with Mark at Kew Green. About the play's début there she wrote: 'Well I understand my first night (sounds so indecent at my age) is August 21st and I thought of staying on another ten days and seeing a few pals. But dearest if inconvenient don't think of me . . . P.S. Please conserve my post which is very valuable— no need to peep however.'

That first night was resoundingly successful and Mark gave an exultant party in his cosy house after the performance with the sort of English breakfast food that Nancy relished. I remember the kedgeree, which I explained to Monsieur Roussin was our substitute for bouillabaisse. Though wreathed in smiles he looked rather puzzled throughout. He must have expected a more boisterous gathering and this was so placid. In thanking 'Dear Old Gentry' for his hospitality, Nancy remarked: 'The comfort of your household—well trust a bachelor for that! Did you see your fellow countryman in the *News Chronicle*, he went for me tooth and nail and ended up I should like to beat Miss M. So I'm dashing for home. Also I've received enough letters to fill a British railway. Fancy, I went into an antique shop in Henley and the two dear pansies who keep it (one a major) dashed at me with my books for me to sign. Do admit.'

She felt more elated after the London production. (24th August): 'I absolutely adored the first night,' she told Robin

Mc Douall, 'so amusing to see a London audience after those old stodges in the provinces! In fact I have enjoyed the whole thing like mad.'

With Robert Morley, Joan Tetzel and David Tomlinson in the leading roles and with ravishing child's picture book scenery by Oliver Messel, *The Little Hut* became a hit in England. Nancy could announce in October: 'I'm entirely taken up with clothes, on account of successful *Hut* . . .' Once bitten twice shy, however, though the bite had proved profitable, and she returned to fiction refreshed by this experimental digression. In March 1951 she wrote to Heywood Hill: 'I'm offered every French play under the sun now! But never again until workhouse looms, because of that awful going on tour . . .'

Home in 'Mr. Street' she resumed the quieter rhythm of work and leisure. She was always ready to see close friends of whom 'the Colonel' was her Parisian mainstay. Evelyn Waugh was assured of a warm welcome though the 'cloven hoof and forked tongue' might appear at awkward moments. 'Evelyn Waugh has been here,' she told her mother (21st May, 1949). 'We went to Chantilly where he quarrelled violently with the Coopers. I just managed to keep out of it I am glad to say and although he had every meal with me except a luncheon with Claudel we ended up on the best of terms. I breathe a faint sigh of relief now he has gone, though I really love him and his company. Diana says I am far too weak-minded with him, but of course it is the only way to keep on terms! He is a real oddity . . .'

'Evelyn is here,' she wrote Heywood Hill (14th May, 1950): 'I was forced by his dreadful behaviour to enquire how he reconciles so much wickedness with being a Christian, to which he rather sadly replied that I didn't realize how much worse he would be if he wasn't one—added to which that he would long ago have committed suicide but for his religion. But I find that he is quite all right with Duchesses so *that* in future will be my clue. It's middle class intellectuals who come in for the full horror of his bloodiness. His new book sounds lovely . . .' And, a year later (8th July, 1951), 'Evelyn got a cable while I was with him asking for 800 words about me for U.S.A. He wrote it at once and it was so beautiful I blubbed, nothing but pure distilled honey. He speaks of the shop "at least one American Sergeant will remember" . . .' (The

Sergeant in question was Stuart Preston, much lionized in London towards the end of the war, an ultra-sociable habitué of Heywood Hill's and a cultured devotee of Nancy. Like me, he wilfully discounted her anti-Americanism). Evelyn's distilled honey, however, was not without a drop of acid, for he wrote that, 'having voted socialist and so done her best to make England uninhabitable, Nancy broke from her chrysalis, took wing and settled lightly in the heart of Paris.'

To her mother she wrote of another visit from Evelyn (15th March, 1952) 'in a very good and mellow mood . . . always wanting to seem very old, cupping his ear whenever you speak and holding letters at arm's length and hobbling on a thick stick. It's so unlike my other contemporaries with their pathetic desire for youth. Well, I must say I should like to keep my waist, my face having more or less gone already.'

Those of us living abroad are accustomed to periodical invasions from England. Hospitable though Nancy was, she managed to defend her privacy. 'A flood of English. One woman said to me "It's very funny, when I ring up my friends here they are awfully pleased to hear my voice but they seem to have engagements every day for a week. I believe the English think that Paris is a social desert where nobody knows anybody else and sits waiting for the visitors to cheer them up. Like some little port in the Red Sea. It's very odd, I must say. Actually there's more going on than I can remember . . ." '

Dinner with the Windsors, for instance, 'in a terrible fix as it is *tenue de ville*, i.e. jewelled jacket costing £600 which I do not possess. All my horrible clothes laid out like a jumble sale and I in tears. (My mother's great saying better be under than over dressed is no consolation at all.) As I wrote those words the secretary rang up and said now it's short evening dresses. Well, supposing I hadn't got one? As it happens I HAVE. (Next day) Duchess in a crocheted straw dress, utter knockout, saying "Oh just the sort of thing you pick up in the village, you know." *What village?*'

After another dinner with the Windsors she reported to her mother: 'We were only eight and I had another long talk with him [the Duke], mostly about King Edward. "Not very nice what that boy wrote about my grandfather*—Christopher

* *Four Studies in Loyalty,* by Christopher Sykes. London, 1946. Referring to the first study, 'Behind the Tablet'.

83

Sykes was it—do you know him? Who are the Sykeses?"

' "Well," I said, "the present one is Sir Richard, his father was Sir Mark and his father was Sir Tatton."

' "Tatton is a Yorkshire name. Do you know how I know that? Well, I was in the Navy with Commander Bower and we were confirmed together and his name was Robert Tatton Bower and it seems that Tatton is a Yorkshire name." "Oh yes," he said, "It was always 'send for Lord Redesdale' at Sandringham if they wanted to cut the trees or anything. What happened to Batsford?"

' "Sold."

' "So where were you raised?"

' "Went into White's the other day and saw a face I thought I knew and by Jove it was Bruce—snow-white and very thin . . ."

' "Yes, I can't remember the time when there wasn't Lady Airlie—now when I saw my mother last week she said, 'I can't take Mabel about any more she's too deaf—I ask who's that? And all she says is what. So I've told her she can sweep in after me at the big functions, but when it's picture galleries and things like that she can't come.' Not bad, he said, from 82 to 83 is it?"

'He's writing his memoirs. I said, "Do tell where you've got to." "Just coming to the deadline."

'Duff [Cooper] went to see him with a compte rendu he wrote at the time (he was in the Cabinet) and they spent the afternoon over it. As Duff got up to go he said, "Well, anyway you've never regretted it, Sir, have you?"

"No by God I haven't. When I see poor Bertie surrounded by all that muck—at least in the old days the Government were one's friends"—

'I'm really too busy to write letters but thought all this would amuse you.'

When Burgess and Maclean decamped to Russia, Nancy wrote again to Heywood: 'Did you LOVE the diplomats? Everybody here thinks they came over to see about their dresses for Charlie's [de Beistegui's] ball and have been too busy with fittings ever since to notice the fuss . . .' In the meantime a French newspaper reported that *La Princesse de Clèves* had had a great success in America under the title of *Love in a Cold Climate*.

CHAPTER SEVEN

NANCY'S MOST ACCOMPLISHED novel, *The Blessing*, was published in 1951, and it is permeated with her joyous love of France and her vision of a sophisticated section of French society. Indeed it is the consummate product of Nancy's liaison with contemporary France. She described it as 'a roman de mœurs—and *what* mœurs—those I see around me'. The plot—how mischievous little Sigi contrives to keep his French father and English mother apart for his own material profit though both his parents are deeply attached to each other —provides a loom for Nancy to weave her funniest jokes and human observations.

Fabrice, Duc de Sauveterre, is resuscitated as Charles-Edouard, Marquis de Valhubert, 'who cannot—he really cannot —see a pretty woman without immediately wanting to sleep with her.' He was also a polished dilettante who had 'a charming collection of minor masters with one or two high spots, an important Fragonard, a pair of Hubert Roberts, and so on. He was always adding to it, and had bought more than half the pictures himself . . . He knew the long, intricate histories of all the palaces of the Faubourg St. Germain and exactly where to find each one, hidden behind huge walls and carriage doorways.' Grace is a more mature version of Linda, for whom 'Charles-Edouard was the forty kings of France rolled into one, the French race in person walking and breathing'. She sees the French through rose-tinted spectacles—how unlike Uncle Matthew! 'She even loved their snobbishness, it seemed to her such a tremendous joke, so particularly funny, somehow, nowadays. She was beginning to love the critical spirit of all and sundry. It kept people up to the mark, no doubt, and had filled

her with the desire to improve her mind and sharpen her wits.'
At times the *mondaine* Nancy waxes lyrical: 'It was one of those
Paris afternoons when, by some trick of the light, the buildings
look as if they are made of opaque, blue glass. Grace wondered
how much Carolyn really did love the stones of Paris. She
seemed not to notice, as they went by, the blue glass façade of
the Invalides surmounted by its dome powdered with gold . . .'

The screen of the narrative flickers with idiosyncratic
sketches. 'By the way, Tante Régine is coming to luncheon.
When I told her you were here she screamed like a peacock and
rushed off to buy a new hat.' Tante Régine musing on modern
youth: 'Poor little things! I'm glad it's not me growing up now.
What a world for them! Atom bombs, and no brothels. What
will their parents do about that—after all you can't very well
ask your own friends, can you? I suppose they'll all end up as
pederasts.'

The superbly drawn English nanny is, as Nancy admitted, a
caricature of her Blor; Ed Spain, 'the Captain', a leading
London intellectual, is based on Cyril Connolly; Mrs. O'Dono-
van who 'liked everything French, indiscriminately and unreasonably', is based on Mrs. Hammersley, whose father had
been connected with the British Embassy under Lord Lyons.
But one is at a loss to account for the grotesque windbag Hector
Dexter: in his case Nancy's anti-Americanism cantered away
with her.

'I'm so *delighted* you like *The Blessing*,' she wrote to me
(15th September, 1951). 'Most of my friends do, but many of
the reviews have been terrible, not one good word. It is selling
pretty well nevertheless, and is book of the month, next month,
in America so we'll see how they take to it. Up to now my
books have done very badly there, with awful reviews . . .'

'. . . I didn't go to the [Beistegui] ball. From early years I've
had a horror of being an unattached woman in Venice. "Oh look,
here comes old so and so, what's the betting she's going to cram
into our gondola—*there*, I told you so." Besides the Colonel,
now a deputy, had to be here and it seemed a shame to leave
him all alone in an empty Paris.

'I saw Winston who talked about a "Mr. Bistinguay". It
seems that Winston was cheered, but much less than "Carlos di
Spagna" . . . As I write I receive the U.S.A. Book of the Month
magazine with a pen portrait of me by Evelyn. Terribly eulo-

gistic, but one or two digs. I don't quite like "bright but patchy culture"!!! An American came to interview me and said did I know many of her compatriots and I said only two, Sergeant Preston and Lady Marriott. Won't they be surprised.'

'Oh the pros and antis, why didn't you keep a list?' she wrote to Heywood in November. 'Princess Olga [of Yugoslavia] who never spares one the cold douche, said the other day "I loved your book—moost people doon't you noo! . . ." It's still selling a thousand a week . . .'

Because *The Blessing* was concerned with fashionable society in France and England Nancy was accused of snobbishness by the inverted snobs. But she had written about the fraction of the world she knew intimately: she was not tempted to investigate its outskirts. To paraphrase Virginia Woolf's remark about Jane Austen, Nancy 'would not alter a hair on anybody's head, or move one brick or one blade of grass in a world which provided her with such exquisite delight'. Whatever arrows a jaundiced reviewer might sling, Evelyn Waugh, her most fastidious critic, had telegraphed 'deep homage'. His soothing message was followed by lavish sales.

In October for a change, she enjoyed a short visit to Rome— 'so much to look at in the warm sunshine, it was heavenly. But I am made for France, and fidget when away from Paris. Also there was nobody but D'Arcy [Osborne, ex-Minister to the Holy See, later Duke of Leeds] to take me sightseeing and he, though very faithful, on the doorstep every morning at eleven, is analphabet and this sort of thing went on: "Now these frescoes are by some very well-known artist whose name I have forgotten." I look in my Baedeker: Raphael. But he is a dear and I mustn't complain.'

Her recurrent itch to tease found vent in a flippant article about Rome which was published in the *Sunday Times*. Other tart impressions of the foreign places she visited were to follow periodically. The tease invariably succeeded. Because she compared the Eternal City to a village 'with its one post office, one railway station and life centred round the vicarage', many Romans were furious. Nor were they pleased by her remark that St. Peter's, 'seen from the colonnade, is very much like a lesser country house'. The Duchess of Sermoneta read the article out loud at a luncheon and destroyed it. What she minded, according to Nancy, was the statement that most of the palaces were

87

for sale. 'Prod despises the social life there,' she told her mother, 'and so would I if I lived there, literal *vacuum* in the upper storey of all and sundry, but for a short time it was highly agreeable, specially as they made such a fuss of me. I've done a spiffing *S. Times* article about it all.'

In January 1952 she told Heywood Hill: 'I've made £10,000 last year, not bad is it, but I need more so that I can go out hunting, it's all I think of now . . .' She meant hunting for antiques. Though badgered for interviews and articles, she was thoroughly savouring the sweets of success and her enjoyment was free from self-conceit. It was all such a breathless surprise.

Disregarding Hector Dexter, some American dames gave a luncheon in her honour. 'Have I boasted about the 200 Gov women ("all keen Mitford fans") who are giving a luncheon for me next Monday? I only hope it's not to beat me up as every one is the wife of a Dexter. Evangeline Bruce the ambassadress is very giggly about it I note . . .'

Particularly she enjoyed contributing a sketch in French to a charity revue. 'Here,' she wrote to me in April, 'we are all busy with our sketches for the charity revue in June. Mine is too lovely; the daughter of un vieux duc who becomes a man and wins the Tour de France. The duc doesn't turn a hair, "nous avons déja eu la tante Éon dans la famille". The Tour de France is in Racinian language and modern journalese—"les anciens rois de la route sont corroucés par les exploits de ce coureur mystérieux, ce Machiavel de la pédale, ce *super-crack* . . ."

'Violet [Trefusis] has retired to Florence to write hers, in the company of two professional dramaturges, this is thought most unfair!'

As with nearly all amateur productions there were hitches. 'I think I shall have to withdraw my sketch,' she wrote in May. 'They want to take out every joke, terrified of offending people, and the compère, on whom all depends, has now chucked the whole thing (not just me). How far they have gone since the *Chien Andalou*. I find it very odd (prudery I mean). I'm saying take it or leave it. Violet too is in trouble and Marcel Achard not allowed to have people in bathing dresses! ! !'

Nancy's sketch, however, was not withdrawn, and she took infinite pains over rehearsals. On 27th June she wrote to Heywood: 'Well, it went off all right I think. But how can one know with the dear French? I received exaggerated adulation from all. If I'd written *Macbeth* it could not have been more, but then so no doubt did Violet and you should only HEAR what they say to each other about her sketch. I think it's a good system, it keeps the moral at boiling point, but of course, it's hard for ONE to know the truth. What I can say is all my actors were perfection, it never went half as well at any rehearsal, so I got an agreeable surprise . . . The whole affair was masterly. Only two thoroughly bad sketches, only one pause and it only went on half an hour too long. The good sketches and all the tableaux vivants and ballets were perfection and there was a tango which made me ill with laughing. So everybody is feeling pleased and monumental sums were taken for charity. Every inch of space crammed and Marie in the poulaille was surrounded by duchesses and most impressed because the ones she didn't know were shown her by another femme de chambre, also M. Dior. I've never seen the tout Paris turn out in such force ever since I've lived here . . .'

Unfortunately the jokes evaporate in translation for as Nancy had to admit, 'the Tour de France means literally 0 to the English'. The sketch had to be altered 'because nobody would act in it if Cyclamen (the cyclist heroine) became a man for fear that one day the Duke of Windsor give a ball and not ask them as a revenge. They couldn't risk it . . .'

A faded typescript of it lies before me. The scene is set in the large drawing-room of a château, empty except for a chair and a table. Patches on the walls where pictures used to hang, two or three empty pedestals or niches.

The impoverished Duke and Duchess D'Espasse discuss their daughter Cyclamen, who instead of angling for a rich husband can only think of cycling—'all due to the grotesque name you saddled her with', the Duke complains. In the meantime three tourists who have paid 100 francs to visit the château are disgusted to find none of the treasures described glowingly in the guide book and want their money to be returned. Cyclamen enters with a racing bicycle and announces that she will retrieve the family fortune by winning the Tour de France under a male pseudonym: 'From today I am Cyclamen, Dauphiness of the Road!' 'She should have been a boy,' sighs the Duke, dreading the vexations in store for him at the Jockey Club on her account.

The angry tourists are refunded, and the steward-caretaker

(who is also the local mayor) lends the Duke and Duchess his television set, so that they may watch the race. The screen lights up and the excited Duchess exhorts her daughter to win: 'Remember our family motto: "I surpass". Courage, Cyclamen! Excelsior!'

The whole scene is mimed except Cyclamen's comments at the microphone and the radio reporter's text. The latter introduces 'this new, mysterious star of the road whose pluck and audacity are astounding,' as Mr. Cyclamen forges ahead of all the super-champions. At every winning post 'he is greeted by a genial American playboy named Homer on whom he flashes his first victorious smile.' Now and then the reporter passes the microphone to Cyclamen, whose incomprehensible remarks about regilding the family coat of arms are interpreted as due to fatigue.

Eventually Cyclamen wins the coveted trophy; is embraced by Homer; and recognized as a woman. Back at the château there is a long queue of tourists waiting to see the room where the new ace was born. 'But she was born at Neuilly,' exclaims the Duchess. 'Mum's the word!' says the steward. 'Already 50,000 francs worth of tickets have been sold at the entrance. There's even a gentleman who wants to buy all the champion's belongings as precious relics.' Cyclamen and Homer arrive and insist on being married immediately.

The Duchess protests but the Duke tells her: 'We must keep abreast of the times, dear.' The marriage contract is produced and the jubilant couple are married by the mayor. The Duchess, overcome with emotion, implores them to have 'lots of baby bicycles', and they pedal off to embark on the tour of America.

Evanescently frivolous, no doubt, this ephemeral trifle, a script for marionettes. What is noteworthy about the original is the giant strides Nancy had made in the French idiom. Her parody of the rhetorical clichés of French radio reporters is close to actuality. The impoverished Duke and Duchess in the empty château and the disgruntled tourists are obvious figures of fun.

I was unable to attend the revue but I was in Paris in July and Nancy gave a party for me. Never had I seen her look prettier; a rose in full bloom. She, too, might have won the Tour de France. *Pigeon Pie* had been republished and Nancy told Mark Ogilvie-Grant (7th June, 1952): '10,000 copies have been sold, so at least 30,000 people now must know all about

90

Vocal Lodge and the butter coloured wig and the wigless pig ... My American agent writes that she has a film offer for *Pigeon Pie*, shall I say: yes on condition that the King of Song [Mark] acts his own part in it?' ... 'Noël [Coward] is here. I got a very garlicky kiss (English people here always stink of it I note) and "Darling I've got such fan messages for you— *Pigeoners*." '

Now the novel which had fallen flat on its original publication in 1940 received better notices in America than her other books. 'It's selling madly,' she told her mother. 'When I think how poor I was when it came out, almost starving (literally really—I used to lunch at Sibyl's awful canteen for 1/- and I can still remember the pain I used to have after it) I feel quite cross, though it's nice at all times to have a little extra money.' To Heywood Hill she wrote in August: 'Fancy, since I left you I've made considerably over £50,000. Do be impressed. Local girl makes good ...' Bertrand Russell had become one of her recent fans and she was greatly flattered when he told her that he went regularly to *The Little Hut*. 'I have always wondered who it is that goes regularly and now we know. Old philosophers.' In November she wrote again: 'I've been asked to send a short autobiographical sketch of myself to a Gov literary Who's Who. They send a sample: "It was during the years of bitter poverty in the hut of old Jabez the Trapper that the poet in me was born". I've said that I was born in the slums of London because my father was a second son and in England second sons are always poor. I suggest that it was during the bitter years before he succeeded that the poet in ME was born. Do tell Osbert [Sitwell].'

Though Nancy had won fame as a novelist she seldom read contemporary novels. 'How I wish I could get on with Miss Compton-Burnett but it's my blind spot,' she confessed. 'So I plod on with Saint-Simon, such a nice readable edition, and the Racine, which on account of the notes is as good as *Punch*.' With her serious addiction to history, above all eighteenth-century history, she was easily diverted from fiction to biography. No adequate biography of Madame de Pompadour had appeared in English—another incentive to embark on such a venture. 'I'm really starting from scratch,' she said. 'I know more about Louis XIV than Louis XV.'

'I'm doing Pomp, very much enjoying it myself though

nobody else may,' she told Christopher Sykes (16th January, 1953). 'I've finished an account of what I think the battle of Fontenoy was like, trying to pretend that I hope the English are going to win. (As both the generals were huns and most of the French troops Irish there can't be any very strong national feelings over it.) I'm rather nervous, never having done such a thing before, and with the fearful example of my poor friend Polnay's book on Charles Edward, so good yet so badly received, before me.'

From 'Mr. Street' she wrote to Mrs. Hammersley: 'On 7th April (1953) I retire to a heavenly pension at Versailles to get on with Pomp. Impossible here—friends are pouring over, brought out by the fine weather and buzzing like bees on my telephone. I think Versailles is just the locale, don't you? (in fact a very important part of the book depends on the geography of the château, which I shall get to understand I hope).' And from Versailles: 'I really am working—two or three hours in the library here and until midnight in my bed, and most of the day— seven or eight hours. Evelyn [Waugh] who came to see me, says it's too much, one shouldn't do more than four, but it suits me. Everybody has their own system. The library is bliss, they have of course everything and all hop round ONE, very different from British Museum or Nationale . . .

'I've got a letter from Binkie Beaumont saying I *must* go to New York, everything paid, with the *Hut*. Goodness! He speaks as if it would make all the difference if I went—how queer— as I said Shakespeare and Oscar Wilde don't go and yet their plays run. I don't think I can ginger myself up to it, really, all alone like that. What do you advise. It's not till October . . .

'One could do worse than to come and live here, only not in winter, I doubt if it would be warm enough for ONE. Also at the moment it is too full . . . The other guests are nearly all American soldiers who are perfectly unbearable but are out all of every day except Sunday. Then there is an ill old mad French-man with his nurse who says sententiously to the company in general "il faut les aimer!" and clinks bottles in a very sinister way. Yesterday the Americans never got up at all—trays of chicken, champagne, vitamin foods and *Danish* butter (why?) went to them at intervals and they came down to dinner in their pyjamas. I work of course every working hour as there is nothing else to do.'

Nancy's eyesight troubled her and she had spasmodic misgivings during the course of composition. 'Getting on famously,' she wrote to Heywood Hill (15th April, 1953) 'except that I am tortured by my eyes which is a bore because if I can't write all day, or read, there's nothing I can do except sit with them shut and that is so dull when one is dying to be AT IT.' And to me from Versailles (27th May): 'I should never have taken it on. I haven't the education—I feel very low about it. However too late now, as in childbirth to STOP.' On 22nd June from Paris: 'I'm still shut up and working very hard and going to no parties . . . I don't want to stir up the telephones. The book is good—best I've done I think, but the public won't like it, reviewers are always beastly about the biography of a novelist.'

The book finished, again she wrote to Heywood (18th July): 'I gave Pomp to Hamishham (who came specially) in the afternoon and met him for dinner and DIED on the way there. "I'm sure you'll find another publisher" was what I envisaged, and only saying it after dinner when I felt stronger. However, one look at his face and I could see all was well. The relief was great . . .'

After 'a terrible month of August, sitting for hours every day in the Lyric Theatre during a "heat wave" (i.e. rather warm, muggy and cloudy)' because *The Little Hut* was being rehearsed for America, Nancy fled to Hyères where she stayed with the affable Chilean Tony Gandarillas. Tony could not exist without opium, thanks to which he was very spry and continued to beguile his friends with cosmopolitan gossip in ripe old age, but I am sure he never persuaded Nancy to share a pipe with him, though she was on tenterhooks about her first biography. 'The book, read by a few souls when I was in London, had a mixed reception,' she informed me in September. 'Cecil Beaton, who read it because he was doing the dust cover, thinks it very bad indeed. However Raymond [Mortimer], *on the whole*, gave it his blessing. So did Dr. Cobban, the greatest living expert on French history, who very kindly consented to have a look and take out some of the grosser errors.'

Nancy had a tendency to identify herself with the characters she delineated, and it gave her peculiar satisfaction to write about a period she appreciated thoroughly. Madame de Pompadour seemed to have been chosen by destiny to become Louis XV's mistress and she was already a queen of fashion

93

when she captivated him. For the next twenty years, until she died at the age of forty-two, she swayed politics at home and abroad, played the role of a female Maecenas, and remained indispensable to the restless and blasé monarch. Undoubtedly Nancy was biased in favour of Madame de Pompadour and Louis XV but this added vivacity to her narrative. She also had a talent for simplification: her language, sometimes verging on schoolroom slang, was far from that of the scholastic historian. The result was a gain in readability, though here and there we may smile at certain colloquialisms.

Madame de Pompadour led Nancy on to Voltaire and Frederick the Great with a backward inspection of the Sun King in between. She had found a subject after her own heart into which she could infuse her delight in the Ile de France, and her book is a prose paean to pleasure—the *douceur de vivre* before the French Revolution. One of the chapters is entitled *Pleasure*. Aware that this was still frowned upon, Nancy wrote: 'People in those days approved of pleasure. When the Duc de Nivernais left on his very serious and tricky mission to London after the Seven Years War, he was described as going "like Anacreon, crowned with roses and singing of pleasure." This was by way of being high praise.' Furthermore, she explained that 'the act of love was not yet regarded with an almost mystical awe, it had but a limited importance. Like eating, drinking, fighting, hunting and praying it was part of a man's life, but not the very most important part of all. If Madame de Pompadour were not physically in love with the King, being constitutionally incapable of passion, it would not be too much to say that she worshipped him; he was her God. She had other interests and affections, but she made them all revolve round him; rarely can a beautiful woman have loved so single-mindedly.'

Before the book's publication in 1954 Nancy admitted to Heywood Hill: 'I must say these months of waiting are very bad for an author's nerves! . . . The worst of living alone (a state which I personally prefer) is that there is nobody to say "oh well, not so bad this and this is rather nice" when one begins to see things en noir. I quite see it wouldn't do at all for a pessimistic character. As you know life generally appears to me in a rosy light . . .'

Later she was to become impervious to the arrows of reviewers, but having put so much of herself into *Madame de*

94

Pompadour she was unduly sensitive. On 13th March she wrote to Heywood: 'I've got a letter from Dr. Cobban saying he'll bet my reviewers have never read an original 18th century document, or any secondary stuff since Carlyle. Wouldn't they be furious at this news! But far the most beastly doesn't come under this category, it is A. J. P. Taylor in the *Manchester Guardian*. In a way I think his review holds more water than Harold Nicolson's and Cyril's—he doesn't object to the history or indeed deign to mention it at all—but the fact that somebody like me should poach on the sacred preserves. He obviously couldn't bear the book. I don't know much about him, do you? Gooch is easily my favourite so far, though I did love Cyril's [Connolly's] for being so funny . . . A few more reviews. Don't say I said this but the fact is none of them know their subject and that is why they seem so˙ confused and contradictory . . .'

Again Nancy had achieved a prodigious success. I remember numerous passengers on the Channel steamer to Calais hugging their copies of *Madame de Pompadour*, as if in preparation for the fleshpots of Gay Paree. Nancy was the recipient of even more fan-letters. 'Oh the horror of fan-letters,' she exclaimed to her friend Alvilde Lees-Milne. 'It's so odd why they should think one should *want* to know their boring reactions to one's work. Like a breath of fresh air was one I got yesterday. "My grand-mother was born Mitford, she married a farm labourer called Potts. In spite of the opprobrium attaching to the name I persist in calling myself Mitford-Potts . . . I live alone in a bungalow and shall soon no doubt be murdered by one of the many people who think all Mitfords better dead. Yours sincerely, Mavis Mitford-Potts. P.S. Please don't think I admire your idiotic books." '

'Every single German publisher has been after Pomp,' Nancy informed Mrs. Ham, 'and I've got a huge advance finally from one in Hamburg. I told Marie-Louise Bousquet who said, *"au fond c'est le seul peuple qui nous aime."* '

Her social life was often harried, as was mine in Florence, by the irrepressible Violet Trefusis, and we had this singular bugbear in common. We called her Auntie Vi and exchanged anecdotes about her for many years, interrupted, in my case, by a definite estrangement owing to Violet's extreme rudeness. Though she possessed a facile wit which depended mainly on

95

punning Violet was a law unto herself, perhaps the most selfish woman I have known, so selfish and inconsiderate that she became a joke, except to a tiny clique of blind adorers who believed she was a daughter of King Edward VII (a role she loved to assume) and treated her like capricious royalty. Mr. Nigel Nicolson's *Portrait of a Marriage* was yet to be written, but if we believed what we were told then, Violet had been courted by all the world's leading statesmen, musicians and poets. It is fitting that Philippe Jullian, author of *The Snob Spotter's Guide*, should write the biography of this super-snob for whom literature was a mere hobby. She was one of those friends who made one prefer a foe. As Nancy, while engaged on her *Pompadour*, complained, 'Violet is literally torturing me, she rings up all the time. I have to leave the telephone on because of various matters to do with the lease—nobody else telephones and I've begged her not to, she doesn't pay the least attention. I'm really beginning to quite *hate* her.'

We had a rhyme:

> Violet Trefusis
> Never refuses
> But often confuses.

'I've got a luncheon party today. Violet arrived for it yesterday,' Nancy told Heywood Hill. 'I was eating a little bit of fish. I said you MUST go away but she tottered to the table, scooped up all the fish and all the potatoes, left half and threw cigarette ash over it. I could have KILLED her. Lady Montdore exactly. Nothing left for Marie and hardly anything for me.'

But there was no escape from the predatory Violet in the small circle Nancy frequented, and it was the same for me in Florence.

'Old Auntie is being wonderful and keeps us all on the hop,' she told Robin McDouall. 'She is said to have bought a house without doors or windows and with only a skylight through which she comes and goes on a broomstick. This *potin de Paris* was recounted to me at luncheon today and I haven't yet verified it. Also she rang up one of the partners at Jullian's whom she has long known but seldom sees and warmly urged that he should spend May and June in Florence with her. He was reeling with amazement when she added she had sent him the manuscript of her novel which, she added, has been a coast to coast best seller in America. *Alors il a compris.* He asked me what her *standing* (this is a new French word) is in the English world of letters. I was really at a loss. I said she is very well known but I think more for her mémoires than her novels—?'

To Alvilde Lees-Milne Nancy wrote (6th February, 1954): 'Last night Philippe Jullian gave his first dinner party. It would have been intensely agreeable but for Violet and the cold. Honestly Violet is the ruin of a small evening—as for the cold, it took 3 hot water bottles to stop me shivering afterwards. He had Peyrefitte, a luscious, rather funny, rather horrible man, J-L Curtis the writer, and the nice fat Princesse de Croy. Violet made up her face 10 times at dinner. I counted.

'Tonight is Beaton Night at the Embassy, a dinner of 38 we are told. So I can wear my ball-dress, oh good.'

Cecil Beaton's state visits were always red letter days. On a future occasion Nancy wrote: 'I went to no fewer than five dinner parties for him—in fact my clothes completely gave out! At the Embassy I sat next to Cocteau who said that Rosamond [Lehmann] is translating something of his, "she must be a *very* old lady now." I said well, yes, about my age. It turned out he has never seen her and thought she was about 80—don't you find it odd? Of course she started very young, with *Poussière* [*Dusty Answer*]!'

'Don't you find it odd?' had become one of Nancy's regular refrains. 'I've seen something of Willie [Somerset Maugham] while he's been here—I've never known him so agreeable. But by a sort of wonderful magic he finds the same sort of people here with exactly the same drawing-rooms as those he frequents on the Riviera. Thumping jazz gramophone and bad modern pictures if you know what I mean. I find it too odd for words—especially as he seems to like and enjoy serious conversation.'

A little serious conversation went a long way with Maugham, who was really more interested in people who could provide him with another plot or a good game of bridge. But he had known Nancy's great friend Violet Hammersley as a child in Paris and he shared Nancy's amusement at outrageous conduct. He expected most people to behave badly, whereas Nancy, in spite of the failure of her marriage, was less cynical. Her hero, Captain Scott of the Antarctic, could not be fitted into Maugham's formula of human caddishness and she remained a secret hero worshipper. She was too warm-hearted to swallow ready-made formulas but she always loved to tease.

A grand opportunity to tease as many people as possible came from an unexpected quarter when Professor Alan Ross of Birmingham University produced an article on polite English usage in a scholarly Finnish journal. Its origin might be traced to Uncle Matthew's dogmatic pronouncements on the subject in *The Pursuit of Love*. To quote Nancy's letter to Heywood Hill, 1st May, 1954: 'My crazy friend Prof. Ross has written such a lovely pamphlet for la Société Néo-philologique de Helsinki, printed in Finland but written in English, on upper class usage in England. Entitled LINGUISTIC CLASS INDICATORS IN PRESENT DAY ENGLISH. It has sentences like "The ideal U-address (U stands for Upper Class) is *P, Q, R,* where *P* is a place-name, *Q* a describer (manor, court, house, etc) and *R* the name of a county . . . but today few gentlemen can maintain this standard and they often live in houses with non-U names such as *Fairmeads* or *El Nido*." (What will the Finns make of it?) Anyway it seems a natural for the Xmas market, illustrated by O. Lancaster and entitled *Are You U?* I've suggested this to the Prof (who may of course think it dreadfully infra dig) and I've told him, if the idea appeals to him to send you a copy and you would perhaps advise about a publisher. It is dreadfully funny throughout because written in a serious scientific style. I'm glad to say *Pursuit of Love* is one of his source books. He is a great new character in my life and a card if ever there was one— U himself, and in my expert opinion he has got everything right but one.'

The first-fruit of this was Nancy's essay *The English Aristocracy*, published in *Encounter*, September, 1955. 'I lovingly cook away at it all day and I think it the best thing I've ever done,' she confided to Heywood. 'It's a sort of anthology of teases— something for everybody. I think it will be safer to be in Greece when it appears . . .'

To illustrate the typical aristocratic outlook on money her case history of the imaginary Lord Fortinbras is like the synopsis of a novel which might have been written by Evelyn Waugh. She denounces those who 'cheerfully sold their houses in London and "developed" their property without a thought for the visible result.' Park Lane, most of Mayfair, the Adelphi, and so on bear witness to a barbarity which I, for one, cannot forgive.' And there is an autobiographical undertone when she writes: 'Divest, divest, is the order of the day. The nobleman used to study a map of his estate to see how it could be enlarged, filling out a corner here, extending a horizon there. Nowadays he has no such ambitions; he would much rather sell than buy. The family is not considered as it used to be; the ancestors are no longer revered, indeed they are wilfully forgotten, partly perhaps from a feeling of guilt when all that they so carefully amassed is being so carelessly scattered.' Some of this is very near the knuckle.

The September issue of *Encounter* was promptly sold out. Copies were annotated by 'furious aristos' and a spate of indignant letters proved that Nancy had hit the mark. 'Oh my post!' she exclaimed to Alvilde Lees-Milne, 'Everybody now is furious—Frogs, Greeks and English—and Geoffrey [Gilmour] says the only place left for me is America where they can't read. One man wrote (to *Encounter*) "I often go to the Guards' Club and there they generally say cheers or something before drinking. Since the article they still say it, but with some reference to Miss M." Can't you hear them: To hell with Miss M-!! Another wrote, to me, "my secretary has just read your article and is so furious she refuses to type a letter to you." I wrote back is your secretary a Duchess?'

The sequel was a booklet called *Noblesse Oblige*, with contributions by Evelyn Waugh, Peter Fleming, Christopher Sykes and Sir John Betjeman (a versification of non-U terminology in unforgettable stanzas), in addition to Nancy's article and Professor Ross's, illustrated by Osbert Lancaster in his happiest vein.

'I loved your U piece,' Nancy told Christopher Sykes. 'I think you must moil a bit more, and invent future U and non-U expressions for things like journeys to the moon and horrid future things of that sort. Atom burns perhaps and tabloid meals . . . You can tease me a great deal more in it—I can take it . . . P.S. Artificial insemination non-U.' But Evelyn Waugh's contribution was rather double-edged, as Nancy complained to Patrick Leigh Fermor: 'Evelyn is anti-*one* and begins, "We must remember that Miss M. only became a hon at the age of 12 and it went to her head and she has been a fearful snob ever since"— and other cruel words. I said Evelyn do put a footnote to say that you love me in spite of all. "That is perfectly evident," he replied. Only to the reader with second sight.'

Evelyn's chief pinprick was directed at Nancy's socialism:

'Alertly studied, your novels reveal themselves as revolutionary tracts and here, in your essay, you speak out boldly: "Hear me, comrades. I come from the heart of the enemy's camp. You think they have lost heart for the fight. I have sat with them round their camp fires and heard them laughing. They are laughing at *you*. They are not beaten yet, comrades. Up and at them again." '

The squib fired off by Nancy in playful mood continued to send hissing sparks, long after Nancy became bored with it. Unfortunately the pother it caused helped to falsify the popular image of her character.

Some of her U-shibboleths she came to take seriously nevertheless, not only in post-prandial argument, and I suspected that her stubborn prejudice against her early novels might partly be due to the inclusion of such non-U words as mirrors ('Every mirror was besieged by women powdering their noses'), mantelpiece ('over the mantelpiece hung a Victorian mirror', 'an enormous Gothic mantelpiece of pitch-pine,' etc, in *Highland Fling*), and notepaper ('Like most people who write for a living he hated writing letters, and moreover seldom had any notepaper in his lodgings,' in *Christmas Pudding*.)

As Evelyn Waugh pointed out, Nancy could be an agitator of genius. She could not resist a childish temptation to shock, more mischievous than malicious. When she was quoted in some newspaper as saying that John Wilkes Booth was her favourite character because he had killed Lincoln, 'the most odious character in history,' as many Europeans as Americans were incensed. Even in her cherished France she could not resist writing an article which infuriated many whose opinion she cared for. This was more than a tease, for she sought to justify the execution of Marie-Antoinette as a traitress. Prince Pierre of Monaco cut her dead and as her dear friend Princess Dolly Radziwill remarked, 'Some doors will for ever be closed against her.' Perhaps Rose Macaulay was thinking of her attack on the luckless Queen when she described Nancy as 'deeply heartless'. Her spirited defence of Madame de Pompadour, whom Carlyle had dismissed as a 'high rouged, unfortunate female of whom it is not proper to speak without necessity,' may strike many as perverse by contrast. I suspect there was a neurotic dichotomy between Nancy's barbed pen and her warm heart.

*

Though she protested that she hated travelling she was easily tempted by an invitation from the Ambassador Sir William and Lady Hayter to visit them in Moscow in 1954 when the Iron Curtain was impenetrable to tourists.

'I still haven't got my visa for Russia,' she wrote to Heywood Hill (1st May, 1954); 'Iris Hayter thinks they are busy reading my books, but one of the secretaries here says it all depends on Burgess!! They've had my passport for an absolute age . . .' Then on 31st May, hurray! 'Well, I'm off. The Soviets went to ground with my passport and the Embassy (ours) said there's only one card left for us to play, you must go yourself and try and get it out of them. But take a book and make no plans for the rest of the day, they will keep you there for hours. So off I went—gave my name—was immediately ushered into a huge room, full of pictures of Stalin, whose occupant rose to his feet crying, "Je vous attend depuis des semaines." It was quite sinister—come into my parlour. I was out in the street again, with visa, in 2 minutes. Then I went to Cook and said can you send me to Moscow, thinking perhaps there would be more difficulties. The man simply looked through a heap of brochures —"Come to sunny Monte Carlo" and so on, until he got to one saying "Come to lovely Russia" and sold me the ticket there and then . . .'

Two weeks later (14th June): 'I'm back having had the most fascinating fortnight of my whole life. I ended up with 3 days alone in Leningrad (at the Astoria!) I think I must write it all down and send it to various buddies—no obligation to read. I can't write for the papers. William (the Ambassador) has asked me not to and anyhow I think I couldn't have. The Russians were *more* than kind to me and it would be a bad return to laugh at them, while if I managed to suppress the laughs everybody would say I am a fellow traveller and so on . . . Nobody knows what *real excitement* is who hasn't flown in a Russian aeroplane and seen the Red Square parade . . .'

Eight years later, when 'much water had flown under the bridges,' Nancy published her diary of this brief visit in *The Water Beetle*. It is studded with observations of significant details and the laughs are not suppressed. Of the aeroplane flight she wrote: 'We shot into the air with the minimum of fuss —no revving, no voice bossing about safety belts—no safety belts either. But we never seemed to gain any height at all and

101

it was "Oh do mind that tree" all the way to Moscow. So I was able to see the endless steppes very comfortably as from a train.'

The Red Army parade was to commemorate the 300th anniversary of the union with the Ukraine. She was privileged to watch it from 'a small stand in the Red Square for members of the *Corps diplomatique* and a few Russian officials . . . Massed bands punctuated by cannon fire instead of drums, endless marching troops, MIGs whizzing between two church steeples; Bulganin, like a toy, standing up in a motor which dashed about from regiment to regiment, greeted by Ra-ra-ra—all as exciting as an air raid and all laid on for the commercial travellers [Malenkov and Co] and me. No other audience allowed . . .'

About the lack of tipping and the apparent lack of interest in money she observed: 'If the love of money is the root of all evil, it is perhaps the root of a certain amount of humanity, too, and this total detachment has something frightening about it. It was the single thing about the Russians that struck me most. Have they always been like this—has communism produced it or is it because there is so little to buy?' According to nineteenth-century travellers they had not always been like this. Lady Londonderry, who visited Russia in 1836 complained: 'The cheating is terrible and possessors of hotels and lodgings seem to regard all foreigners, especially English, their lawful prey.' Evidently cheating has been sublimated into the realm of international politics: it has risen in scale and prestige.

Nancy's comments on Russian women—'super-govs'—; on a dress show in one of the big shops; on the pictures in a gallery of Russian art; on Lenin's tomb; and her conversation with a woman from the State publishing house, are hilariously Mitfordian. ' "How many copies would you sell here of a popular novel?" I asked. She replied fifty million. N: "How absolutely wonderful. I can't wait to come and be a Soviet writer."

'Super-gov (clearly not taking to the idea): "This has its good side and its bad."

'N: "Well it can't have a bad side for the writer. Do tell me the name of a book which has sold like this."

'Super-gov.: "*Cement.*" '

A far cry indeed from *The Pursuit of Love*!

Back in 'Mr. Street', Nancy summoned a few friends to a caviar feast but nobody ventured to ask her about her recent voyage. Paradoxically, caviar produces an atmosphere of *luxe, calme et volupté* in which it is almost painful to introduce the subject of Soviet Russia. In any case Parisians are more parochial than we are and prefer to converse about topics nearer home.

It was suggested that she print her Russian diary for private circulation but she was warned that some unscrupulous journalist might get hold of it and use it. She told Heywood Hill, 'as nearly all my friends are unscrupulous journalists this seems a danger which I can't risk'. And as Nancy was very much 'in the news' her diary had to wait.

Having visited Prince Yussupov's country house, now a museum near Moscow, she was interested to meet him at dinner with Dior. 'Goodness the lies that man tells,' she exclaimed to Heywood. 'He pretends his house—the one I saw —was looted and all the objects sold abroad and that he has often seen his furniture etc in museums and shops. But you can plainly *see* that everything in that house has always been there, nothing missing and all is of wretched quality. I sat listening with great impatience to a stream of obvious inventions and a lot of dreary mystical stuff thrown in. I must say he is exceedingly handsome . . .'

The sizzling repercussions of *Noblesse Oblige* led to further interviews that were not altogether distasteful. Nancy was informed that 'it has now reached the large non U public and the orders from provincial booksellers are beating all records. Christopher [Sykes] has made a very good joke—he says the great interest taken in the Titanic was because she was a U-boat.'

To Heywood Hill she wrote (12th April, 1956): 'Now for the U book. An absolutely blissful person flew over to interview me about it called Scott James? Fitz James? *Sunday Express*. Terribly beautiful and elegant. Evelyn says those nice ones are always the worst . . .' And later in the year, to Alvilde Lees-Milne: 'A sort of red-brick young man came to see me last night, by appointment, to get stuff for a profile for some American paper. He is English. He was ready to kill me, I could see, and was primed with hundreds of disobliging questions, why are you such a snob and so on. In the end he became

103

slightly tamer and was forced to admit that Evelyn is nastier than I am. He says people HATE my books so terribly, he had poked about in them and found a great many deplorable passages which he produced in triumph. Stayed two hours—I was a jelly.' A banner headline appeared in a newspaper DOWN WITH U! and John Sutro flourished it with mock pomposity in Nancy's courtyard. A long article in a Dutch paper described her as Nancy Mitford Schrijfster, femme du monde, enfant terrible. 'Gracious, what is *schrijfster*, one asks oneself. The Dutchman who sends it writes to me describing a visit to London. "I liked best an afternoon in some club where Stephen Spender and 25 other poets recited their poetry" . . . What club? Not White's, I'll bet . . .'

In the meantime 'Pomp', as Nancy nicknamed her maiden biography (which Gaston Palewski said should be called *Pursuit of Kings*) had appeared in a French translation and received a flattering ovation. One of the articles about Nancy described Heywood Hill's bookshop as *'une librairie de Mayfair où les fils de Lords donnaient des rendez-vous clandestins à la Bohème de Chelsea.'* Apropos of which Nancy remarked to Heywood, 'Quite a good idea for the basement—no?' The basement of 10 Curzon Street was then reserved for children's books. And the Dutch translator of *The Pursuit of Love* asked whether he could call 'Hun's [*sic*] cupboard "the cave of the nobles".'

CHAPTER EIGHT

ADAME DE POMPADOUR had launched Nancy into the midst of eighteenth-century France before the Revolution and even while she was 'thinking up a few teases for *Encounter*' she wrote to Heywood Hill (21st March, 1955): 'I've at last got a vague idea for a book. Voltaire's love affair with Madame du Châtelet. I must say it's a shriek from beginning to end—especially the end, and I think I could make something short but amusing of it . . .'

A reluctant excursion into the film world intervened. She informed Patrick Leigh Fermor (15th August, 1955): 'I was offered, I must say enough money to live on for a year, to translate a film on Marie-Antoinette. Quite all right until you realize that every gesture has to be written down—"she is about to pick her nose but changes her mind and scratches her leg instead." So the labour is endless. It amuses me to do the dialogue but there are pages of directions to every sentence of dialogue. The film itself, written by two nice clever Frenchmen, Delannoy and Zimmer, is first class, but they are having a terrible time with the star, a horrible little man like a jockey. He is Fersen, and considers the part is not *strong* enough, and he wants Lafayette's lines as well as his own. I said, at one of the endless, stuffy meetings we have every two or three days, "whatever you do and whoever acts in it the person who will steal any film on Marie-Antoinette is Louis XVI because he is the only interesting character in the story." Very ill received. How I loathe all actors—it's a lesson really never to work for films or stage. Then the great panjandrum is a Scotch peasant called Clark, one of the romances of industry, who seems to own the British Isles. He came for a lightning visit and said to me all in one breath, "After this I'm going to sign you on to write a film, like *Cavalcade,* on the British in India, and then on the ordinary little people of France and Britain and then one on the dying crofters of Mull." All very ME, I must say. He said I can consider myself booked up for the next three years. He then buggered off to a meeting to discuss building tourist hotels in Russia—leaving me to receive general felicitations. "He liked you—!!" My present contract comes to an end in October, thank heavens!

'So you see no jokes. I sit alone in a lovely empty Paris— so empty you'd think there had been myxamitosis, and work really all day. I have to do ten pages a day and it's a lot.'

In January 1956 she started, 'in a very desultory way,' on *Voltaire in Love,* which in my opinion is the best of her historical productions. In February she informed Mrs. Hammersley: 'I've really begun a book at last, rather a relief to have taken the plunge. Voltaire and Madame du Châtelet—it's been simmering for some time as you know. I'd rather do a novel, but not unless really inspired. Colonel on my side—he says how many novelists have written more than three or four good ones? Very few. I am quite pleased with my last three— no use writing dreary pot-boilers and lowering the level, do you agree? . . . I worked out of doors for hours today.' During its composition she was lucky to secure the sympathetic support of Mr. Theodore Besterman, the editor of Voltaire's letters including those to his niece Madame Denis, hitherto unpublished, proving that he became her lover five years before the death of Madame du Châtelet, his acknowledged mistress.

In one of her teasing letters to Mrs. Ham (26th March, 1956) ending with 'Some fiendish love, Horror', Nancy mentioned that she was also collaborating with Miss Lucy Norton on a translation of Saint-Simon—'she to do the work and I'm to write a sort of running commentary. She's quite first class I think (a real translator, not one of those who sits up in bed scribbling away with no reference to the text. Not one of those Isle of Wighters if you know what I mean). We expect to make thousands (horror touch of sheer genius).'

Evelyn Waugh arrived in April, 'which means downing tools again.' As she could not get on with her work in Paris her old crony Victor Cunard suggested that she come to Venice.

But even Venice was too social; the neighbouring island of Torcello offered her the right combination of 'heat and quietness' she longed for. From Torcello, chez Cipriani, she wrote to Mrs. Ham on the Isle of Wight (2nd June) that it was 'the most perfect place for work I ever was in (except of course the other Isle) . . . The waiters here are sweet. They are like wonderful nannies, think I don't eat enough and try to stuff me with food. The result is I've only just escaped a first class liver attack.'

Recalling Ruskin's purple passage about Torcello in *The Stones of Venice* ('Mother and daughter, you behold them both in their widowhood—Torcello and Venice . . .') and the very ancient history of its Cathedral, Campanile and Baptistry (visited briefly by hurried flocks of tourists) it was incongruous to visualize Nancy there 'working terrifically' on the seventeen-year liaison of the cynical and worldly Voltaire. 'I've come to a sort of half way house with my book,' she told Heywood Hill (7th July). 'It's better than I thought. Uphill work though, compared with Pomp. It is . . . one long succession of rows which are almost impossible to disentangle or render amusing.'

'I've got an idea for you,' she wrote to Mrs. Ham. 'Why not translate Voltaire's *Lettres Philosophiques*—sometimes called *Lettres Anglaises*—which he wrote when he got back from England. They aren't letters but short essays on Quakers, Parliament, the drama (*Shakespeare n'a pas une étincelle de goût*) and so on—screamingly funny and not a long book. If my book did well it would give them a fillip . . .'

Though Nancy resisted social blandishments in Venice and the Lido on this occasion, Victor Cunard had unwittingly set a new pattern for Nancy's existence: henceforth she went to Venice during part of every summer and it became as much of an annual treat as Fontaines les Nonnes, to which she looked forward in September. As she wrote to Mrs. Ham: 'I found a postcard from you written a year ago saying "everything looks very bad." It looks a good deal worse now doesn't it! But I pin all my hopes to Fontaines, *ses eaux, ses agréments, ses jeux, son clair de lune*, etc. etc.'

Back in Paris—'lovely and hot again so my spirits, which move with the thermometer, are up'—Nancy went on a sight-seeing tour of all Voltaire's houses. Mr. Besterman's edition of his letters was a constant stimulus. But in Paris interruptions were inevitable. 'Book goes slow but smashing, or at least I think so but then I always do. Violet [Trefusis] telephoned. As she can write books without working she doesn't understand the necessity, for those less gifted, of doing so.' And again (to Alvilde Lees-Milne): 'Sacrée Violette! She rang up and said you must give a luncheon party for me, so I weakmindedly did. It went very badly, with Denys Cochin saying Cocteau is a blague and Picasso se fiche du monde and silly old Vi pretending to be shocked and wounded. Very funny that it is now the young generation who says all that. Well afterwards she said that she is going to *show you Spain*—strongly hinting that she has a lover there in the bull-fighting trade. Carmen Trefusis . . .'

The telephone, although disturbing, had some humorous compensations. 'So funny, a friend who had better be nameless, rang up and asked if I could find out from the Jebbs [Lord and Lady Gladwyn] anything about le petit Y, with whom her daughter is in love. So I had ages with Cynthia [Lady Gladwyn] who had nothing but good to say—then rang up Mme X who listened rather impatiently and then said Yes, but has he ever had a woman? Oh how I screamed—so typically French! I said really I can't ask the British ambassadress that. Or can I?'

From Fontaines she wrote in October: 'I seem to have moved in here for life—Mme Costa turns a deaf ear when I speak of going away and as I am perfectly happy I stay until Colonel's return. . . . The Chabots, Yolande and Jeanne are here. After meals we do nothing but talk about the pictures of les petits. *"Moi je préfère la p'tite." "Eh bien non, pour moi le p'tit est plus ressemblant."* ' Some of us would have thought this rather dull but it suited Nancy who saw it all through rose-coloured spectacles as usual. In the evenings she played bridge, which she considered 'a vital element of country life because one can't chat all and every day'. About bridge she wrote: 'It's only the English who get cross and, as a rule, only those who can't play for nuts. I play a certain amount here and never see crossness. I believe it's generally because the person is cross with herself but won't admit it. I've noticed in life there are three things nobody will admit they do badly, playing bridge, talking French, and driving a car . . . Riding used to be another.'

She was still working hard, though she dare not mention the subject to her pious hostess who spent most of her time on her knees in church. Her private thoughts revolved round Voltaire who, as she twitted Mrs. Ham, compared translations to servants who are sent to deliver a message and say the opposite of what they were told to say. 'Three Abbés and one Bishop was the bag on Monday. Not bad?' They would have been shocked, however, had they been aware of Nancy's literary preoccupations.

'The complete works of the devil, Voltaire, are hidden under the back stairs and I smuggle the volumes up to my bedroom like a schoolgirl with *The Green Hat*,' she told me. 'Haven't dared confess I am writing about him! Everybody here is between 80 and 100 so they regard me as young and beautiful and rather dashing—it is very nice.'

With her partiality for military heroes which was to lead to her last book on Frederick the Great, Nancy was charmed by 'dear Monty'—Field-Marshal Lord Montgomery. As Lord Gladwyn relates in his *Memoirs*: 'One of our social triumphs was to effect a conjunction between Nancy Mitford and Field-Marshal Montgomery. Monty had started the ball rolling by saying to me one morning out of the blue: "Read a novel the other day. Hardly ever do. By a woman, too. You wouldn't know it, I expect. It's called *The Pursuit of Love*, by Nancy Mitford." "Monty", I said, "Nancy is one of our oldest and dearest friends. You must meet her!" "Well, haven't much time. But if you like. Short lunch." Nancy, suitably approached, had said "But, darling, he's divine. So *Roman* and *Shakespearian*. Of course I should be charmed." So they were next to each other at our narrow table and, needless to say, both being of great intelligence, they got on like a house on fire. Afterwards, when I was Ambassador, we usually had, at the end of each summer season, a jolly lunch *à quatre* under the big *marronnier* in the Embassy garden (now dead). And, always, it was the greatest fun.' After one of these occasions Nancy reported: 'He said the French haven't fought since Napoleon. I said what about 1914? Yes, but they cracked up in 1918. Well the Germans cracked up worse. The only time I've seen him without an answer. So I said in a buttering voice, But all depends on the leader, as YOU know. He beamed again. He *is* a baby . . .'

Nancy devoured the biographies of generals with gusto. 'You must read Sir Philip Magnus's *Kitchener*,' she told Mrs.

Hammersley. 'It's one of the funniest books I've read for years. He was an absolute brute and a fearfully incompetent general so *why* was he the idol of our race and nation? But funnily enough one gets rather fond of him towards the end. Certain things in common with Monty it must be said . . . Do tell anything you know about Kitchener. Did you ever see him? I can think of nothing else now. What a good writer, Sir Philip Magnus.'

Much as she enjoyed visiting friends and relations in England, she wrote to Alvilde Lees-Milne in a despondent mood (5th December, 1956): 'I shall never be able to leave these walls again. The nervous strain of finding not only no cabs on the rank but none in the streets even occupied ones. (All gone it seems to get labels to stick on their wind screens, what sort of labels?) The nervous strain I continue has aged me by 25 years. I stood crying by the gentlemen's and a very grumpy cabby, on his way to relieve himself, said I could sit and wait in his cab. He was clearly very constipated indeed and took *hours*. Finally I arrived ten minutes late and was the last passenger—it didn't matter but it was the torture of not seeing any taxis at all. My cabby said he'd been a Communist ever since Lord Fisher had kicked him off a pavement when he was seven saying go back to the gutter. I was half fascinated and half in such a state of worry that I couldn't make him go on and tell more—

'Faithful Air France the only fliers—BEA passengers were being herded to Victoria to catch a train poor brutes. I was back here by 3—got a taxi at Orly who told me all is absolutely normal for the moment . . . Heavenly present from Dior as usual. I'm still pondering over that film [the film on Marie-Antoinette]. P.S. Two Frenchmen in the plane were discussing the prodigious avarice of les anglais. I shrieked.'

During the last war Nancy had smiled bravely through danger, discomfort and inconvenience, but ten years later in time of peace her nerves were more easily frayed. She still looked so young and slender that I could never realize we were born in the same year: we were both in fact middle-aged and Nancy complained of the low stamina which forced her to husband her energies. She reserved her vitality for her work, her gaiety for her friends. When Marie-Laure de Noailles gave her spectacular costume ball on Mardi Gras, 1956, Nancy confessed to me: 'I can't face it. You see fancy dress balls (or any balls however memorable) are no good to me because at 11.30 I drop off my perch. A sort of natural Cinderella. So I'm lending my pretty fur hat to Jean de Baglion to be Baglione in and fleeing to Roquebrune . . . Malcolm Bullock said to Violet, what are you going as [to the ball]. She said Lady Hester Stanhope. He said, pretending to have heard Esterhazy, "what, the Esterhazy of the Dreyfus Case?" How I shrieked! Tony Pawson goes as Byron (!) Diana Coo Mrs. Siddons (very good). Then all London is trying to get asked and it will be interesting to see what happens as Marie-Laure is not one to be put upon is she! Paul-Louis Weiller as François I by the way . . .'

Nancy's *Encounter* mail continued to harp on the same string. 'Furious Scotchmen, furious Baronets, furious friends saying how vulgar I am. Willie Maugham always says toilet paper, so realizes HE is not U, etc . . .' But Nancy also received 'perfectly serious letters from people saying things like, "I am descended from Alfred the Great's sister and I would like to congratulate you on your splendid stand for people of our sort." '

To Mrs. Hammersley she wrote: 'As for U everybody I see says how tired they are of it, etc, to which I reply then leave it alone. But they *can't*. It's really too extraordinary.' 'No,' she declared, 'I'm not got down by U., only the cuttings which have got out of control since every sort of local or trade paper speaks of U and me on any and every pretext.' It was a relief to turn to Voltaire and Madame du Châtelet.

Between 'working like a maniac' and getting to grips with Monsieur de Voltaire, Nancy was also being televised in January 1957: 'I'm having *such* a time with the television people. They've already spent two whole afternoons here, and the French Eurovision two more and coming again today (cables and so on). It's to last half an hour, did you ever hear such a thing? I'm dying of fear. The men are very nice to you, rather I suppose as the warders who hang you are nice, and they may have to drag me in the end like Mrs. Thompson. One of them said, "My father sends his love." "Who is your father?" "The Archbishop of Canterbury". Colonel says he'd better say nephew, in France! . . . Oh the T.V. What to wear is such a problem. No black or white allowed and nearly all colours look black except sky blue, which of course I haven't got.'

111

Nancy was titillated willy nilly by the parerga of her profession.

To her mother she confessed: 'I really don't think I've ever been so frightened—the preparations were simply terrific. Nobody allowed to park at this end of the street from midnight the day before, police in the street for 24 hours, twenty men in the flat and courtyard all day from 9 a.m., a sort of railway from the street (I had to send flowers to all the neighbours). A huge crowd in the street all day, Mme Brand [the concierge] *dans tous ses états* explaining what it was for (I wish I'd heard her). I had a terrific tummy upset and couldn't eat anything all day. But once it had begun I didn't mind in the least! What was very unnerving, all the people concerned, interviewer, producer and so on were at least as nervous as I was and showed it more. Somebody said the life of one of them is about that of a bomber pilot—after four years they can't do any more, the strain is too great. It is supposed to be a technical triumph to get it over from France . . . Ouf! Thank goodness it's done.'

Conscientiously she pursued her new protagonist to Geneva whence she informed Mark in April: 'I'm here to do a bit of work at the Musée Voltaire. This is a nice calm town rather like what I had imagined Athens to be before I went to that city of the plain . . . There's a lot of new (unpublished and unsuspected) Voltaire stuff, very luckily for me *ça tombe bien*. I've been goggling over it. Also, as all can be said nowadays, there is the Hyde Parkery at Frederick's court, details of which may surprise some people.'

Mr. Theodore Besterman gave Nancy his paternal blessing. 'Besterman is NOBLE,' she told Lady Redesdale. 'In spite of the fact that he himself is to write a life of Voltaire he has let me see all the new letters which entirely change the story and which he could have easily kept dark until I'd finished and nobody would have been the wiser. It must have been a temptation—I don't know that I, in his place, would have behaved so well.' And to Mrs. Ham she wrote 'Besterman, who is noble, has read more than half my book (all I've done) and says greatly to his surprise he only found one error of fact. As I had suspected, the pleasure he took in the T.L.S. review of the letters was mitigated by the reviewer's total ignorance of the subject. But I suppose of English people only he and I really do know the subject in tiny detail, it is so huge and so complex

7. Nancy—from a drawing by William Acton

Nancy from Mogens
Xmas 1947

8. Nancy in 1947—from the painting by Mogens Tvede

that nobody would trouble unless working on it . . . The new letters, to the niece, which prove he was sleeping with her for years, never suspected, are simply hair-raising!' And again to Mrs. Ham she wrote on 3rd May: 'I was sitting up in bed writing my book when I suddenly finished it! It has gone off to be typed and I am free to write a few letters at last . . . I feel the need of non-petrol air.' Ten days later: 'John Sutro has taken off my typescript to Hamish Hamilton so I feel like somebody who has lost a particularly tiresome child . . . Poor Madame Denis, she'll turn in her grave as I'm awful about her.'

Unlike many a greater poet Voltaire drained the full cup of popular triumph during his long lifetime. Some have considered his seventeen-year liaison with Madame du Châtelet a great love affair, but romance shrivels in contact with a genius so icily intellectual. With Voltaire there were no delicate shades of emotion. The swiftness of his wit was winged but his nature was flawed by squalid pettiness. His relationship with Madame du Châtelet was mainly a matter of convenience and prestige. The Newtonian lady required more physical attention than the middle-aged poet was inclined to provide and Nancy portrayed her as a semi-comic bluestocking. While Voltaire cohabited with her he became the quintessential French *homme de lettres* whose influence spread far beyond his study and her bedroom. This was Nancy's theme, though Voltaire escaped from the latter to that of his buxom niece Mme Denis—under the pretext of impotence.

It was no mean feat for a free-lance historian to depict such paradoxical celebrities—the ruthless opportunist, the cranky valetudinarian destined to prolong a premature old age, and the aristocratic highbrow of whom Frederick the Great was jealous. Nancy steered her way through the domestic labyrinth with colours flying. Her stronger partiality for Louis XV and Mme de Pompadour could not prejudice her against this less exalted pair but she failed to make either of them sympathetic. In this case she could not identify her protagonists with personal acquaintances though she detected certain traits of Voltaire in at least one contemporary littérateur. 'I couldn't get fond of Emily, try as I might,' she told me. 'To me she is like a much cleverer Violet [Trefusis]. I think the only woman in their set whom we would have liked was Mme de Boufflers. Can't help loving Voltaire, for the jokes, and old Stani of course.' She quoted Lord Chesterfield with approbation when he sent his son to Paris to learn 'that ease, those manners, those graces which are certainly nowhere to be found but in France'. And she exclaimed with sincere fervour: 'Oh happy age, when everything made by man was beautiful, when the furnishing of an Hôtel Lambert could as safely be left to a clergyman and a district-nurse as, nowadays, to a Ramsay or a Jansen!'

Like our friend James Lees-Milne ('Old Furious' or 'Grumpikins') Nancy found little to admire in modern art or architecture. Her Slade School enthusiasms for Epstein, the Spencers and the Nashes had waned: Coysevox and his successors had firmly supplanted them.

She lunched and dined out a little more frequently since *Voltaire in Love* was off her chest. 'There was a screamingly funny Anglo-French literary luncheon,' she told Mrs. Hammersley (21st May, 1957). 'All the Anglo ladies including Rebecca West and Mrs. Priestley were got up (freezing day) in chiffon and picture hats. It was supposed to be for young (*sic*) writers to exchange views. I had to exchange with young Priestley in a vile temper because Gram Greene was at the grand table and he wasn't, and André Chamson (80) furious because Lacretelle was. I did have a horrid time, though I rigoléd *intérieurement* [giggled inwardly] like anything.' The luncheon was followed by a performance of *Titus Andronicus*: 'a more disgusting play I never saw, tortures, murders, mutilations in every scene, culminating in a woman eating her own children in a pie. The French, who of course didn't understand a word, received it with wild enthusiasm. Couldn't help thinking of Voltaire who said that Shakespeare was a great genius *sans une étincelle de goût* and that no people love a hanging so much as the English therefore naturally they also love his plays.'

During the tenure of Lord and Lady Gladwyn the British Embassy was again a second home, as in the heyday of the Duff Coopers, and Nancy particularly relished an exclusive dinner with Field-Marshal Montgomery. 2nd July, to Mrs. Hammersley: 'Dined with Monty and the Jebbs, just the four of us, you know how he always rather fascinates me. We talked about generals having luck. He said, "I had luck when Gott was shot down." N: "Perhaps it was lucky for us too." M: "Yes it was. Gott was very much above his ceiling—he would have lost Egypt." John Marriott says this is quite true and it was Providence who shot down Gott!'

In July, on her annual visit to Venice, she wrote to Hugh Thomas, 'the sea there is warm like a bath and the only out of door water I can bear to swim in (in Europe, I mean). The social life, before the tourists begin to arrive, is extremely agreeable. You see the same people every day so conversation is no effort and their houses are of unparalleled beauty though not generally very well arranged. Then all that boat life is so good for the nerves. I think it's far the best place for a holiday, it seems to combine *tous les agréments*.' And to Mrs. Ham: 'I'm having a lovely time, very social but that's less tiring here than in Paris and I can bear it. An angel called Contessa Cicogna has taken me in charge, brings me every day to the beach in her launch, feeds me, this morning sent her maid to pack and unpack (change of hotels). It naturally makes all the difference to one's pleasure . . . The Graham Sutherlands were here, they can talk of nothing but the Royal Family, I was surprised . . . He said he vastly prefers Simon Elwes as a painter to Annigoni. I think I do too. Willie [Maugham] turned up, very spry but deaf and that tires him. No Ear Aid. He'll strike a hundred, I guess.'

From now on Anna Maria Cicogna became, as she said, 'the pivot of her Venetian existence,' and that her life there continued to be so agreeable was mainly due to her. 'I always lunch and generally dine with her and all the nice Venetians are there, plus a few travellers. She is almost perfect I think—calm, punctual, affectionate, clever, and sometimes very funny. The Venetians, like all Italians in my opinion, remind one of English people far more than the French do. Not as neurotic as the English though. Anna Maria said, which made me think of Farve, Andrew and so on, "My father [Count Volpi] used to say if only these young men would do nothing they would be very well off, but they will either gamble or go into business and then of course they lose everything." I must say they still seem very rich, living in their enormous palaces with thousands of nice servants . . . I went to the Biennale to see the modern pictures. The thing now is to tear a jagged hole in the canvas and then roughly darn it. I'm afraid I laughed—to the fury of the reverent young sight-seers.'

To be taken in charge by Contessa Cicogna was to enjoy

Venice from the inside as it were. It was not the Venice that is usually seen by tourists staying in hotels. I can corroborate Nancy's praise of this generous Venetian who contributes so much pleasure to those fortunate enough to know her. Nancy's old crony Victor Cunard, a Venetian by adoption who was familiar with most aspects of Venetian life, with the genealogies and problems of the natives as well as of the foreign residents, was another magnet. His extra-dry humour appealed to Nancy's, though it was fraught with infectious malice. He had read the proofs of *Voltaire in Love* and 'removed many a dreadful gallicism'. And Prince Clary who had lost his great family estates in Bohemia during the war, was a beehive of recondite anecdote, especially about the Hapsburgs and Central Europe. Here she invariably found a congenial and stimulating circle.

'With the Italians,' she wrote, 'rather like the French at Fontaines, I absolutely love them and then I do long for somebody to discuss them with you know. I went to Freya Stark for the week-end at Asolo but she's only interested in Arabs. She says Asolo is peopled with Pen Browning's illegitimates, isn't that amusing!' (Pen was the only son of Robert and Elizabeth.)

Usually she stayed in 'Anna Maria's garden house which is a dream of comfort and has a view of San Giorgio Maggiore from the bed', and she prepared to leave 'when all the smart folks are crowding in and the nice little family beach life broke up'. 'How I love this place,' she exclaimed, 'more and more. I feel so well here too. I'm sure Venice and Paris are the only towns one could bear to live in nowadays.' Always sensitive to literary and historical associations, she wrote that it had been 'very moving to dine in Lord Byron's lovely stuccoed rooms by candle light in Palazzo Mocenigo, quite unchanged, with a lot of jolly, rather silly Italians, just as he so often did, and see the same view from the balcony [whence one of his mistresses threw herself into the canal]. How I thought of him, longing for Brookses!'

Local gossip was fomented by farcical rows between wealthy women of a certain age, but these were scarcely Venetian. 'A dinner given by Momo [Lady Marriott] and sabotaged by Daisy [Fellowes], who is supposed to have got Momo so jittery that the *placement* was quite mad. Three women too many. Our Betters. Then Momo riposted by stealing Daisy's hair appointment and trying to steal her evening coat. As they are all too old for love now it's the best they can do I suppose. What will they steal and sabotage in the Next World? "She took my appointment with St Peter!" '

Undeniably it was a Venice de luxe that Nancy revelled in with a novelist's eye and a wistful appreciation of all the beauty now being threatened by so many factors, such as soil subsidence, a rise in the sea level, and a diminished hydraulic resistance at the lagoon's three outlets in the Adriatic.

'Though I suppose Venice is less spoilt than almost anywhere in the world, horrors assail one on every hand,' Nancy wrote to Sir Hugh Jackson in 1962. 'The silence broken by splashing noises is replaced by the engines of motor boats which stink of petrol, and then no young Italian would think of walking about without a small wireless in his pocket bellowing jazz at full blast. Oh dear, I do think that when we die we shan't have nearly so many regrets as somebody like Mazarin, the world is becoming so vile. There is no English colony left here, rather sad, I should think almost the first time in history. There are some delightful Russians and Austrians washed up here after the wars and a very agreeable small society . . .' The society, she told Alvilde Lees-Milne, 'is a hard nut to crack, as everybody is rich enough not to be impressed by good cooks and so on. At the same time they simply love a new face if it pleases them . . .'

She was alarmed by prevalent rumours of a motor road along the Zattere and skyscrapers between the Carmine and Piazzale Roma. 'They say it's almost certain now. I think Unesco ought to do something, but of course they would only get excited if the works of Henry Moore were threatened. Alphy [Clary] says the more foreigners protest the more the Itis say we are not a fusty old museum, we are a great wonderful modern country like America. Oh the brutes.' And in another letter (17th April, 1961): 'While the English mourn over thirsty doggies Venice is doomed. Bauer, pushed by Colonel (pushed I like to think by me) has been conducting a resounding campaign in the *Figaro*. Alphy is very pessimistic, but perhaps the circumstances of his life make him so. The motor road will run under his nose . . .'

Nancy also visited Contessa Cicogna in Tripoli, where she reigned over a ravishing little oasis from which she has been ousted by the present régime. 'The house and garden are a sort of Paradise, and the garden the only one I have ever fully approved of—about three acres I suppose of brilliant flowers in squares, like a Persian carpet or a patchwork. But I was awfully ill there as a result of vaccination and the Arabs gave me the creeps . . . We were always about fourteen and when I wasn't languishing—seven days of high fever and I'm still very thin—I adored it.

'But the high spot was the Bosphorus where I went from there and spent a week with my great new friend Ostrorog. He has got a pink wooden palace with its feet in the sea, a cross between Venice and Russia, and he showed me Constantinople which I suppose nobody alive knows as he does since he has lived there all his life. I can safely say I've never enjoyed a visit more. He is on the Asiatic side, next village to Scutari (which is utterly unchanged since the Lady of the Lamp) and you go everywhere by boat and the Bosphorus is unspoilt—nothing but large villas and palaces in parks and little wooden villages on the sea. Such pretty boats, never a speed boat. Then there is such a charming life there, all based on French civilization—servants, the lingère from Scutari who looked after me (he has only men in the house) all brought up by *les bonnes soeurs*. The neighbours sit about like in Russian plays, languidly reading the *Figaro* . . . As much as I detested the Arabs I loved the Turks.

'Then I had a nice week in Athens though a bit too mondaine. Lovely bathing. Now the grindstone and I don't move again until I've handed in the m.s.—around Christmas I guess . . . Saw Auntie [Violet Trefusis] yesterday . . . As she always has to go one better she said she once had a burning affair with Ostrorog and got in the family way. I said goodness Violet, where is it? She muttered something about a bumpy taxi.' (26th June, 1964, to Alvilde Lees-Milne).

*

Peter Rodd had faded into the background of Nancy's existence. He had followed many a circuitous trail in directions ever more remote from Nancy's and they no longer had more than mixed memories in common, bitter rather than sweet. 'To enable old Prod to get married, which he seems to want,' Nancy was willing to divorce him as secretly as possible 'in the hopes of avoiding much publicity'. Her marriage was dissolved without regret, probably with relief, in 1958. All her love had been lavished on 'the Colonel', since their meeting in London during the war. Absent or present, and he was often absent on behalf of General de Gaulle, he remained the centre of her life until she died. He admired Nancy and was deeply attached to her, but he had always been candid about not falling in love with her. He was a devoted comrade on whose sympathy, advice and intellectual refreshment she could steadfastly rely. Theirs was a very special and happy liaison—so happy that the thought of marriage did not enter into it except, perhaps, in dreams. For Nancy, in her heart of hearts, was also a bachelor in spite of her marriage. She often repeated that she preferred to live alone and I think she was sincere. I suspect that she would have subscribed to La Rochefoucauld's maxim: '*Il y a de bons mariages, mais il n'y en a point de délicieux.*'

CHAPTER NINE

NANCY PAID ANNUAL visits to her parents who had chosen to live apart in their old age—Lord Redesdale in a cottage at Otterburn, Northumberland, and Lady Redesdale at lonely Inch Kenneth off the Isle of Mull in Scotland. True to form, her father had borne his misfortunes stoically. The loss of his only son Tom, the sad end of his daughter Unity, the break with Jessica, and the disintegration of the British Empire, were sorrows that had left their scars on this rugged old soldier. Besides he had grown very deaf. But he was proud of Nancy's meteoric success. He enjoyed her jokes even wryly at his expense, as she enjoyed his eccentricities, though she said she felt like Captain Scott of the Antarctic when she crossed the Channel to visit him. She could still laugh at his 'Uncle Matthew' mannerisms. 'Have you read the Queensberry book on Oscar Wilde?' she asked her mother (9th January, 1950). 'It's the best of any I think and would amuse you as old Lord Queensberry is so exactly like Farve, or what he would have been under those circumstances.' 'My old father-in-law [Lord Rennel]', she added, 'a terrible prig, knew Wilde well (and pretended that he knew nothing of *les mœurs* which I don't believe) but said nobody has ever been so brilliant in the world.'

Already in May 1949 she had written Lady Redesdale: 'I had a letter from Farve saying he is waiting for the end in great comfort, well I suppose we all are, in a sense, waiting for the end, but I was so impressed that I wrote and offered to go, but he says don't. I wonder if I ought to really as he seems to have quarrelled with everybody else almost and is lonely I suppose.'

In September she decided to fly to Redesdale Cottage, whence she wrote: 'Farve has become a good time boy—nothing but cocktail parties. One was given for me here last night—ten neighbours—can you beat it. More in character: "I was showing a blasted woman over the garden"—pause—"I thought it was Lady N"—long pause—"Well it was Lady N. She rang about twenty times—at last I went to see what it was and I said oh I thought you were a van." However she didn't come to the party.'

In June next year he returned her visit and she gave a party for him in 'Mr. Street'—'a cocktail party which Farve absolutely adores. It went on from five to eight solidly, but he was spryer than ever at the end. Old M. de Lasteyrie came. I said are you pleased about the elections. "Oh! you know when it isn't the scaffold I'm always pleased." He then told Farve about his two grandmothers being beheaded. Farve said "I rather liked that relation of Joan of Arc".'

Somebody having asked her if Lord Redesdale were connected with the Parisian Baron de Rede, this became a standard joke. 'Barons Rede and Redesdale have but little in common,' she told her mother. The former 'lives but for luxury, beauty and social life—a less lively Cedric. He looks like a tie-pin, thin, stiff and correct with a weeny immovable head on a long stiff neck.' Whereas Baron de Rede collected works of art her father was inclined to sell them. 'I went last week to see one of the grandest collections of furniture, etc. here, belonging to Comte Niel,' she wrote (18th May, 1951). 'He showed me two celadon carp mounted for Mme de Pompadour (Mlle Poisson) and said "we'd give anything to know where the other two are." "Sold by my father in 1919," I said sadly. "How *could* Monsieur votre père have borne to sell them?" How indeed! I suppose you don't remember who bought them?' Nancy imagined that her father would have been far happier living in Canada than in the Cotswolds. 'But how ghastly it would have been for us!' she exclaimed. 'Farve writes every Xmas and every birthday saying *how* I wish I could give you a present but of course it's impossible. Why?'

Half in jest she had adopted many of his verbal expressions, as when she summarized Venetian life in August: 'super-sewerage and a ball every night.' Her affection for him was tinged with nostalgia and muffled in laughter: 'I've found an old postcard from Farve addressed to Miss Blob M. e.g. Blob-Nose which he always called me. Reminds one of something?'

When he died in March 1958 she wrote to Mrs. Hammersley: 'I feel rather sad and mooney about the past, though I don't think he enjoyed life very much latterly.' And from Redesdale Cottage, Otterburn, 22nd March: 'The cremation this afternoon—by no means such a gruesome ceremony as I had imagined—the coffin goes down in a sort of food lift. Beautiful service, beautifully read in a real not parsonic voice by a canon something. It took twenty minutes. But everybody is rather cross now—I've got Carlyle's *French Revolution* mercifully and retire into that . . . The will is quite dotty, but nothing much to leave . . .'

Earlier in the year she had enjoyed what she described as her 'visits to the major novelists'—L. P. Hartley, Evelyn Waugh and Anthony Powell. 'The food of all three about equal (not good). Leslie had the warmest house and warmest heart. Evelyn by far the coldest house and Tony Powell the coldest heart but the most fascinating chats and a pâté de foie gras. He raked up some old characters from my past . . . that was all very interesting. I find all these writers take themselves very seriously and Tony Powell speaks of *Punch*, of which he is literary editor, as though it were an important vehicle of intellectual opinion . . .' Nancy had not seen an adverse criticism in *Punch*. 'When I went to stay with Tony he began by saying he was so relieved I'd suggested coming because afraid I might have minded the article. So I read it under his nose and of course shrieked—so he was relieved again. I love that sort of furious criticism showing that somebody is in a real temper. The Americans aren't nearly so amusing, but intensely serious and favourable.' Apropos of the latter, 'I was asked to appear on American TV everything paid *and* 500 dollars and my publisher begged, for the sake of the book. No fear. I'm writing an article for *Harper's Magazine* (not *Bazaar*) on Why I hate America. Their title. Enjoying it terribly, venom pours from pen.'

Never having seen America, Nancy's venom poured from blind prejudice. In this respect she was a chip off the old block: Lord Redesdale's hatred of Germans had vanished as soon as he visited their country. Fortunately the Americans were more entertained than angered by her diatribe, which did not affect the sale of her books in the States. Nor did it affect her friendships with several Americans, each of whom she insisted was a phenomenal exception. In April 1949 she wrote: 'The beautiful, gay and charming Evangeline Bruce is to be American ambassadress here, we are all enchanted. I think she'll make an Embassy rather like Diana's was, a thing which is badly needed here.'

The Gladwyn Jebbs (Lord and Lady Gladwyn) who in Nancy's opinion transformed the British Embassy in Paris, did not arrive till later. Nancy informed Mrs. Hammersley on 4th July, 1954: 'The Jebbs are a success *beyond all hope*. I've never heard the French—the monde, the intellectuals, the politicians, and the man in the street so united in praise of anybody. They can't do wrong. You don't know the pleasure this is to me, apart from the fact that the Embassy is fast becoming the centre of all fun. Under the Coopers it was brilliant, but fearfully criticized too, whereas the Jebbs seem to have the knack of pleasing everybody. Cynthia has developed in an extraordinary way you know. I've seen a lot of her alone— she is so good and at the same time surprisingly worldly wise. Really she and Iris Hayter are something to be proud of. I see your eye glazing with boredom as you read this.'

While in Paris Nancy did not consort with many French writers. A few she met now and then at social gatherings: Jean Cocteau was the most ubiquitous of these. She sat next to him at embassy dinners but never became intimate with him. Prodigal of poetic images in iridescent flights of conversation as well as in ballets, films and dramas, it was remarkable how long this verbal magician had woven his spells in the Parisian limelight. While he seldom failed to scintillate, embassy dinners must have been to him what pub-crawling would have been to Nancy, who could only see his funny side, a fraction of the real Cocteau: 'he told me he has a godson and at Christmas he felt rather guilty about this child to whom he had never sent a present, so he went off and bought a beautiful big pink mechanical rabbit. He received a very cold letter—*il paraît que mon filleul est colonel.*' She saw more of Philippe Jullian, the talented Anglophile writer and illustrator who designed modish covers for her books, and Philippe's rarefied circle of dilettanti. When she spoke of 'the monde, the intellectuals, the politicians', it was chiefly of 'the Colonel' she was thinking.

Did English writers take themselves more seriously than their colleagues across the Channel? The first thing that always strikes me about France, even in railway stations, is that literature is taken far more seriously there than in England: you need only glance at the publications on display. Most French writers even subconsciously aspire to become members of their classical Academy. Their social behaviour may be flippant but when they speak of their *métier* they become earnest, with a profound respect for the precise values of words and shades of meaning. Their conversation is usually more sparkling than that of English writers but they are unlikely to 'talk shop' at embassy dinners.

How seriously did Nancy take her own writings? Despite her distaste for solemnity she devoted immense patience, care and industry to the composition of her books. Her innate modesty should not deceive us. In the brief articles she wrote for newspapers she remained an expert agitator: she stung if she did not draw blood. This was just what editors wanted, but readers have developed thicker skins in the last decade.

We happened to share an exceptional interest in the Bourbon family, of whom she wrote with perspicacity: 'Licentious or bigoted, noble or ignoble, there has seldom been a dull Bourbon. They were nearly all odd, original men of strong passions, unaccountable in their behaviour . . . Bourbons steal the picture whenever they are in it.'

She had been engaged on a bracing introduction to Miss Lucy Norton's selection and translation of the Duc de Saint-Simon's Memoirs when she was overjoyed by General de Gaulle's return to power. Her letters to Mrs. Hammersley bubbled over with excitement: 'We cried with happiness—after so long it seems unbelievable . . .' 12th June, 1958: 'I dined in the company of La Tour du Pin who smuggled Soustelle out of Paris. His line of talk made my hair stand on end. "We are all going into the Maquis against the General". It's the old story—no human beings are so idiotic as the French *right*. I dined with the Bourbon-Bussets last night, all the gilded youth (never have I seen such diamonds) all strongly for the General and I think underestimating the fascist danger. I know something about fascists and feel exceedingly nervous. The next few months are going to be tricky.

'They say Chevigny wanted to go to Colombey and arrest the

General. The army told him don't count on us, the police the same, the garde républicain the same, and finally the local gendarmerie. They say, like Ney bringing Napoleon in an iron cage. It has all been very much like the retour d'Elbe—the enormous shadow looming—everybody saying no no and then crumbling at the sight of the man.'

18th June: 'I thought of you, Mme Costa and the Maison Dior during La Tour du Pin's récit of how he smuggled Soustelle out of Paris. A young Mme du Four, living in the same immeuble as Soustelle, was induced to hide him in the back of her motor and drive him out. She goes in and out many times a day and the police knew her by sight. So when all was fixed she said (so French) what shall I wear? My tailleur from Dior hasn't come yet! However, it did come, in time to figure. When they'd got him out they made one of the chaps in the plot take her to a film so that for at least two hours she wouldn't be able to tell her friends!'

20th June: 'J. telephoned, *"Vous êtes contente des événements— comme nous tous?"* Do you remember the face she used to make if one mentioned the General? *"Surtout pas"* and so on? And always cracking up le Maréchal? Oh do admit. Now she pretends they've all longed for de Gaulle with an aching passion ever since the war. I said O but I did feel rather furious! Colonel is here for the 18th June of course. He looks so well and happy. I went to the Champs Elysées—an immense crowd crying *"Merci"* as the General passed. The Colonel says "he is amusing himself". Malraux said to Cocteau: *"il est devenu si rusé"*. But Colonel says nonsense, he always has been *rusé . . .'*

Nancy's aged friend Mme Costa was a firm Gaullist, but this was 'most unusual in her world, Catholic, royalist, *bien pensant*, Action Française . . . The cry generally goes up: "I vote for the General with both my hands so as to avoid shaking his". They vote for him because "who else is there?" But they hate.' Nancy concluded 'it's not the jeunesse dorée who are against the General but sort of forty-year-old ultra-Conservatives.' This was probably true of her fellow guests at Fontaines.

After July in Venice and Rome, where the temperature rose to 101 degrees and Nancy saw two women carried out of the Vatican, 'evidently dead', she confessed: 'I sigh for the land of the cypress and myrtle—I loathe the oak and the ash.' In August she visited her mother at Inch Kenneth, Isle of Mull, where she 'caught a powerful Scotch germ which simply floored me and drove away the health so expensively acquired in Venice. I must say northern climes do not suit me.' To Mrs. Hammersley she confided: 'Muv says she lives here because there are no tourists. But her eye is glued to a telescope and as soon as a tent appears on Mull she sends a boat and the amazed occupants are press-ganged over and given a vast tea. Yesterday two jolly Lesbians in trousers were the bag . . . The deaf aid has been discarded for good and so it is yelling and even then hardly being heard. But anyhow she never used to listen to one, so not much change.'

With her mother an exchange of letters was easier than conversation. They wrote to each other often and Lady Redesdale kept Nancy's letters in separate envelopes. She must have enjoyed them, for it is obvious that Nancy took trouble to amuse her with descriptions of the people she was seeing and comments on what she was writing and reading as well as current events. They were the best substitutes for talk, and they read like talk: 'Did I tell you about the lady who discovered her maid had never been to a theatre and sent her off for a treat to one. *"Eh bien Madame—n'est ce pas—le rideau se lève et voilà des gens qui discutent leurs affaires de famille. Moi je suis partie."* I told Mme Costa who said when she had a box at the opera she used always to take a seat for her valet de pied until he begged her to excuse him and let him wait outside with the others because he found it so *ennuyeux*!'

Mindful of her mother's views on health and distrust of modern medicine, for 'she did not really believe in illness', Nancy fed her with tit-bits about doctors and medical fads: 'Louis XIV's doctor, who lived to be over a hundred, always said the reason fish live to be so old is that they are never exposed to *courants d'air*. He slept in a sort of leather envelope head and all so as to be quite away from them . . .

'About doctors. I heard a woman in the Ritz saying: *"on lui a fait des soins si terribles qu'il en est mort dans la nuit."* I've just read a life of Louis XIII who was literally killed by doctors at the age of 42. Several times he seemed on his death bed and they gave up their *"soins"* upon which he always rallied. This was put down to the prayers of the Paris convents—nobody put two and two together. Richelieu who adored him urged the doctors to more and more terrible *soins* and stood over him to

see that he did all they said. You know he was married for 23 years before Louis XIV was born. At the beginning Anne of Austria had several miscarriages—then they became very much estranged. Finally the courtiers got them into the same bed by a trick and alerted all the convents within reach—the nuns prayed all night and Louis XIV was the result! . . .

'Momo [Marriott] just back from U.S., tells me that as well as a blood bank they now have a bone bank and you can ring up for a big toe joint or a new collar bone. I knew you'd enjoy that . . .

'Have you heard of Gaylord Hauser? He's an American who, like Uncle Geoff, lives on wheat germ and honey and, unlike Uncle Geoff, has made a fortune out of it. The menus are to make you cry, all the things ONE hates most, but I've no doubt there's a lot in it. He's having a wild success here in the American set—can't believe the French would ever take it up. I do think it's a shame Uncle Geoff didn't cash in first.

'I'm told Americans now have blood transfusions for everything, even after a late night. I'm sure it's just what I need: horrors!'

When Lady Redesdale went to assist a pregnant neighbour in an emergency Nancy gave full rein to her fantasy: 'I so screamed at the idea of you, dissembling your nervousness, acting as midwife to this poor lady. (Knowing your aversion to antiseptics I see she is foredoomed to death by septicaemia.) Then of course you must shake the child to make it breathe and if it is a *blue baby* send to Oban for an iron lung—if a *monster* (elephant head or three legs) it's your duty to do away with it— if *quins*, your fortune will be made. Goodness! In any event I should think there will be a lot of unwelcome publicity. Coroner's frank words to peeress, mother of seven. Were the instruments boiled? Unfortunately no provision for so-called mercy killing exists in the law of this land. Etc, etc. If I were you I should hurry her into a clinic *now*, before it's too late.'

Presumably Nancy had sent her mother the Gide-Claudel letters, for she wrote: 'I must admit the idea of your being entirely on Gide's side is the funniest thing I ever heard in a long life. Well I have no moral feelings, specially, about all that, but I couldn't help being on Claudel's side for his strength, single-mindedness and the beautiful French he writes.'

'The Marquise d'Harcourt was a hundred this month. She

127

said to her daughter, "What are pederasts?" "Oh Mother I really can't tell you." "If you can't tell me when I'm a hundred when can you tell me?" She was ordering a dress for the birthday party and said to the dressmaker, "I expect *my* clothes to last quite ten years".'

Characteristically there were intermittent teases: 'I did love the photograph (of self as child). What a furious face—of course everybody was so unkind to me it's a wonder my temper wasn't ruined for ever. When I think of modern children —how the voice must never be raised and how they are hurried to the psycho-analyst's sofa for the least thing, I don't know why I'm not raving in an asylum.' . . . 'You know how my childhood is hidden in a cloud (so terribly unhappy that Nature has mercifully caused me to forget it).'

But Nancy's teasing could go too far in print, and Lady Redesdale was offended by the references to herself in *Blor*, the portrait of Nancy's Nanny which she considered one of her best writings. By way of apology Nancy wrote to her mother: 'Oh *goodness* I thought it would make you *laugh*. I always feel one's young self is like a completely different person one can view quite objectively and laugh at—in my case at least this is true. Of course one can't very well write about a Nanny and leave out the mother and for the modern reader one must explain the complete difference between mothers and children in those far off days from now. If I did a portrait of you (which I won't) you would come out quite different from the oblique view seen, as it were, across Nanny. In any case everybody knows you are Aunt Sadie [in *The Pursuit of Love*] who is a character in the round and is you in middle life exactly as you were . . . It's one's eccentricities people love one for.'

Did Nancy's conscience prick her? She continued in a second letter: 'I've read the piece again. Of course the trouble is that I see my childhood (in fact most of my life) as a hilarious joke. But *nobody* could take this seriously—bobby in the nursery— Titanic—and so on—all clearly a caricature, what's called Meant to be Funny. If you seem to have been rather frivolous so was everybody at that time. Edwardian women are famous for having been lighthearted. The tone of the whole book is meant to be light, frivolous and satirical . . . Voltaire used to say *qui plume a, guerre a,* too true.'

Lady Redesdale was not instantly mollified, for Nancy wrote

again: 'Anything which *now* seems odd or unfortunate in my childhood wasn't your fault it was that of the age we lived in. Children were not considered then—or at least girls weren't. The Duc Decazes and my neighbour Bagneux (French equivalents of Farve) *loathe* Paris. They both live here, groaning, in order to educate their children. This could not have happened in the England of your (and my) young days. To state that it did not happen is not to reproach you but the whole social structure. I carefully said in the essay that the relationship of parents and children is quite different now.

'But the person who appears completely vile is *me*!! . . . No more efforts at autobiography. I've learnt my lesson.'

Examining Nancy's references to her mother objectively, one can understand Lady Redesdale's failure to be amused. Nancy's humour could be lopsided on occasion. True, she often laughed at herself. 'Somebody wrote (did I tell you?) Voltaire doesn't love Nancy, Nancy go home, on the Embassy garden gate. Said to have been Ed Stanley. How I shrieked!' (to Alvilde Lees-Milne, 6th November, 1957). She was not in the least offended by her sister Jessica's remarks in *Hons and Rebels*. On the contrary, she liked the book though her family could not speak of it. Her instincts might be mischievous but not malicious. The suppression of a painting by Derek Hill is a case in point.

Derek had been so captivated by the refined bone-structure of Nancy's bosom-friend Princess Dolly Radziwill that he longed to paint her portrait in spite of her reluctance to pose for him. Christian Bérard persuaded her to yield. Derek first produced a sketch in oil and then a larger portrait after two or three sittings. The latter, though unfinished, was exhibited at the Leicester Galleries in London, but the sketch was left in an ante-room for a relative to look at. At the private view Violet Trefusis trotted up to Derek and said, 'I've bought a picture of yours.' Derek naturally asked her which. 'The sketch of Dolly.' 'But you can't do that without Dolly's permission,' Derek protested. He was protesting to a blank wall. Violet insisted on clinging to her purchase which the model had never seen. 'Give it to Dolly for Christmas,' he proposed, 'and I'll give you any other picture you may choose in return.'

Violet duly sent the sketch to Princess Radziwill on Christmas Day and the parcel was opened before her guests at luncheon. An awkward silence followed while the gift was inspected. Nancy spoke up: 'It's so unflattering that you'll have to burn it.' Whereupon it was consigned to the flames in the cheerful fireplace.

Derek was horrified to hear of the fate of a creation he cherished—'perhaps not flattering but forceful, like a Goya'. The blame was divided between Violet and Nancy: in fact Violet had been the *agente provocatrice* and I have little doubt that she had bought the sketch with malice prepense. Baroness Alix de Rothschild took up the cudgels on Derek's behalf. 'Legally you can't destroy a painting by a living artist,' she told Nancy. 'He has a right to sue you.' 'I wouldn't mind if I'd published a book and the manuscript were destroyed,' Nancy answered. 'Do tell Derek I can't wait for the *procès*. What fun we'll all have!'

In the meantime Nancy sent Derek (*Maître* Hill as she dubbed him) a match with a Christmas card inscribed 'love from Savonarola'.

There was no lawsuit but there was a sad sequel. Derek kept his word and presented Violet with a landscape view from L'Ombrellino, her Florentine villa. When he visited her in 1965 he decided to revarnish it. 'Leave it at Doney's' (the fashionable tea-shop), she said, 'and I'll send my butler to collect it.' Six months later Derek received a note from Violet: 'Why did you see fit to steal the picture you gave me?' 'You asked me to leave it at Doney's. I have done so,' he replied. But the butler never called or Violet clean forgot, and the painting was washed away in the flood of 1966.

The unfinished portrait of Princess Radziwill was included in a retrospective exhibition of Derek Hill's work and to compensate for her loss of the original sketch Violet bought it.

Some time later Nancy, unabashed, remarked to Derek: 'Cher Maître, I've done it again!' But in this case the picture's destruction was not complete. She had cut off the arms and legs of Norah Auric's portrait of 'the Colonel' to fit the head into an oval frame. She had signed it, moreover, with the artist's name spelt wrong. Consequently she was not popular with modern painters except Bérard and the more traditional Mogens Tvede, who has left a charming portrait of her in water colour. Tchelitchev said of her: 'Her face is so small I couldn't get it on to a postage stamp!'

As her books were her main source of revenue Nancy was sensitive to reviews, but she told Mrs. Hammersley: 'Very good to have one or two blaming reviews among the praise, nothing better for sales.' Though she preferred reasoned abuse to uncritical adulation she was nettled by Mr. A. J. P. Taylor's review of her *Madame de Pompadour* in the *Manchester Guardian*. Mr. Taylor had written: '*Pursuit of Love* characters have appeared again, this time in fancy dress. They now claim to be leading figures in French literary history, revolving round Louis XV and his famous mistress, Madame de Pompadour. In reality they still belong to that wonderful never-never land of Miss Mitford's invention which can be called Versailles as easily as it used to be called Alconleigh . . . Once more we have the secret words, the ritual of society, and the blunders of the uninitiated . . . Certainly no historian could write a novel half as good as Miss Mitford's work of history. Of course he might not try.' Commenting on this to her friend Lady Harrod, Nancy wrote: 'In a way it's a compliment when the historians bother to say keep off the grass—which is really what it amounts to, as they can't pretend my facts are wrong.'

She was gratified when Dr. Cobban included her *Pomp* in the bibliography of his 'History of Modern France', and delighted when Sir Lewis Namier congratulated her on her review of Dr. Gooch's *Life of Louis XV*, which contains her trenchant remark: 'Dr. Gooch also furiously takes him to task for loving women. Oddly enough, some men do.'

Naturally she was susceptible to praise. With regard to *Voltaire in Love*: 'I hardly like to tell you that my book is a triumph in America—not one adverse word and the anti-English *Time* has given it what they call a "rave".' Again to Mrs. Ham she wrote: 'A Swiss woman publisher has just been to see me about doing 10,000 *Love in a Cold Climate* in a Swiss edition. She said, "I must tell you I have rarely seen anybody with an expression of such *pure goodness* as you have". I said I would pay her fare to Isle of Wight if she would go and repeat these thoughts at Wilmington, Totland Bay.' (Nancy told me that this best-selling novel was advertised in Cairo in a list of pornographic literature as 'How to make love in the cold'.)

The Swiss publisher was not exaggerating, for Nancy did have an expression of pure goodness as even her photographs show. Her pranks were due to an innocent love of fun, unaware that their effect might be devastating. While she did not court publicity she was shrewd enough not to discourage it. Somerset Maugham had advised her to answer fan letters, of which she received bushels. Among these was one from 'a woman saying she had seen a young girl sitting crying on a suitcase at Victoria, whereupon the passers-by began quoting to each other (all strangers) from *Pursuit of Love*.' Another told her: 'as soon as I'd read *Pursuit of Love* I rushed to Paris where I very soon married a Frenchman and we've got a daughter called, of course, Linda.' Such letters were often exhilarating.

She valued the critical opinions of her friends, some of whom, like Raymond Mortimer and Cyril Connolly, also happened to be book reviewers, but she considered that few of them were qualified to deal with French subjects. 'The English ignorance on French matters never ceases to astound,' she wrote to Mrs. Ham. 'Betty Chetwynd said the other day that when one has lived here a few years one sees that even the pundits like Harold Nicolson and Cyril [Connolly] don't really know as much as they pretend to. Raymond [Mortimer] is another matter, he *really does* know.' After Evelyn Waugh, Raymond Mortimer became her chief literary mentor, who patiently read her proofs and corrected errors.

Since her research on Madame de Pompadour Nancy had a hankering after a house of her own at Versailles. In January 1959 she heard that the house she coveted had suddenly come on the market. 'There are such pros and such cons,' she told Mrs. Ham. 'But I'm in favour of letting fate carry one along up to a point. The Rue Mr can never be mine and I long for something that is.' In February, 'the Versailles house hangs in the balance and I desire it more and more. Perhaps I shall get it but it will take most of my savings if I do.' The house hung in the balance for another seven years. Remembering the days of her poverty, she confided to Lady Harrod: 'The Colonel roars with laughter when I save up for my old age and says, "when you were earning £5 a week in the bookshop I never heard about your old age", which is rather true, but there was nothing much I could do about it then, except hope! Violet [Trefusis] tells them all here that I'm an appalling miser—all very well for her with a huge capital sum in Canadian dollars! If one could count on the Bomb it would be different.'

The delightful apartment in Rue Monsieur suited her

exactly. 'I do love pretty little things that lie about doing nothing in a room,' she remarked, and she had filled her rooms discreetly with pretty objects. The only drawback was the vicinity of noisy children. As she complained to Mrs. Ham (19th March, 1959): 'When I see *Fillette dans le coma depuis 4 jours* I do so wish it could be all the children in this courtyard who literally drive me mad. Talking on this subject with my late hostess Mme Lambert, she said, "Take Anne de G. (a lovely heavenly creature aged 25 with three babies), if she couldn't have a large family she would feel there was nothing in life for her". No doubt there are such women—how could they be ordered to limit their families? Of course in the end everything will work out as it always does . . .

'I'm more than thankful to have no children, much as I minded at the time.'

Yet Nancy enjoyed the society of the young. When young Henry Harrod and two Eton friends went to Paris on their own she gave them 'a marvellous luncheon with champagne' although she had intended to see nobody. 'They all came to luncheon yesterday,' she told Lady Harrod, 'so sweet and funny and hungry. As I'm not answering the telephone they *came* and of course I couldn't resist their dear Woodley faces seen through a curtain. Absolutely loved them.' And she was vastly diverted by her nephews who gave her fresh ideas for her next novel.

Intensely loyal to her old friends, Nancy had to admit that she had outgrown many chums of her girlhood. Mark Ogilvie-Grant was the closest of these: him she had never outgrown. Each of them recovered their youth when they wrote to each other, long intimate letters full of private jokes and whimsical affection. But Nancy felt about many others as she felt about Mark's cousin Nina Seafield, who announced that she was coming to live in Paris: 'I love seeing her once a year but as a neighbour NO.' And Hamish Erskine, with whom she had wavered on the verge of matrimony in her twenties, what a gulf had widened between them since the period of *Highland Fling* (dedicated to Hamish)! She wrote to Mark (6th December, 1958): 'Poor sweet passed by on his way to Elizabeth Chavchavadze. She says he's been asleep ever since he got there. He has written a piece for some book on snobbishness! and is furious because they only gave him £5. I suppose he thinks, like all amateurs, that writing is well paid. It is, if you scoop the jackpot, but otherwise sweeping crossings pays better. I got a letter from a poor fellow (unknown to me) who has published two novels and lives in Spain. He says he can only eat once a day "which sounds more amusing than it is". Ay di me. He wants to come and live here, I've begged *not*. It would be once every two days, and less amusing than ever. Golly life here is expensive.

'To go back to poor sweet, one does wonder what he uses for cash. Then he *is* so silly. He was sitting here—I said now I advise you to go and catch the train. Oh no, it would mean waiting at the station. So he misses the train. Two expensive taxis, a telephone call to Bourgogne, and another night in an hotel, and another taxi in the morning. Made me cross. Quite a fiver I guess.' For a season Daisy Fellowes (the Hon. Mrs. Reginald, formerly Princess de Broglie) had offered Hamish a sinecure as social secretary but his insouciance had exasperated her until she dismissed him with, 'Good-bye, Hamish, we shall meet next summer.'

Nancy often visited Mark in Greece as she had formerly at Kew Green, usually in June before proceeding to Venice. Her article 'Wicked thoughts on Greece', in which she attacked the American School of Classical Studies and the Stoa, 'said to be "of Attalos", but really of Mr. Homer A. Thompson,' was the fruit of one of these visits. In compensation she admired the excavations at Olympia and at Delphi, where 'the ruins lie in their own wonderful background and tell their own wonderful story'. Above all she admired Hosios Loukas, 'the Byzantine church in its almond grove on a mountainside,' hoping that 'Mr. Homer A. Thompson will never get there'. This led to a heated exchange with Mr. Thompson in which Nancy had the last word. She returned to the charge in an essay on tourists, who were harmless on the whole with one exception: 'Some Americans, who had probably seen the Victor Emmanuel monument on their way through Rome, generously decided to present the Athenians with its equivalent which they call the Stoa of Attalos. It is ghastly, but does not matter much, since Athens is past praying for.' As the genial painter Peter Mitchell, a 'good American' friend of Nancy's, remarked: 'However correct the excavations and restorations were, they hardly added up to a Hubert Robert.' Nancy wanted to see ruins with the eyes of Hubert Robert, forgetting that they had originally been painted in bright colours.

While Mark was Nancy's Athenian guide Patrick and Joan Leigh Fermor showed her the islands beloved of Lord Byron, opening her eyes to their unspoiled scenery, and to an existence relatively primitive and serene. Professor Alan Ross's pamphlet on 'Upper Class English Usage', read aloud while Nancy was visiting the Leigh Fermors at Hydra, seemed even more comical in such surroundings. Patrick, who has written so vividly about his Grecian adventures, should also record his conversations with Nancy. He and Joan were living in the house of Niko Ghika the painter during one of Nancy's visits. He tells me that they were looking after a neighbour's dog called Spot, 'who barked incessantly at some visitors, and accepted others in silence. During a maddening call by some people we hardly knew the wretch never stopped barking for a second. "Out, damned Spot!" I can hear Nancy wailing to herself with eyes rolled up dolorously, and when they left she said: "I'm afraid old Spot is an unerring Non-U indicator."

'Bidden to some feast at Spetsai, we caught the steamer with Niko. He was praising Le Corbusier, and Nancy said, "But I can't *bear* him!" All the time the steamer's gramophone was playing a deafening non-stop tune, rather like a roundabout at a fair, which, to tease Niko, gave rise to an improvised song which we both sang mercilessly:

> *Corbusier! Corbusier!*
> *Tout est si propre et si gai!*
> *Les pannes d'ascenseur*
> *Nous laissent tous rêveurs,*
> *Mais, quand même, vive Corbusier! (e poi da capo)*

Lots of verses. For years, the phrase *"tout est si propre et si gai!"* surfaced whenever a particularly squalid or mournful scene came in sight. She couldn't bear the lateness of meals—"nearly as bad as Spain! It's all right for *you*, reeling drunk all of you, but what about poor abstemious *me*? Well, inner resources I suppose. I'll just think about Voltaire, or Madame de Boigne, till a crust appears . . ."

'After Mark ("Old Gent"), her favourite Anglo-Athenian was certainly Roger Hinks, then head of the British Council there, though he suffered bitterly from anti-us emotions during the

Cyprus troubles. One day he said: "I'm off to Italy to see some proper painting, and by painting I don't mean the daubed planks that masquerade under the name here! They haven't an inkling of *chiaroscuro* or *morbidezza*." (This occasioned a song by Paddy to the tune of *Giovinezza*, which began: "*Morbidezza! Morbidezza! Chiaroscuro! che bellezza!*")' Nancy's nickname for Hinks was the Old Turkish Lady. Eddy Gathorne-Hardy was another congenial spirit.

Paddy describes a later visit when, 'we were living in a rather wretched house at Limni on the west coast of Euboea, with an amazing view over the sea to the snows of Parnassus. There was no room for a guest that you could call a room, so Mark brought her to stay with our neighbour, Aymer Maxwell, a delightful Galloway laird, very civilized, rather eccentric, very amusing, an angel in fact, always in a bit of a stew about what he gravely called "my staff"—rightly, I must admit. It was an immediate click—"I adore Sir Aymer, and I love Bleak House!" —(the house had belonged to the English overseer of a magnesite mine, now abandoned; it had a certain charm with a touch of the dak bungalow about it, only bigger and more rambling, lit by petrol lamps and candles). There are several other English residents, revelling as usual in minor feuds and gossip, not to mention labyrinthine complications, slander and conspiracy among the local Limniots, and subtle playing of one foreigner against the others, then *vice versa* in every possible permutation. Nancy was fascinated: "I quite see. A Euboean Cranford . . ."

'We had most of our meals in an out-door taverna among the trees, which is full of shaggy resin-gatherers from the mountains in summer, pals of Aymer's and of ours, and often tight. There is a great deal of unsteady dancing in the evening, lurching and retsina-spilling and not very tuneful song. At one moment when a stumble had brought down a whole Indian file of dancers in a sottish and Breughelesque heap, Nancy murmured "*Arcady*", heaving a sigh of mock rapture, followed by a round-eyed pitying look, then a bell-like peal.

'Aymer took us for idyllic sails in a charming yacht he has called *Dirk Hatterick* (after the Galloway pirate in *Guy Mannering*) . . . to the Boeotian shore, up the coast towards Mount Pelion and the Gulf of Volo, to a small island with a tumbling monastery that he thought of buying, dropping

136

anchor in deserted and brilliant blue-green bays, bosky to the water's edge with cistus, rosemary, lentisk and thyme under reflected emerald green pines and the tall spurs of Mount Canodilli; always with Parnassus afloat and glimmering in the west. She loved it. They were very happy days. But once, on a short outing when we were due back for luncheon on shore for some reason, instead of on cushions on the deck, it grew later and later . . . Nancy closed her eyes with a sad sigh and made the French sawing gesture across her tummy with the edge of her hand. "Nancy, you think of nothing but meals." "Try to be nice." Then: "Early and light, early and light, are the luncheons the Limniots love."

'She came down here (to Messenia) with Mark soon after we had finished building the house . . . I can't remember any separate fragments of chat, only endless talk on the pebbles in the bay below, and lying on the terrace; and a journey down to Mani to look at the San Gimignano-like towers, and a picnic on a flower-covered ledge in the masonry of the Arcadian Gate in the ancient ramparts of Messene, which undulate across the valleys like the Great Wall of China. Sleep under the branches was broken by voices: a carload of Germans looking at the titanic fallen lintel that half bars the great portal. We watched them unseen in our eyrie, and unspeaking till they drove away. A wild and marvellous spot.'

Perhaps there were moments when Nancy remembered that she was directly descended from William Mitford, the historian of Greece.

CHAPTER TEN

'I'VE BEGUN A novel—still at the sticky stage but I think it has possibilities,' she told Mark in August, 1959. The novel was *Don't Tell Alfeed*, wherein the professor of Pastoral Theology at Oxford is suddenly appointed Ambassador to Paris. This gave Nancy yet another opportunity to hold her mirror to the corner of the world she loved: Paris and life at the British Embassy.

'Uncle Matthew' reappears, now grown old, 'stiff and slow in his movements; wearing spectacles; decidedly deaf;' and the tale is unfolded by Fanny, daughter of 'the Bolter' and wife of the professorial Ambassador. The Valhuberts and other Mitfordian figures are introduced and the narrative is interspersed with her private reflections on various aspects of French life and dialogue apparently transcribed verbatim. Lady Leone, the bewitching former Ambassadress, creates some preliminary confusion by digging herself into the entresol flat of the Embassy and refusing to leave. Further confusion is caused by an influx of the Ambassador's progeny: his bearded elder son David with a pregnant wife and adopted Chinese infant, on their way to cultivate Zen Buddhism in the Far East; and young Basil, a ruthless exploiter of the package holiday industry which has recently become so notorious.

David informs his mother that he can't approve of her way of life. 'I hate the bourgeoisie. In Zen I find the antithesis of what you and Father have always stood for. So I embrace Zen with all my heart.' The adopted infant was 'named after the great Zen Master Po Chang. We dropped the Po . . . It was Po Chang who placed a pitcher before his followers and asked them "What is this object?" They made various suggestions. Then one of the followers went up to it and kicked it over. Him Po Chang appointed to be his successor.' The more practical Basil regards 'carting out the rubbish' in the role of package tour operator as his 'career, his work, his future'. He assures his bemused mother that 'the Foreign Office has had its day— enjoyable while it lasted no doubt, but over now. The privileged being of the future is the travel agent.' Nancy's Basil seems destined to develop along the lines of Evelyn Waugh's Basil Seal.

The outrageous offspring of poor Sir Alfred and Fanny Wincham steal the show, but they also strain the plot and one's powers of credulity though Nancy took pains to record the barbarous idiom of the juvenile. After Lady Leone vanishes from the scene fantasy whirls off into farce as in Nancy's earliest novels. However, her roseate vision of Gay Paree is undimmed: she has not become cloyed. 'A Paris dinner party, both from a material point of view and as regards conversation, is certainly the most civilized gathering that our age can produce, and while it may not be as brilliant as in the great days of the salons, it is unrivalled in the modern world . . . I am always struck by how easily a French party slides down the slipway and floats off into the open sea. People arrive determined to enjoy themselves instead of, as at Oxford, determined (apparently) to be awkward. There are no pools of silence, all the guests find congenial souls, or at least somebody with whom to argue.' She concedes that diplomatic hostesses are boring: 'They might have to deal with unexpected dialogue and that would never do. The conversation must run on familiar lines, according to some well-worn old formula'. But the diplomatic hostesses belonged to other nationalities.

Even if we don't happen to be hungry our appetite is whetted by the description of lunching with the Duchesse de Sauveterre in her country house. 'We began with brochet. Why is brochet so good and pike so nasty, since the dictionary affirms that they are one and the same? Then partridges, followed by thick juicy French cutlets quite unlike the penny on the end of a brittle bone which is the English butcher's presentation of that piece of meat. They were burnt on the outside, inside almost raw. Boiled eggs suddenly appeared, with fingers of buttered toast, in case any- body should still be famished. Then a whole brie on bed of straw; then chocolate profiterolles.'

(It is amusing to compare this with the genteel English repast described in her early novel *Christmas Pudding*: 'Presently Lady Joan (or Miss Felicity) would appear, and several pretty, fluffy girls in printed crêpe de chine, and they would all go downstairs to a meal consisting of egg rissole with tomato sauce, cutlets with paper frills round the bone, hard round peas and new potatoes, followed by a pinkish jelly served in glasses with a tiny blob of cream on the top of each portion.')

As for Americans in Paris, 'they are dreadfully unhappy: they huddle together in a sort of ghetto—terrified of losing their American accent.' Surely such Americans as Natalie Barney, Julien Green (de l'Académie française), Stuart-Merrill, were almost as French as the French: they thought and wrote in that language. But Nancy must be forgiven her pet prejudice.

To her old crony and ex-partner Handasyde Buchanan, an astute critic as well as a brilliant bookseller who sold hundreds of her books, she wrote nervously on 1st September, 1960: 'The new Mitford runaway (we hope) comes out in November. Raymond [Mortimer] has just helped with the proofs and he likes it. I was beginning to wonder if it isn't awfully bad as the few who have read it have hardly commented. Anyway Cecil's [Beaton's] jacket is lovely . . . Do tell me when you read *Alfred* (I suppose you'll get a proof) what you think.'

Handy's verdict must have been reassuring for she wrote again on 7th September: 'You were a duck to write—one so thirsts for opinions at this stage and I feel yours is honest. I think Lady Leone's bit is less successful because it's at the beginning, before I've really established the characters. At the same time it gives me a chance to do so and to say a few things about embassies and *the* embassy and the life there. Of course I couldn't really let myself go about Lady Leone who has been so good to me.

'Raymond liked the children best, which rather consoles me for you liking them least . . . I got all the tourist horrors from our consul in Venice, Mr. Lane, who says he spends most of his time hanging about death beds. The rest of the bus-load goes inevitably on and he has to cope with dead and dying tourists—he loathes it. All old folks are called *Son et Lumière* here. I've simply bagged the joke.

'Who's who. Except for the obvious ones, most of the characters are mixtures. Northey is Cristiana Brandolin talking

140

like Debo. Basil is my Diana's Ali. Philip is quite made up and so is David. Bouche-Bontemps (I got the name off a tombstone, and the name Jungfleisch too) is any French politician over about fifty. The young ones are thin, priggish and Protestant. Grace is more or less me. Katie and Mrs Trott are real, at the Embassy, I think that's all?

'Raymond says he has done a lot of house-maiding to the proofs . . . I long for Debo to read it and have asked if Hamish Hamilton could send her a copy—if not she might have yours when you've all done? Perhaps you could angelically ask Hamilton if he has sent one? And my mother, if at all possible. Really she should have it first. P.S. Les Iles Minquiers are boiling up again—one of the evening papers has had headlines two days about them and how unfairly we got them, etc. Gladwyn says I may have been prophetic and the new ambassador may have to cope again!' In an undated note to Handy Nancy added as an afterthought: 'Robert Byron used to say I had a tendency to farce which must be checked. I've always tried to do so . . . I suppose *Alfred* had a farcical side, one might say though there was nothing in it that doesn't happen in the papers almost daily.'

To Christopher Sykes, who was repelled by the character of Northey, Nancy replied: 'How too funny about your hating Northey. I couldn't make up my mind about her. The first ending of the book was Northey telling Fanny that she had been to bed with all the followers. "Not Bouche-Bontemps." "Oh yes." "And Mockbar?" etc, etc, yes to all. "Well, darling, don't tell Alfred."—"Oh but Alfred as well—" Then I thought it wasn't in character so I altered it. I was rather shaken by the all-in-wrestling, which she announced with a cruel gleam which I suppressed. I suppose she has so much sex appeal that *one* is rather in love with her even and wants to present her in a favourable light. Perhaps as you so cleverly suggest, a sequel had better show her up as entirely evil. Oh how I wish I were good at plots. P.T.O. I'm sure my best novel is *Love in a Cold Climate*—(I think *Voltaire* is the best book) . . .'

Within a year she was telling Mark Ogilvie-Grant: '*Alfred* has sold hard on 50,000 which is a relief because he had a very bad press. It shows, what one knew really, that that doesn't matter at all.' And to Mrs. Ham she wrote (3rd July, 1961): 'I've sold *Alf* for a film, greatly to my surprise. I expect you will jump for joy on hearing this news. So I've got a little money to see me through the impending war. Where should we go for it? Isle of Wight perhaps?'

This was Nancy's last novel, and its popularity proved that stories of high life, or life in high places, were still in favour with that Anglo-American reading public which is reputed to be puritanical and egalitarian. Like Proust, but for more romantic reasons, she continued to believe in the social supremacy of the Faubourg St. Germain. She deliberately shut her eyes to the seamier side, the frequent banality, stupidity and shallowness of the fashionable society she glowingly described. I have encountered denizens of the Jockey Club quite as tedious as Nancy's American puppets. The 'gentle game of pat-ball' of diplomatic hostesses may have caused her swerve from fiction to history, from the Ouida-ish dukes of her day-dreams to the genuine dukes of Saint-Simon, more interesting and far more fantastic than their Proustian descendants. To Saint-Simon she turned as a catalyst with evident relief.

Though she was shy of appearing on television, Nancy braved it to promote the sale of her novel and described the ordeal to Mrs. Hammersley (3rd November, 1960): 'I was very much put out by them dragging in my poor sisters—didn't know they were gossipy like that. Then the questions—why do you live in Paris? One can't very well say because it's twenty times more agreeable than living in London. The odd thing is, however feeble you are, it sends the sales whizzing. I sold half as many again last week. I think the public feels that you are in some way sanctified if you've *been on telly.* Also I didn't ask for a first class to go back as it wasn't at mealtime, but as soon as I showed my nose at London Airport they transferred me into first class for nothing! I've never been so amazed. But can you tell me why anybody watches? It seemed so deadly dull—a woman with a lot of dogs—a young man cross with the critics and pontificating about his play. Too mysterious.'

The sound of her own voice reminded her of 'all her aunts rolled into one', so she suggested that Mrs. Ham might act as a substitute: 'I offered you up as a human sacrifice to one who wished to record my voice in order to have a document illustrating upper class usage, fast dying out. My voice when recorded sounds merely irritating. I told him that you have a pretty speaking voice and he'd better ask you. Osbert [Sitwell] whom

I saw in London fully agreed. Do co-operate, I think it's such a good idea.'

Melodious, cooing with a hint of mockery, girlishly giggling, Nancy's voice remained that of a well-bred débutante who had not aged since the nineteen-twenties. One could not imagine that she was already in her fifties. But the deaths of many old friends in rapid succession depressed her. 'How fast'—to paraphrase Cavafy—'the snuffed out candles were multiplying.' In her 'horror-comic' vein she wrote to Mrs. Hammersley, who had offered to bequeath her a bronze bust of herself: 'I'd rather have your diamond brooch (than bronze bust). Do let's always be truthful. Your image in my heart but your brilliants on my breast . . . Simple souls see God before we do, you must console yourself with this thought . . . Don't forget BROOCH please (in will) . . . All my friends seem to be dying in middle age.'

Her cherished Victor Cunard was dying at Asolo: 'I go up there every other day, missing the beach, three hours altogether in broiler buses . . . I think it was partly brought on by the madness of Nancy Cunard [his cousin]—I mean by her going mad. She went to an hotel at 3 a.m. and when the night porter aged ninety showed her her room she ordered him to sleep with her. She then set fire to a policeman. She is now in a bin where she writes heartrending letters to poor Vic. Do write to the old boy.' 'It's a great worry and also not much fun panting up there,' she confessed to Mark, 'because he's in such a bad temper. I always thought people on their death-beds lay with angelic smiles saying I forgive you—not old Vic who has cooked up every grievance, over a friendship of 25 years to fling at my head.'

The loss of other friends in the same year, 'all in different ways irreplaceable,' made her gloomy and she wondered if she could bear to return to a Venice without Victor, whose brother Sir Edward had long been an invalid. In August 1961 Nancy wrote: 'I've just done my good deed for the year—went to the Gare de Lyon at 9.20 a.m., met Edward Cunard and brought him back here until his next train went at two. He's on his way home to Barbados by ship but will he survive the journey? He is a dying man.'

In the meantime he had done an unpardonable thing from any biographer's point of view. He informed Nancy, as if the news would console her: 'Victor kept all your letters from the 1930s—I spent the whole afternoon tearing them up.' Nancy confessed to Mrs. Hammersley that 'it was a blow, as I've never kept a diary and they would have been so useful', which proves that she had a book of memoirs at the back of her mind. To me she said that her letters to Victor were the best she had written: they were probably the most revealing, though I doubt if she unburdened her heart to him as to Mark Ogilvie-Grant. Nancy mentioned that she had bought an exquisite Louis XVI meuble with drawers to keep her letters in. To sort these out will be the task of her future biographers. I dread the survival of mine, which were never intended for publication.

Another good deed for 1961 was when, as she told Mrs. Ham, 'I went to talk to 150 girls of twenty doing advanced studies are you impressed? For some reason I wasn't really frightened and it was very enjoyable. The Professor who took me said "voilà—je leur ai donné un bon petit Noël!" ' (A photograph of a similar occasion is reproduced here.)

Like me, Nancy received innumerable questionnaires about our friend Evelyn Waugh. In October 1960: 'An American who is writing a book about Evelyn uses me as principal adviser. Such questions as, is Freddy Furneaux-Smith (*sic*) Sebastian? Why didn't you and Diana Cooper become Catholics? Did Tony Last go abroad to read Dickens because he couldn't visualize life with Diana Cooper? simply pour in. Without telling actual lies I don't discourage his notions. "We are to visit Garsington which will be great for us. All those places where the bright young set used to have fun!" ' . . .

'I said to the Wid (Mrs. Hammersley) "Look, the swallows are going." "I can't imagine why they ever come." Oh dear, nor can I. Luckily I got boiled in Venice before the weather turned there.'

Luckily, too, while so many friends were failing her aged hostess Mme Costa was still going strong. From Fontaines Nancy wrote to Mark, 18th January, 1961: 'I was ordered down here by Mme Costa and gladly came—after about a month in Paris I stifle. It's funny—ten years ago I used to think they were the oldest people in the world here. Now Mme Costa is 86, and M. de Rohan Chabot 94. He still says "enfin sole" when it appears, on Friday. The maid, Thérèse, is 93 and Jeanne Rödel's mother 95. The two latter keep nearly dying and then coming to again. One is lapped in luxury and for some reason never bored at all . . .

'How I wish I had a farm—I always do when I'm down here in this rich beautiful country . . . I think country life is preferable to town life only if one can have a big house like this and unlimited servants (here there are eight and a wonderful daily). Otherwise one might get lonely. The alternative would be to farm oneself, but I don't think these farms ever come on the market. The farmers round here are immensely prosperous and collect incunables in their spare time! Most awfully nice people. No doubt we shall both end up in towns despite all these day dreams!' (To Alvilde Lees-Milne).

At all seasons she rhapsodized about existence at Fontaines: 'If this place is ideal in the autumn, it is fairyland in the spring . . . I never heard such a dawn chorus—the cuckoo is here though not yet the nightingale—nests everywhere, and the larks! On our moulin walk they are literally deafening: seen from the moulin the house is buried in blossom. Oh how I crave to live in the country—but where?

'The *Sunday Times* have offered me £500 (most I've ever had) for a piece on French country life. I propose to describe Fontaines exactly, only all names disguised. I don't think Mme Costa would mind, do you? If I ask her beforehand it makes such a thing of it. After all people are for ever describing their friends, en clair, in mémoires. Of course you (Mrs. Ham) will figure largely—Suez, etc—Mrs. H I thought. Please comment. I'll let you read it first if you like.'

The resulting *Portrait of a French Country House* was reprinted in her most personal book of essays *The Water Beetle*, dedicated to Mrs. Hammersley. 'I do hope we shall all meet in the next world,' she told her, 'though Evelyn predicts Limbo for me.'

The next world: for the time being Nancy was perfectly satisfied with this one in spite of occasional grumblings, not meant to be taken seriously. Fundamentally sceptical, she longed for evidence of an after-life. Who better than Evelyn Waugh, a staunch Roman Catholic, would enlighten her about his faith? 'I wrote and asked Evelyn exactly what happens to us when we die and he wrote four pages of minute detail,' she informed Mrs. Hammersley (13th June, 1961). 'I bet you don't know. I asked a whole table of R.C.'s here and they hadn't a clue (as English tourists always say about everything). Very interesting what he tells.' (23rd June, 1961) 'I've put Evelyn's masterly exposé into the archives. Briefly it is this. We die and are judged at once. Saints (?) go straight to Heaven. Sinners straight to Hell. The rest of us get varying sentences in Purgatory. At the Last Trump those still remaining on earth are judged. Those who are serving their sentences have to join up with their bodies (like finding one's coat after a party. I hope the arrangements are efficient). The only bodies who rose again at once are Our Lord's and Our Lady's. The body (the good) is US because we do not, like the Mahomedans, believe that body and spirit are two separate things. I wrote and asked Evelyn why, if the body is us, we are not told to take care of it but on the contrary encouraged to tease it. He said that Cyril Connolly's idea that the body ought to be fed on foie gras and covered with kisses is not regular—the body must be mortified. Oh yes—the end of the world is also the end of time. Isn't it interesting! I can hardly wait.'

The unpalatable facts of death were forced upon her with disconcerting frequency. Much as she 'minded'—and she was easily moved to tears—she deprecated the display of grief. 'I shall be very much surprised, and rather cross, if you die before me,' she told Mrs. Hammersley. 'You know how you are always dreaming of my demise—well, I dreamt it the other day. Marie had laid me out and people were défiléing past my bed and I heard the Colonel's faithful Pauline saying "elle n'a plus son joli sourire". Are you in floods, heart of stone?'

About her own demise she could speak light-heartedly, especially to one much older than herself. But from now on the consciousness of absences became intensified, for so many of her close friends, Mme Costa, Princess Dolly Radziwill, Tony Gandarillas and Mrs. Hammersley, were older than herself. Since 'that Russian injection for eternal youth' Tony Gandarillas had 'suddenly begun to look a hundred'. The shock was greater when they were of the same age, or younger. To Alvilde Lees-Milne she wrote (8th February, 1962): 'You will be sad to hear that George and Elizabeth Chavchavadze have been killed, motoring home from the funeral of Lulu's brother. Thank goodness they were killed outright. Poor George had already had one bad accident and no doubt ought to have given up driving. Oh dear I *mind*. It so happens I've seen a lot of Elizabeth lately—she was such a comfortable friend—George seems to have run into the back of a lorry which braked suddenly to avoid two colliding lorries . . . (12th February) It was all very terrible—ghastly details—but the thing is they were killed at once. Poor Denise [Bourdet]. The only paper that could be found had her telephone number so she was rung up at 5 a.m. to be told two people were dead and who were they?

'The funeral was the most beautiful I ever was at. Russian and R.C. priests together in perfect harmony. Russian choir. One felt transported and consoled. A huge turn-out of course, every friend, and true sadness. (When I think of C. of E. funerals—what Debo calls the utter ghastly drear of them—I feel it would be worth turning R.C. to have one like Elizabeth's!) Of course the two coffins made it particularly moving. They were buried at Passy. Who next? Dolly without a doubt. I mind *terribly*.

'I shall have to go over soon and see Mama. The bother is they won't let me back without being vaccinated which terrifies me. Stupid I know. So I must put by some days to be ill before coming . . . (17th March) It seems old Blighty, as well as everything else, is now a dangerous smallpox area and they won't let me back unless I'm vaccinated . . . Marie is terribly against and keeps bringing in the paper to show me photographs of people who have died *dans d'atroces souffrances* of vaccination (not of smallpox!) . . . Our splendid Bardot got on to television and described exactly what happens in the slaughter houses and there's a terrific fuss. 30,000 people wrote to her and the ministry is obliged to act. I love her for it.'

Evelyn Waugh had dedicated *The Loved One* to Nancy, knowing that she shared his appreciation of the horror-comic, an English blend of the farcical and the macabre—in her case at a discreet distance. She recoiled from the formal lying in state of friends and shunned the *chapelle ardente* for which the practical French had a cult she could not comprehend. It amused her none the less. When the famous Misia Sert died her friend Princess Dolly Radziwill had reported: 'Mlle Chanel was there doing up the corpse. "Alors, Coco était en train de faire ses ongles—j'ai trouvé ça très bien de Coco, seulement je te dirai—elle l'avait un rien trop maquillée." Literal *Loved One*.' And after the demise of Comtesse Edith de Beaumont, 'she lay in her ballroom in white lace and everybody popped in here after. "Pour moi c'était le dernier des bals", said one, and another,

"White lace, such a good way of using it up. I never know what to do with old lace." '

If she were plunged in gloom, she quickly rose to the surface: no use repining. The reticulated pattern of her existence varied slightly from year to year: visits to her mother and sisters in England, Scotland or Ireland, to Mark Ogilvie-Grant in Greece, to Contessa Cicogna in Venice, to Mme. Costa at Fontaines, and sometimes to Princess Dolly Radziwill or Tony Gandarillas in the South of France.

All of Nancy's friends remarked that she and her sisters seemed never so happy as when they were united: they would rush together with screams of delight and with neither eyes nor ears for anyone else. Patrick Leigh Fermor recalls: 'It was tremendous fun being with three of the sisters together. They would gang up by twos against the remaining one for teasing purposes—more in pious commemoration of schoolroom usage and custom than anything else. When it was Debo and "Woman" (Pam) against Nancy, they would call her "the Old French Lady" or *"Poor* Nancy, she's a frog you know!" If Nancy should ever use a French word in conversation, automatically and expressionlessly Debo would say *"Ah oui!"* or *"Quelle horrible surprise!"* often both, e.g.: Debo: "Come *on*, old French lady!" Nancy (appealing to a third party with a sigh): "Poor child, she's wanting, you know. *Un peu toquée . . ."* Debo: *"Ah oui? Quelle horrible surprise!"*

'When Nancy and Debo combined against Woman, both would imitate her rather idiosyncratic way of talking, which I think she loved. The basis of Nancy's onslaughts on Debo, when her turn came, were accusations of illiteracy (unfounded, in my theory, because, though never *seen* to read, she's so full of surprises that Xan Fielding and I determined long ago that she must be a secret reader: cupboards full of books discovered after decease, we suspect, like all the empty bottles found after a secret drinker dies.)

'When young the great thing was, by appealing to Debo's love of animals, to wring her heart until tears rose to her eyes— "welling up" was the expression used, just as "mantling" means to blush ("Did you well up?" "I'm not sure, but I think I mantled.") Debo was nicknamed "Nine", as if she had not developed since that age. Nancy would wring her heart and make her well up about a poor little spent match, alone and unloved in a match box, etc.

'At Lismore Nancy found a postcard in the village shop, depicting in sombre colours an old Irish peasant sitting sadly and pensively on the right side of a grate. "Look, Whistler's Father!" she exclaimed. It was wonderfully apt in colouring, style and position, and Nancy sent off a score or so to various friends.

'In Fermoy, Co Cork, she was spell-bound by a wax dummy in a dress-shop window, discoloured, flyblown, with horse-hair shingle moulting, wearing a 1925 cloche hat and a low-waisted short skirt of the period, and half-melted, so that the figure was stooping over in a drunken lurch. Whenever plans were discussed she said, "Do let's go and have another look at that lady in Leigh Fermoy!" She and Eddy Sackville and I went to see a marvellous garden belonging to Mrs Annesly at Annsgrove (Cork). There was some giant gunnera like mammoth rhubarb, dangerous, man-eating looking plants. Later, when someone came under unfavourable comment, Nancy said, "The fiend! Let's throw him to the gunnera!" In the same garden I sat on a bench which promptly came to bits. "Look what the boy's done now!" Nancy said. I pointed out that both legs were rotted hollow. She looked and said, "Ah well, perhaps there were faults on both sides . . ."

'It was nice hearing Mitfordese in so unpolluted a flow— "When do they *loom*, the fiends?" "No sewers to dinner today, I trust." "It'll all loom in the wash, I dare say." The fire was getting low. Nancy peered at the grate and said weakly, "I note no bellows." At a picnic on the edge of a wood a huge fire was built, whereupon Nancy gathered a small handful of sticks, threw them on and sat down firmly, saying "No Mohican *me*." '

In a short article about Ireland Nancy wrote that she had not been prepared for the primness of Dublin, nor for the plainness of the colleens. 'Where are the shawls and petticoats and pretty bare feet? They must have gone to Hollywood.' In reply to her enquiries about the Little People a keeper told her that the Russians were driving them away and nobody saw them now. But she found the country-house life unremittingly pleasant— 'the guests move in for a long stay with their dogs, their children, their fishing rods and needlework'—and concluded: 'One is happily back in the nineteenth century.'

149

Already she was consulting Sir Hugh Jackson about another subject she had in mind, the embryo of her *Frederick the Great*. 12th October, 1961: 'Might not *Frederick's Frenchmen* make an amusing book? Of course the démêlés with Voltaire have been described, better than I could, by Carlyle and Macaulay, still the modern public may not know much about them and there are other very funny episodes one could describe (rather improper I fear, but still—!) I think if I went slowly my eyes would stand up to it. Do tell me if you like the idea.'

In April 1962 she wrote to Mark: 'Stoker's [her nephew Peregrine Hartington's] reports from Eton . . . say he seems to think he is a character in one of his aunt's old world books [*Don't tell Alfred*]. Debo couldn't think who this aunt was. I go to Lismore on 27th and oh would that ye were there.

'Have you read Isherwood [*Down there on a visit*]? Now at last we know what goes on in Greece. Unworthy, to say the least . . . I'm muddled about plans. I dined with Turkish Fred— got a cab to go home—said allez à la rue Monsieur, to which the cabby said numéro 7 et vous êtes la célèbre Nancy Quelque- chose. It's all right—old Tony had once taken me back in that cab and done a bit of boasting on the way home. Are you shrieking?

'Colonel is back in the Government goody gum trees as Ole Nole [Coward] would say. I went to a farewell for your large handsome café society friend whose name I have never under- stood. Too late now. Busy with my book (thoughts on Greece etc.) so adieu.' The little book of great thoughts, as she des- cribed it, was being 'cooked up' for the autumn.

In May she wrote again from Derreen in Killarney: 'Have you ever been here it is beautiful beyond compare. A thousand trees lost in the gale seem to have made no impression whatever —the ones which haven't been cleared away have got rhodo- dendrons and ferns growing out of their trunks. What a climate! . . . Went to a shopping centre and purchased a china plaque with in Irish lettering "Everybody's Queer but Thee and Me". Now who can I give it to? Takes a bit of thought.'

To Mark again, from Paris, 27th June: 'Busy correcting Homer Thompson proofs which can't fail I think to annoy that wretched old Philistine. I go to Venice tomorrow till end of July . . . I'll be here I hope all August when Decca comes.'

As usual 'Venice was divine, only the time whizzed at a

terrifying speed and I seemed only just to have arrived when five weeks had gone and it was time to come back.' Paris in August was 'heavenly, hot and empty though not quite as empty as it used to be, people are getting wise to the niceness unfortunately.'

From Fontaines she wrote to Alvilde Lees-Milne on 20th October: 'So heavenly here, I'm still in a cotton dress can you beat it! Mrs Ham is here and all the usuals—the Jockey Clubites arrive this evening with news from the great world. All madly anti the General and simply furious because he threatens to go. They say it's his duty to stay—how does this fit in with Gallic logic I don't dare ask them. I sit rigolering intérieurement . . . Did you know that Marie Stuart was the same height as General de Gaulle? Nobody ever says this as one is never told that Charles I was a dwarf but I think it's so interesting.' 26th October: 'For about two days the wireless tried to make one's flesh creep and I spent my time preventing the old ladies from hearing the word Cuba. Quite easy as all they care about is the Concil [Vatican Council]. Then Holy Dad blew the gaff by broadcasting an appeal for peace.

'Do you know what young people here call anybody over forty? E.L. Stands for *Encore Là* [Still There].

'I went to a circus last night and noted that, whatever anybody may say, the lions and tigers simply *love* it! So that's a weight off one's mind.'

At about this time a Cambridge don rang up Sir Malcolm Bullock and said: 'You know France, does General de Gaulle write his own speeches?' 'No,' said Sir Malcolm, 'Miss Nancy Mitford writes them for him.'

The 'little book of great thoughts' was christened *The Water Beetle* and embellished with jocose illustrations by Osbert Lancaster. Beginning with the bravura portrait of her nanny Blor and ending with her conversation piece about Fontaines les Nonnes, it is the nearest Nancy floated towards an autobiography. *Inter alia* it contains a moving tribute to her hero Captain Scott of the Antarctic, the diary of her visit to Russia in 1954, her defence of Louis XV (with whom one suspects she identified the Colonel) and her candid admission: 'I like fact better than fiction and I like almost anything that makes me laugh. But my favourite book falls into neither of these categories: it is *La Princesse de Clèves*'. Apart from her inclusion of

151

Byron among the supreme entertainers there is no mention of any poet. Here we have the essence of Nancy within a small compass, 'gliding on the water's face/Assigning each to each its place'. It is a highly individual bouquet, and it still reads as if the flowers were freshly picked with diamonds of dew on their petals.

In a post-script to her account of Fontaines, disguised as 'Sainte Foy', Nancy added that she showed it to a French friend who said, 'My dear, if the English think we all live like this, they will never join the Common Market.' I said, 'Don't worry at all, the English don't believe a word I tell them; they regard me as their chief purveyor of fairy tales.'

True, her commentaries on the Parisian scene had much of the charm and fantasy of fairy tales and as soon as you read them you longed to cross the Channel. She dwelt fondly on the apparent lack of change: 'The *bouquinistes* by the river; the donkeys in the Tuileries gardens; the lace blouses, in the shop on the corner of the rue Duphot, which I coveted as a child and still covet now, but which have a curious remoteness like blouses in a dream; the falling cadence of the glazier's cry as he walks the streets with a huge pane of glass on his back; Madame Bousquet's salon on Thursdays; the pink electric light bulbs at Larue, rapidly diminishing, alas, as they can no longer be replaced; the flock of goats milked in the street . . . George of the Ritz bar; the outside platforms of the buses; the insides of the taxis which must, one feels, be the very same that took the troops up to the Battle of the Marne . . .' But the cost of everything has soared since her description of wines in the 1950 catalogue of Etablissement Nicolas where a Pouilly Fumé 1929 was advertised for 10s. a bottle and a Porto Imperial 1848 cost £2 10s., and one doubts if everybody in Paris still has some connection with the *haute couture* which always fascinated Nancy.

The houses she visited 'glittered like a miniature Wallace Collection' and the women were generally 'glittering with jewels'. There was ball after ball, with champagne flowing from 14 buffets and women in huge romantic crinolines. Her letters after settling in Paris are full of them. To Mark Ogilvie-Grant: 'Marie-Laure is having a Scotch ball—real bagpipes, Strip the Willow, all the cissies are off to Scotch House for their kilts. We want somebody to teach us the reels—why don't you come in that capacity?' And to her mother: 'I'm just off to a fancy dress ball in black tights, little velvet jacket and beret and a *dear* little black beard. Nobody has talked of anything but this ball since Xmas so of course excitement is at fever pitch! The Colonel keeps ringing up to say he is against the beard, but I am firm! Dolly Radziwill is my wife in black and white and her wonderful jewels and we are King Sigismund and Queen Barbara. Bébé [Bérard] is Henry VIII surrounded by his eight wives, nobody likes to tell him there were only six.' Again, in January 1951: 'We are all entirely concentrated on Marie-Laure's Fête de Village ball. Momo [Lady Marriott] arrived off the Queen Mary last night and I said I've got the most vitally important things to tell you (i.e. how she must come in our group) and she screamed with laughter, saying in New York they think it's dangerous to go to Paris now, and wonderful to be greeted like this. Diana Coo wanted me to go with her as a tall ridiculous English woman with everything just wrong, so I'm going in the village school with Cora Caetani, as the school negress. Violet [Trefusis] is to be la veuve du village, followed by the ghost of the husband she had murdered (Antonin de Mun). I'm sure they'll be wonderful. Then all the musicians are to do a music hall which will certainly be divinely funny as they are all clowns at heart. Isn't Marie-Laure a good old girl to give this lovely party and such a sensible idea as no outlay for dresses required. We have all got pale blue overalls with white collars, awfully pretty, and sailor hats—£2 the lot.'

After a while Nancy became surfeited with such entertainments and preferred reports to the reality of Carlos de Beistegui's ball in Venice which gave rise to so many legends. It was even announced on the French radio that the *entrée* of M. Lopez would cost £50,000 and include two elephants. 'The £50,000 may well be true,' she wrote, 'since M. Lopez and his suite of twenty are to represent the Chinese Embassy to Venice in the eighteenth century and will sparkle with specially woven material covered with real jewels. But the elephants are a legend.' A young couple who, for fear of Communism, had sold their estates with the intention of emigrating, were said to have spent all the proceeds on their *entrée* at the ball, and 'a lady who advertised for a dwarf to accompany her in the role of Spanish Infanta, arrived home to find her hall filled with rich dwarfs of her acquaintance who had not been invited . . . No society people left Paris before the middle of August, they were too busy trying on their dresses. When finally they got away a yacht race round Italy ensued, since there is only one good mooring in Venice for a big yacht. It is to be hoped that these ships will not suffer the fate of the Spanish Armada, as in that case the ball would be deprived of its most splendid *entrées*.' The guests of the great ball trickled back to Paris 'like survivors from a battle. Each has a tale of daring to recount, each gives the impression that it was a damned close-run thing and would never have done without his or her particular *entrée*.'

By contrast with such elaborate festivities Nancy wrote from Fontaines les Nonnes: 'Yesterday we visited a convent full of old Marquises whose husbands had told them to take orders when widowed. I couldn't help thinking how it wouldn't suit English Marchionesses! Oh how different we are, it's really extraordinary.

'An old man I know said to his girl the other day, "I've an offer of marriage for you." "Mais Papa, you know I don't want to marry." "Well, in any case I wouldn't have advised you to accept, as the young man is blind." "But that makes a great difference. If he's blind I can lead a life of sacrifice—I accept," and now they are married. She'd never even seen him!'

But for a dash of Ouida I do not think it too far-fetched to find a parallel, *mutatis mutandis*, between Nancy's descriptions of the Parisian scene and Mary Russell Mitford's of *Our Village*. She had the same constitutional buoyancy of spirits, the will to be happy, and 'a tendency to body forth images of gladness' which Anne Thackeray Ritchie noticed in the early Victorian Miss Mitford. And as Lady Ritchie observed in her introduction to *Our Village*, 'There is one penalty people pay for being authors, which is that from cultivating vivid impressions and mental pictures they are apt to take fancies too seriously and to mistake them for reality.'

Among Nancy's steady correspondents was an old gentleman whom she did not meet personally but who remained a faithful pen-pal until she could write no more. Sir Hugh Jackson had known Paris intimately in the serener days before the First World War; he had a specialist's knowledge of French history and he shared Nancy's sympathies and antipathies to an unusual degree. He had offered to look up historical sources for her out of the blue and from the many letters she wrote to him it is obvious that she valued his opinions and advice. She was an avid collector of early twentieth-century French postcards and she exchanged several of these with Sir Hugh Jackson who had a similar collection.

'How I love the cards you send me of old Paris,' she wrote him. 'So amusing that the original colour of the stone has been restored so that the buildings look now as they did then. But the great difference is the emptiness of those days—now you can't either drive or even walk up the Boulevard des Italiens for the milling mob. I do wonder why there are suddenly so many people?' Again: 'I love your cards much more because they are real. The Madeleine is that colour again instead of the black mass which I knew . . . Thanks awfully for the lovely coloured one . . . Can't now remember which you have had. Splendid Restaurant (outside Gare St. Lazare)? And the lady catching the bus? They are getting less nice and one never sees the heavenly one départ pour la chasse any more . . .'

Among the cards was one of a strange machine entitled *Distribution automatique*. What was it distributing? she queried. The heavily clad ladies in front of it offered no clue. Horse-drawn omnibuses, women in enormous hats, bemedalled and moustachio'd officers, 'lovely and solid', as she said, reminiscent of the Marquis de Soveral; the *mairie* of Marcilly like a painting by Utrillo ('Isn't this France all over? Built in 1904?') Behind one of the Chambre des Députés she wrote: 'Anyway it's a nice card, of the sort we like, and shows how few people there used to be so short a time ago. This place now is an immovable jam and the pavements black with people. What a bad idea it was to reduce infant mortality.' Of the Place de l'Opéra she wrote: 'I bought this ages ago to show you the Opéra now it's clean. The cab drivers all think it's the most beautiful building in Paris!' Apropos of which on 1st April, 1962: 'The French wireless gave out that Malraux is to pull down the Opéra and put up a palace of modern music, designed by Le Corbusier. They gave an infinity of dreadful details. I boiled. It went on all day at the times of the news until finally they said Poisson d'Avril (April fool)! You can't imagine how clever and funny it was. It seems they were besieged with furious telephone calls.'

The postcards exchanged with Sir Hugh Jackson evoked the world of Marcel Proust, whose biography by Mr. George Painter enthralled Nancy: 'He has a way of writing about people we have all known as if they had been dead 1,000 years which is very whimsical! But on the whole he hits them off pretty well.'

Nancy told Patrick Leigh Fermor that she wrote to Mr. Painter saying 'had he noticed that Proust is practically the same person as Voltaire and he replied "This is supernatural," and that he'd thought of that the whole time he was writing it. It's true. I wish he'd now do the same for Voltaire.'

Perhaps the fact that Nancy never met Sir Hugh Jackson personally enabled her to open her heart to him about her literary projects as she seldom, if ever, did to other friends, myself included. Their correspondence started in 1956 when Nancy had reviewed Dr. Gooch's irritating *Life of Louis XV*. 'Why are nearly all the books written about France so unspeakably bad?' she had exclaimed then. 'Do read Gooch if you want to spit red buttons. He even scolds the poor man for *not* punishing the people who went to Chanteloup. What, I wonder, would have been said if he had punished them! One Rohan Butler of All Souls is doing a huge life of Choiseul and Marcus Cheke one of Bernis. I wonder what we shall think of them?'

She had contemplated visiting Madagascar with Raymond Mortimer—a strange idea for one who enjoyed an occasional change but disliked distant journeys and was bored by travel literature. 'Well, no I never went to Madagascar,' she told Sir Hugh (18th April, 1963). 'It seemed to cost about £1,000 and there are many things I would like better, at that price. So I stayed cosily by my wood stove and had the laugh of those who utterly despise this form of heating. Gas flickered, oil failed on account of frozen canals, coal likewise, and my good old stove continued with its nice glow, delicious smell and friendly ticking noise. Neither I nor my bonne had a cold the whole time. Luckily I'm never lulled into expecting mild winters to go on succeeding each other and always lay in a phenomenal quantity of logs . . . I don't think I can manage Frederick [the Great]. My eyes are no worse but no better than when I wrote Voltaire and I can't face the pain. So until I can think of a subject for a novel I must do easy pot-boilers. I've been commissioned to do a picture book of Versailles—refused at first because there are so many, then thought it could be amusing to describe the various happenings in the places, opposite the photographs? I'm off to Ireland now and will begin when I return. Oh the famine book, it was just TOO MUCH. [A book about the Irish famine.] I went yesterday to see a film called 1914–18 which is two hours of documentaries taken at the time and is fascinating beyond words—so brilliantly put together. That is too much too, and my brother-in-law who came (and who was in the war) has been sad ever since, thinking of all his dead friends. Goodness, what times we have lived in! I don't like much what I read of England at present either and still less what I *see* when I go there in the building line. But all the young people I meet—friends of my nephews—are wonderful. They must be the hope of the future. (I mean the sixteen-year-olds not those dreary Angries).'

CHAPTER ELEVEN

INSTEAD OF GOING to Madagascar Nancy attended a royal wedding—that of Princess Alexandra to her Ogilvy cousin, which she described to Mrs. Hammersley (28th April, 1963): 'The wedding was splendid and I greatly enjoyed it but *oh* the get ups I never saw worse. I'm sure English women are dowdier than when I was young. The hats were nearly all as though made by somebody who had once heard about flowers but never seen one—huge muffs of horror. In front of me a green satin top hat with pink carnation dangling. The dresses and coats not only didn't fit but had not been ironed. The colours of the year are pale green and pale brown, very often mixed. Joan Ali Khan, next to me, had a paisley satin coat green and brown, a green net and bow on unbrushed hair and blue satin shoes and she was quite one of the best. Muv in black velvet, lace and diamonds, was marvellous she looked so pretty. The angelic police let her car stay outside so that she got away before anybody.

'The bride is a *true beauty*. Queen of Spain rather splendid, the Queen excellent, though in washy green which I do hate— Princess Anne quite lovely—the Foreign Royals very pop-eyed.'

Lady Redesdale, aged 83, did not long survive this happy event. On 14th May Nancy wrote from Inch Kenneth, Isle of Mull, to Mark Ogilvie-Grant: 'Muv is failing—we are all here —it is very poignant . . . Two days ago she seemed to be going —she said perhaps, who knows . . . and said goodbye to everybody and said if there are things in my will you don't like do alter it. I said, but we should go to prison! and she laughed (she laughed as she always has). Then she rallied and here she still is—we long for her to go in her sleep quietly.

'Of course we are half the time in tears and the other half shrieking, as you may imagine . . . For two days we were storm-bound and in the middle, in a short moment of calm, wonderful Mr. Ogilvie Forbes (wish it were Grant) came over, settled into the bothy and will stay. Did you ever hear of such kindness!'

On 19th May, to Alvilde Lees-Milne; 'It's very sad here but of course cheerfulness breaks in. In fact my mother said to me, what are they all doing downstairs? I said shrieking. She said funny sort of funeral party—we haven't laughed so much in our lives. Three times she has nearly gone and there have been touching almost unbearable farewells but then she rallies and seems much better. The doctor thinks it can't be long but admits that one never knows. We never leave her alone with a nurse and take the nights in turns—two adorable Scotch nurses.

'We are fifteen here and were all women with one boatman until, when we had been storm-bound for two days, running out of loo-paper, an intrepid neighbour rolled over in a rubber ball— he has moved quietly into the bothy . . . It is terribly like the life of Scottie (her hero of the Antarctic)—the room we live in simply *is* the hut and our eyes are ever on the boats hoping for mail. Jokes get sillier every day. Smashing grub and great comfort . . .'

On 21st May, to James Lees-Milne: 'We all wondered if, when the time comes, you would write about Muv in *The Times* as you did for Tom? It would be good of you and greatly appreciated if not too much trouble. You have known her for so long. Happily she now sleeps the whole time—the last few days were truly dreadful. We have been here nearly a fortnight and each day is supposed to be the last. It is very hard to detach oneself from the body, evidently. The good Scotch doctor doesn't force us to keep her alive in horrible artificial ways—the nurses say it would be very different in a hospital.'

To me she wrote later: 'The extraordinary beauty of the Scotch scenery, the fact that we were among friends and that all which has to be done was done by her own crofters, softened the horror of death, I shall never forget her departure from her island, over a glassy sea, bagpipes wailing and the men in the boat talking softly in Gaelic. Better than the London Clinic, all the same!'

'I really think I shall never be able to cry again,' she told

159

Mark. 'I'd had doubts about going to Venice in such deep mourning but Dolly [Radziwill], my mentor, says it is quite all right to do so. I'd like to have two or three weeks there and then take a boat to Athens and then a boat home, a thing I've always longed to do.'

In retrospect Nancy ruefully confessed that she had never loved her mother, for whom Mrs. Hammersley and Mme Costa had been emotional substitutes. Eldest children are seldom a mother's favourites. I suspect she was more deeply attached to her father. 'Uncle Matthew' was a flesh and blood character whose violently virile foibles were endearing to so feminine a daughter. But even if we are no longer young, we feel younger and in a sense more secure with a living mother to turn to and, in Nancy's case, to laugh with. She often reverted to the jokes they would have shared, as when she read Anne Fremantle's memoirs: 'I was riveted to note that Anne's mother, Tiny, was seduced at the age of twelve by an uncle of Muv's at Madras. Oh dear, Muv would have liked that and now too late . . .'

In the meantime Princess Radziwill was failing and Nancy was worried about her: 'If Dolly dies I really am done for as she's by far my most intimate friend.' Her beloved Mrs. Ham was 'wreathed in black merino and gloom . . . "One or two very tiresome things have happened this morning." "Oh dear, does nothing nice ever happen?" "Never".' Mrs. Hammersley was to die next February.

The 'picture book on Versailles' was approached with cautious hesitation. Nancy mentioned it again rather casually in a letter to Sir Hugh Jackson from Fontaines (11th October, 1963): 'When I was in Venice I thought that perhaps masked naked men, orgies and unlimited spying are an accompaniment of maritime powers in decline. Certainly the whole Ward affair comes straight out of Casanova, except that Keeler would have been a nun and Ward the abbé de Bernis. I went to Samos from Athens when poor Ward was in a coma—no papers on Samos— at last I made a friend go to the police station to find out what had happened. "Dr. Ward is dead. You have lost a fine man!" Samian wine, by the way, is delicious. Yes, I had a cloudless six weeks and felt quite guilty about friends at home. A slight bore in Greece is that one is discouraged from swimming from a boat as there are sharks. This is quite new and said to be Nasser's fault, he is supposed to beckon them through the canal to eat us all up. I don't greatly fear death but it would be too ridiculous—even one's greatest friends would laugh if one were eaten I feel!

'I am writing a little pot-boiler on Versailles, to be illustrated. One of those boring books millionaires give each other for Xmas. The publisher asked for it and I've nothing else on hand so said all right.'

This was the germ of *The Sun King*, another feat of which Nancy had reason to be proud. Though she approached the subject on tiptoe it engrossed her for the next few years. She had been enchanted by Versailles while writing *Madame de Pompadour* and a recent visit to the palace at night illuminated by candles as of yore had been a magical, almost mystical, experience. Again she longed for a house in the vicinity. 'I sometimes wonder if I don't mind about places more than about people,' she told her sister Debo. 'If I do I am a sort of human cat I suppose. I only wish I'd never taught myself to look at architecture as it brings more pain than pleasure nowadays.' But Versailles never ceased to give Nancy pleasure, even when she was in physical pain.

On 3rd January, 1964, she told Alvilde Lees-Milne: 'I am working and have to be surrounded by about 60 books which lie on the floor and drive old Marie mad for dusting purposes. I'm doing what will become almost a biography of Louis XIV via the King at Versailles. The trouble is it's all so fascinating I keep going off at a tangent and have just spent a week on Mme Guyon who one can't say has much to do with Versailles! . . . Old Marie retires in October—*don't*! The idea of showing a new person how to light my stoves without setting the chimney on fire wakes me up in the night. And then the chat. You at least know how to cook but think of me starving sadly to death. I went to the kitchen to learn but pulling the vitals out of a dear old hen is beyond my powers—I don't feel hungry enough, it's not like when one was young.'

Fortunately the indispensable Marie stayed on with Nancy for many more years. Lesley Blanch, who also lived in Paris at the time, has reminded me that Nancy was entirely helpless in the kitchen.

' "I simply can't," she would sigh. If Marie was out she could not even make a cup of tea. Once, I recall, we were deep in talk, and it was raining and dark, and she who seldom if ever ate anything at night, at home, said she would love me to stay on, but

161

Marie was out and so—what to do? I suggested I might cook an omelette. "Dearest, I don't know where anything is . . ." We went to the kitchen, and found an absolutely empty frigidaire, Marie's habit being to buy exactly what was needed each day, and no more. Nancy seemed helpless, hopeless, unaware of a store-cupboard, where were the matches, the gas jet . . . and also impervious to any pangs of hunger herself. Though she tucked in and much enjoyed a good blow-out, such as she offered at her lunches. She always seemed to enjoy my cooking efforts, and was a rewarding, second-helps guest. She took much trouble to train Marie. I would not think her in any way a voluptuary— that is, one profoundly aware of the pleasures of the senses— except perhaps for some foods—dishes Marie soon learned to cook beautifully. Together they would pore over the little Larousse cookery book. Marie had I think begun life making hats, and that inbred French hand, so light with ribbons, straws and feathers, was presently transformed to soufflés and such . . . Apropos Nancy's helplessness in domestic affairs she described to me an evening she had spent with her mother in Rutland Gate: the servants were out and the cook had left a macaroni cheese ready, with instructions to put it in the oven for half an hour or so. This in due course the ladies did, but neither of them had thought to light the oven, and were quite puzzled to find it stone cold and uncooked when they took it out.'

My recollections of luncheons in rue Monsieur are dappled with the sunshine Nancy evoked with her lilting voice and trills of laughter while Marie handed round a savoury stew or a succulent sweet. As soon as you crossed her threshold you were greeted with a scent of fresh flowers: you felt relaxed and stimulated at the same time. 'Good-breeding,' said Fielding, 'is the art of pleasing in conversation', and Nancy possessed this art, the nature of which can only be gleaned from her writing, especially from her correspondence. Table-talk, the essence of which is spontaneity, the impromptu interchange of topical news, impressions and ideas, is almost impossible to recapture, and Nancy's remained ultra English in its fleeting allusions spiced with puns and nicknames. Her speech was animated with tender superlatives: she warmed one with gentle irony and she bounded from banality with the lightness of a gazelle. She had none of the airs of a self-conscious literary lady and she seldom

162

referred to her writings. In spite of all the books she had to consult she was surrounded by neatness and order: there was a complete absence of clutter.

While in Paris she was apt to become the victim of her hospitable impulse: she could concentrate better in Venice or at Fontaines. As she confided to Mark (19th March, 1964): 'I'm trying to work and not really succeeding owing to a procession of compatriots—you know how unsettling that can be. They never want to see each other, that's their last idea, and expect me to whistle up cohorts of fascinating frogs. Poor old Marie is wilting.' No doubt her compatriots hoped to meet the originals of Nancy's Gallic heroes. Among the compatriots were several fans, including journalists who needed taming or even 'buttering' for as Lesley Blanch remarked, she had a keen sense of publicity and an instinct 'how to retreat, tease, drop a bomb, become indifferent, absent. She had decided on her line, how to present Nancy's façade, behind which one caught glimpses of another Nancy.' To Mark she confessed: 'I write tenderly to all fans, having been strictly told by Willie Maugham that I must. It costs a fortune in stamps, I can tell ye.'

Mentally refreshed and physically 'boiled up a little' after a trip to Tripoli and Istanbul—outside Contessa Cicogna's Garden of Eden in Tripoli, she wrote, 'one finds old Ireland to the life. The muezzin, who has a loud speaker, sounds like the Beatles IN one's bedroom,' while the Bosphorus conjured memories of Miss Nightingale, with 'pretty old houses, a cross between Russia and Venice in design',—and returning via Athens, Nancy started to grapple with something more ambitious than a picture book on Versailles though, as she told Mark, 'my book is to have 400 illustrations: it's the new idea of publishing.'

Having taken the plunge she wrote to Sir Hugh Jackson (28th September, 1964): 'I'm boldly writing a book about Louis XIV—that is, not a biography exactly but describing the various things which amuse me in his reign. First Versailles and how it was built, then the Poisons, then St. Cyr (which will appear in *History Today* I hope), Lord Portland's embassy. A chapter on doctors. And so on . . . But I'm having trouble, rather, with the publishers who think they won't be able to sell it, after the success of Cronin—and want me to allow it to be one of those picture books. Don't know what to think. If I say yes it can't come out for two years which seems horribly long. St. Germain en Laye is called that because Louis XIV was born there . . . If you have any thoughts on the 17th century do impart them.'

And to Christopher Sykes she wrote (16th December, 1964): 'Oh how I would like to talk to you for hours about the Tyrant. Between ourselves he was awful. Always supposed to be so good at picking wonderful people, but when those picked by Mazarin finally died off they were succeeded by dud upon dud. At the very end, when he ought to have been fussing about what kind of Constitution he left poor dear little *good* Louis XV it was the Constitution Unigenitus that occupied his thoughts.

'He was very brave, and that one likes, and a true aesthete— not a false note that I can see there. I like la gloire and all that side of him. But in human relationships always dreadful. He loved to laugh however, and he loved Lord Portland and so do I (their great scream was anything to do with the Duke of Savoy).' [Hans Willem Bentinck, first Earl of Portland, William III's ambassador to Louis XIV, was an ancestor of Christopher, who had looked up sources for Nancy.] 'There's such a book to be written [about William III and Bentinck.] As I've pointed out in mine, the English thought they were getting honest Dutchmen and were not pleased when W. of Orange and W. Bentinck turned out to be the finest flowers of *French* civilization. Macaulay excellent by the way as per (though I note he falls down over the great House of Sykes) . . .'

Eventually she became convinced that the interest of her book would be enhanced by well chosen illustrations: 'I'm sure people now need pictures with their reading matter and indeed they are the greatest aid to memory. I read an illustrated *Histoire des Français* and for the first time I really sorted out Philippe-Auguste, Charles VII, etc. etc.—comes from seeing their faces, their homes, their coats of arms, etc. My book is going to be too beautiful thanks to clever Mrs. Law [who selected the pictures]. Also Rainbird is perfect about money and his favourite pastime seems to be writing enormous cheques for one.'

Nancy had often mentioned Saint-Simon in her conversation and letters over the last decade, and her enthusiastic article on 'The Great Little Duke', first published in the *New Statesman* (1955), was reprinted in *The Water Beetle*. 'Oh he *is* a lovely

164

Duke!' she exclaimed to Mrs. Hammersley, who was then engaged in translating Mme de Sévigné's letters. 'I don't think Sév could have known him really, he'd have been too young. What a pity—his remarks about the Grignan family would have been worth having—I know he did speak of her but only just. Did Sév really say Racine *passera comme le café*? Somebody said the other day that it is one of those apocryphal sayings—did you find it in the big edition of the letters? I'm nearly sure I saw it in that book you kept urging me to read when I was trying to profit by your company—but perhaps it is part of the new material signed Violet Hammersley.

'My article is really an elaborate tease on Harold Nicolson— rather dangerous ground! But I couldn't resist . . .'

A week later (22nd November, 1955): 'I've been living in the past. Saint-Simon has led to Macaulay, all of whose French passages are taken shamelessly from him. The article went off yesterday—it makes me shriek but will infuriate such as A. J. P. Taylor I fear . . .'

A week later (29th November): 'My (intensely brilliant) Saint-Simon will be in N.S. on Friday. If the proofs don't get to them in time you will chuckle over: "it was during a treat at La Trappe." I so adore the idea of a treat there, don't you? that I quite long for it to stay in. It is all designed as a tease on Harold N.—fearfully unwise, that elephant never forgets, I feel sure!'

Saint-Simon had not only led to Macaulay, he had led to an investigation of the whole period which interested Nancy more and more, and to Versailles, "the outward and visible sign" of the Sun King's power. In 1957 Nancy told Sir Hugh Jackson: 'I plan to end my days at Versailles. It is a ville-musée and one won't be for ever made wretched by new hideous buildings replacing old friends. The tourists are like ants, they follow a trail and two yards off the trail you never see one.' Again in 1960: 'I long to live at Versailles and am looking for a house there—not very easy to find. The other day I went for a walk there and I'm delighted to be able to tell you that our wonderful M. Malraux has had the car park at Trianon moved out of sight. Thank heavens—it ruined all. How I hate motor cars more and more and love M. Malraux who is the saviour of old Paris.' When she wrote of Louis XIV: 'For years before he lived there Versailles was never out of his mind,' she was identifying herself with him. Her longing to live there increased while she was writing about it.

Of the palace Nancy stated: 'He [Louis XIV] built the greatest palace on earth but it always remained the home of a young man, grand without being pompous, full of light and air and cheerfulness—a country house.' Against this architectural background she recounted the chief episodes of his reign with zest and humour, never mincing her words about its scandals and abuses, about the Affair of the Poisons and the absurdities of Saint-Cyr. She tried to see the King's mistresses through the eyes of their contemporaries but with all her good will she could not make them alluring. With the exception of the pathetic Louise de La Vallière, at least they were not dull, and the ascent to power of Scarron's widow remains mysterious in spite of the well known facts. In the long run one dislikes Mme de Maintenon less than her flamboyant rival. Nancy described the Mortemart family as a French version of her own: 'Among themselves they used a private language. They were malicious, but good natured; they never really harmed anybody; they liked laughing and had the precious gift of making other people sparkle.' Her innate prejudice against the medical profession boiled over in her chapter on 'The Faculty', and she could discern little progress between then and now: 'In those days, terrifying in black robes and bonnets, they bled the patient; now, terrifying in white robes and masks, they pump blood into him. The result is the same; the strong live; the weak, after much suffering and expense, both of spirit and money, die.' Though she could hardly sympathize with Le Nôtre's aversion to flowers, and she had to concede that Le Brun, a decorator of genius, was a second-class painter, Nancy was entranced by the harmony of their achievement in collaboration with Le Vau.

'I think old Louis (XIV) has fixed me up for life—no need to bother with Frederick [the Great],' Nancy told M. Jacques Brousse, who was translating her books into French. And indeed the fifty-four years reign of the Sun King provide endless subjects for biography, fiction and drama. Nancy wisely concentrated on Versailles as the symbol and focus of the civilization she preferred. Considering her addictions to the florid Macaulay and the rambling Carlyle the straightforward simplicity of her approach betrays her originality. Amid so much purple she does not even attempt the purple passage. She allows the extraordinary facts to speak for themselves. Her style is devoid of decoration yet in her account of his long reign, beginning in gaiety and glory and ending in a dismal parade of premature deaths, she does succeed in building a prose monument to Louis XIV.

Cyril Connolly had observed of *Voltaire in Love* that Nancy had 'evolved a technique for regurgitating packages of old letters in palatable form which any historian might envy,' and in composing *The Sun King* she perfected this technique. Hers is surely the most entertaining introduction to the subject in English. From a French point of view she was batting on a well-worn pitch: this was the great century of Racine and Molière as well as of Louis XIV and in spite of Lytton Strachey's defence of Racine against English detractors he is still insufficiently appreciated in England, and many of Nancy's sources were unavailable to English readers.

Nancy was a Marathon reader, yet when we remember her trips to Tripoli, Turkey and Chatsworth, and the procession of callers at 'Mr Street', we wonder when she found time to write as well as read.

From Fontaines she wrote: 'There's a great deal of talk here about adopted children because a young man, adopted at three weeks by rich and delightful, perfect in fact, people has suddenly murdered a taxi-driver. Ordered him to come by telephone, made him drive to a lonely place and killed him, all obviously premeditated. The psychiatrists say, and I think it may be very true, that it's most important that the child should know *who* his real parents are, otherwise he thinks they are the Emperors of China and lives in a kind of resentful day-dream. I know this would have been so in my case had I been adopted—as it was I always felt I had come down the wrong chimney and ought to have been Anastasia or Princess Mary.'

In February 1965 she was 'on the last lap' of *The Sun King* and her faithful Marie had decided to stay on another year, 'glory be'. 'Book over for the moment, being typed. I go home tomorrow to correct it,' she wrote to Mark from Fontaines. 'So came down here to breathe a little cold fresh air and delicious it is, with hot sun in the day. I have Mrs. Ham's room now but she never turns up for a chat—it's a shame, she would so much have enjoyed the funeral notes [Sir Winston Churchill's]. I dined with Randolph two days after it—he is on his way to

Morocco to write his book—and he was full of lovely tales, mainly about the Duke of Norfolk who must be a genius. It seems Woodrow Wyatt said to Randolph one can only be thankful the Duke isn't secretary of the Conservative Party. Indeed his enormous gifts do seem rather wasted.

'Elizabeth Longford's *Queen Victoria*—screaming with laughter over it for days—it's too good. The beginning especially perfect: one feels as the sixty years drag on that Elizabeth gets a tiny bit fed up with all the piffle and certainly one does—the end is far less fascinating. Isn't it extraordinary that, surrounded all her life by sophisticated men of the world, she never budged from her pristine naïveté! The Dixons' [British Ambassador's] last glorious act was keeping the embassy flag at full mast when the General's, next door, was at half for Winston. Several thousand people telephoned (so my friends on the exchange told me) and were informed that the flag is only lowered for Royalty. After this they left, unsung, and no doubt Anglo-Frog relations will look up. See you in March?'

In May she visited friends and relations in Ireland and wrote from Cooleville House in Tipperary to Sir Hugh Jackson: 'I've come here from Lismore and am feeling very much better. It's the petrol fumes I think which do one so much harm in spite of the fact that I sleep on an old garden, giving on to the vast garden of Denys Cochin, so am luckier than most. We have got an owl and a great variety of birds left over, I always think when I hear the chouette, from the days of Clovis and long before that . . . Raymond Mortimer is the other guest here (Sackville is our host) so we have lovely chats about all the things you and I like . . . The French television had such a funny hoax on April 1. They explained that it is French week in London and they showed the statue of Nelson being removed from Trafalgar Square and replaced by one of Napoleon, while *les amis de Nelson*, a lot of old gentlemen in top hats had a pitched battle with the Peelers. Everybody believed it (seeing is believing). Alas I haven't got the instrument so didn't see it but it sounded hilarious. They always have lovely poissons d'avril. . .'

'Dublin society is really most agreeable,' she continued. 'I was with my nephew Desmond Guinness who has got a pretty house called Leixlip Castle. We went to the opera, in the Italian

Ambassador's box; we went to the sale of Castletown; we lunched and dined out. It is all, I imagine, rather like life in Florence a hundred years ago. But oh alas the climate! Not one gleam of sunshine the whole time I was there. But for that I might almost be tempted to live there though I doubt, now, if I'd be happy anywhere but in France. Certainly one would feel nice and rich in Ireland, it's incredibly cheap. Castletown fetched the price of a nice Paris flat—with about 500 acres of land thrown in and several old masters which some enthusiastic ancestress of Lord Carew had stuck to the walls!'

And from Leixlip Castle Nancy wrote to her sister Debo: 'The Alice in Wonderlandery is total which for only two days is funny. Viz.—yesterday afternoon an American family arrived. Pa, Ma and daughter. Teeth. Mariga [Guinness] said, "You're the friends of Mr Macklehenny."—"No, no, we're not his friends. Me (hopefully) "His enemies perhaps?"—"Oh no, we're sure he's dourling."—Mariga (looking out of the window) "Here comes your enemy Mr Macklehenny." Americans (fearfully agitated) "But we're *not* his enemies, we're sure he's a lovely person." Mariga. "May I introduce Mr M.—Mr and Mrs Marikovsky?" Americans reproachfully "O'Leary." So it went on. Nobody ever knew why they had come. Vast car.'

The Pursuit of Love was being converted into a musical comedy by Mr. Julian Slade and it sounded promising when he played it to her on Mme Costa's piano. Eventually it was performed in Bristol (in May 1967) but the critics damned it with faint praise. They agreed that it was 'mildly pleasant' and that the cast 'did an excellent job', but the show lasted for three-and-a-quarter hours, contained 23 numbers, and was evidently in need of cutting. 'Almost every character comes from the same well-heeled section of the upper-crust and after a time one longs to hear a fresh accent,' one complained. He concluded that 'a mountain of effort had gone into producing a molehill of a musical.' Another wrote that Mr. Slade had 'only skimmed just enough of the cream to hold the tunes together; and yet it is still funny and still moving, though not half as moving as the book is.' Unfortunately the money could not be raised to take it to London, where it might have had a warmer reception.

Delays over production are always trying to an author and

169

Nancy had to wait until October 1966 for the publication of *The Sun King*. 'No it won't be one of those huge books,' she told her sister Debo, 'quite all right for reading—but will have hundreds of pictures which I love because you can prove your point with them—viz. the Dauphin's wonderful rooms, all destroyed, you can show what they were like, also everybody's *face*, so important.'

The tantalizing part of such delays is that other books on the same subject are liable to be published in the meantime. In November 1965 Nancy wrote to Sir Hugh Jackson from Fontaines on paper with a little mole stamped in gold as a crest: 'Do you like this paper—it's for staying away. The mole is my emblem. Mme Costa de Beauregard, my hostess, used to have lovely writing paper with a little train and a telegraph post and an envelope in the corner but now one is given plain white sheets, very dull.' (Apropos of which she told one of her sisters: 'Auntie, writing about my mole, says when she was young the peasants called them cunts, "a word one never hears nowadays." She's not in the Tynan set, obviously.') 'I've taken the liberty to tell my publisher to send, if he can, if he has a spare, the page proofs of my book to you as I long to know what you think of it. They are loose but quite handy to read—excellent print—uncorrected of course.

'Erlanger's Louis XIV is out—far the best thing he has done but I was shocked to see that he has published a letter from Mme de Maintenon which is well known to be a forgery. Voltaire and Racine's son were the first to denounce as such a batch of her "letters" published by La Baumelle—apart from their statement of the way in which La Baumelle went to work (he stole some real letters and published them mixed up with fabrications of his own), the style of the false letters is utterly unlike hers. So—Erlanger must know it. I wait with interest to see if anybody shows him up! Very foolish of him as the rest of the book is admirable, though he is too spiteful about Mme de Maintenon.'

More impatiently she wrote next April: 'They are still printing my wretched book and have been for months and now I see another one on the same subject is coming out—it's all too boring, that will make three with Erlanger's deplorable effort which has been hailed as one of the twenty *greatest books on history*. I really think the French have gone mad, but of course I can't say so except to you or they'll think it's sour grapes.'

Despite her professed aversion to modern travel Nancy continued on her round of summer visits, in June to stay with Mark in Athens: 'I've ordered an air ticket . . . really life has become too exciting to bear. Fond love, old architect of les menus plaisirs,' she wrote him. Athens would be perfect, she said, 'if not so hideously ugly . . . Seven hours in Rome airport seemed endless . . . The clock seemed to *stick* instead of carrying one swiftly towards the grave as it generally does.'

In July she returned to her beloved Venice. 'All friends pleased, I think, to see one but the number is terribly diminished. I had a long talk with Vittorio the bagnino [bathing attendant] which consisted in him reciting the names of the dead and me saying Oh Vittorio every now and then and crying. It's Victor [Cunard] one misses so much. Alphy Clary, my other great friend here, is tortured by arthritis and can't come to the beach any more. Rome airport seemed for ever . . . No paper backs one could bear to read—dictionaries of sexology—lives of the First Ladies and so on. I think of all the dead, except relations I miss Robert [Byron] the most, closely followed by Victor. It's the jokes . . .'

In September she visited me in Florence and we were joined by Christopher Sykes, a friend since her childhood, who had written a masterly appreciation of Robert Byron. We laughed most of the time but alas, I cannot remember specific jokes. The only fiasco was a dinner with a kindly American couple who had restored their ancient villa in sumptuous style. 'It's like a grand hotel,' she remarked. 'It may sound silly, but I like, specially in houses, a certain degree of shabbiness—couldn't tell you why.' Nancy shook hands with the butler, who had previously been with a Venetian family and was proud to welcome her, but, as the hurt hostess told me later, Nancy had not deigned to shake hands with her. During dinner another guest explained too audibly to her ignorant neighbour that Nancy was one of the famous sisters, one of whom had been a Nazi, another a Communist, and I fear Nancy overheard, for as soon as dinner was over she complained of a racking headache and said, 'I really must be going.' And off we went before the coffee was served. Otherwise, as she wrote me, Florence was 'perfect heaven, everything I like best . . . Oh Italy, there's nothing like it!'

Nancy received frequent messages and a telegram from Violet Trefusis insisting that she visit her villa L'Ombrellino, 'the most beautiful in Florence,' but Nancy had no desire to do so even in Violet's absence. She was happy enough on the sunlit terrace of La Pietra and there was a surfeit of more interesting sights. After her return to Paris Violet 'summoned me to her bedside and put me through such a fearful exam on the Ombrellino that in the end I had to confess I hadn't been there. It was like this, Did you go into the house? No, of course not as you weren't there—we saw the view. How could you have seen it without going into the house? But Violet, from the terrace. How did you get to the terrace? And so on, my replies getting feebler and feebler. I ought to have done ten minutes' prep with you first. She is very cross indeed but more with me for daring to go to Florence behind her back than anything else . . . Violet is madder than ever. She said to a friend of mine, whom she has just met, do you know who I am? (I said the answer should be the Man in the Iron Mask?) I am the daughter of Edward VII *but don't tell anybody.*

'I found the proofs [of *The Sun King*] and a re-proof for having gone away and so I must bury myself in them. The book, read thus, seems exceedingly dull I'm sorry to say.

'G.P. is now on the board of les musées de France. I say his first deed must be to hold a sale—la vente P.—of everything which isn't shown, the money to go to foreign writers living in France. "Are you mad?" he says. "Violet would get every penny." Very true, no doubt.'

From Fontaines she wrote to Mark, then employed by Shell in Athens (15th November, 1965): 'While writing three books of history I've become awfully good at research and now my enormous talent and industry are entirely directed to finding teases for ye . . . My drawing-room is a vision now with new curtains and a new bonheur-du-jour [small writing-table with drawers] on which I spent most of the pittance bequeathed by Uncle Matthew. How I wish Shell would employ me at £1,000 a day including free rides in cars and free chocs—oh how I do wish it. My work, gentle tease, is purely voluntary . . . Came here hoping to sit in autumnal sunshine but this morning I note the wandering snowflake . . . P.S. Cyril's [Connolly's] name for Cecil [Beaton]: Rip Van Withit.'

Nancy had spent her waking hours at Fontaines pulling up and burning nettles, 'so you see on est plutôt abrutie.' Home in Paris, 'I refuse all invitations and hug my stove.'

CHAPTER TWELVE

IN 1966 NANCY definitely decided to buy herself a house at Versailles. The rent of her apartment in 'Mr Street' had been raised exorbitantly and she longed for a place of her own: this was the leitmotiv of her letters throughout the year.

'Vilely cold, tons of snow, everybody falling down, oh how I hate the winter,' she wrote to Athenian Mark. 'The American who lives upstairs gave me a huge white azalea and then, while I was still sort of dazed by it, ordered me to go and see some American dancers with him tomorrow . . . I rather love this sort of weather in the country when one can plunge about like where the saint hath trod. Here they half melt the snow with salt so the streets are icy canals up to the knee and virtually uncrossable—pavements are solid ice. *Oh no.* Old Marie hates going out so I've just been to get tomorrow morning's milk for her.'

To Alvilde Lees-Milne she wrote at the same time: 'My Italian friends are here [Brandolinis] and, as at Venice they come and take one to the Lido, here they come (same time, 11) to take one to the Bois where we plunge about in snow instead of sliding on grey ice as in the streets. It's awfully agreeable, I greatly love them . . . L'oiseau de pluie [Rainbird the publisher] writes about twice a week with suggestions for a new book—practically every stock figure of the fancy dress party has been evoked. But I've no desire to write anything at present— I'm loving total idleness . . . Louis comes out on 1st October . . . Have you read *The Group?*—[by Mary McCarthy]. Screamingly funny. What people of horror Americans are. If you ever see Paul Taylor and his Company, flee the land. I was taken last night, Théâtre des Champs Elysées. They are huge American spastics who galumph about the stage on bare dirty feet to the tune of modern music. No décor of course. Theatre quite empty—the chap who took me said gloomily Parisians only like dancers in spangles and ballet shoes. So do I.'

29th January (to Alvilde): 'All the beauties here give interviews about their *knees*, which they rub with various substances such as wine or snow. Are your knees dry? Oh dear, another thing to fuss about in the morning, rubbing one's knees. I begin to long for the eternal disembodied state so soon to be upon one. Oh *but*, the resurrection of the body? The knees will be drier than ever after a few million years . . . I lunched with L'Oiseau de Pluie yesterday—Mrs Law is still part of the set-up. He offers me Casanova (Colonel screamed) no thanks!'

'We are having a lovely scandal here—one hangs on the wireless hour by hour. Le récit du concierge du coquet immeuble where the body was found, after which the wife (we think in name only) says "il est parti faire un tour parce qu'il avait la tête comme un chaudron." They said Figon was such a nice change from the last locataires—Asiatics. Five hundred people have put in for the flat (though the body has only just been removed—pools of blood) because it sounds so cosy. "*Molto* cosy," as Brando always says. Then the English, it seems, have been cheating like hell in the Monte Carlo Rally. What has come over the old land—first the bridge champions and now the drivers—ay de mi.'

Mme Costa de Beauregard died in February and Nancy was deprived of 'almost my greatest friend here and a second home.' Fontaines had been a perennial haven, a favourite provincial microcosm of la vieille France. No doubt Nancy had embellished it in her imagination, availing herself of happy accidents of atmosphere and obliterating any chance discord or blot. She had depended on it as a spiritual health-resort. Her other greatest friend Princess Dolly Radziwill was failing and, as Nancy was wont to exclaim, 'How I hate new people!' After sixty it is less easy to make new friends—it is like learning a new language— whereas old friends increase in value.

The premature death of Evelyn Waugh was another irreparable loss: he had been so much more than a literary arbiter. To Christopher Sykes, who was also devoted to Evelyn, she wrote: 'Oh Evil! When has one been so sad? *Daily Telegraph* obituary vile. I'm so tired of hearing that he was a sort of lower class milk deliverer who got on in society by pushing—such rot if one knew his family . . . I haven't sent my piece (in French) to Auberon because I never think they care for the other Evelyn being mentioned, but I was obliged to do so as she was the reason why I knew him almost before any of us did—and of course she is the clue to so *much* . . . I think I'm going to move to Versailles, where I've at last found a house. It's such a step, I feel on the brink of a cold plunge.' And on All Souls Day, 1966: 'I think of Robert [Byron] today—my brother Tom, Victor Cunard, Mrs. Hammersley, Evelyn and Roger Hinks. The fact is it's people one has jokes with whom one misses—the loving the good and the upright much less. What an awful thought. Robert is still the person I mind about the most.'

Before the reign of Chaos and Old Night descended Nancy decided to uproot herself. On Easter day she informed Alvilde: 'My plans are, I go with the Brandos to Debo [Chatsworth] for about ten days on 2nd May and to Greece and Venice middle of June to August and otherwise shall be here . . . I've found a dear little old house at Versailles which is just the very thing and will buy it if I can be sure that a skyscraper won't go up under my nose. There's a nice garden (800 metres) at present very private. Unfortunately it's in the quartier de Montreuil, further from the château than I would have liked, but of course that makes it cheaper. Also, enormous bait, a sweet maid longs to stay there. There's a self-contained flat with bathroom for such as you (if you deigned) and Debo.

'Violet [Trefusis] is now quite off her old head. She tells everybody that she had a long affair with the Colonel. He has written her a sharp note: étant donné que vous êtes la seule femme à Paris à qui je n'ai jamais fait la cour. Then she has got a ghastly American in tow . . . She says he's the son of the man who wrote *Le Guépard* [Prince of Lampedusa]!!! Wretched Alice, aged 80 and ill, is still made to cook and wait hand and foot. I lunched there—never again. Vi spat out a great lump of food and with it still in her hand took some salt—she is too vile. She said to Cristiana [Brandolini] if you will introduce me to those good-looking Italian boys I see going to your flat I'll introduce you to French intellectuals. So Cristiana asked her in after dinner and she arrived with the horrible American and Philippe Jullian! . . . One has only to know about other people's lives for one's own to seem completely perfect . . . Troyat's Tolstoi . . . I'm living in it—best book I've read for an age.'

Nancy also informed a mutual friend, Robin McDouall: 'Violet wrote a thumb-nail sketch of herself in *Figaro Littéraire* as follows: "Vaste salon dans la rue du Cherche Midi. Merveilleuse cuisine. Très beaux bijoux. Très liée avec la cour d'Angleterre. L'Egérie de Philippe Jullian. Ecrit ses mémoires." She asked me for a title for her mémoires (I thought she had already written them) and was not pleased when I suggested *Here Lies Mrs Trefusis.*'

In fact Violet had been advertising her memoirs and cogitating the title over the last decade. The title was the crux of it and everybody offered suggestions: 'I think of calling my new book of mémoires either *Queen Fausta* or *No Moss*'. Looks round at the company. 'What do you say, Mr Coop?' Nervous young Yank: 'Well Mrs Trefusis I think perhaps I would choose *No Moths.*' '*Moths*, Mr Coop? Have you never heard of a rolling stone?'

When Violet heard of Nancy's plan to live in Versailles she said: 'Nancy's making a big mistake. She thinks society will run all the way out there to visit her. They won't. At least no Frenchman will. It's much too inconvenient!' But Nancy was tired of random callers and she could always count on seeing her true friends. As she told Mark (25th April): 'I'm not really social and in any event never dine out. I so long to see blossom in the spring, mists and mellow fruitfulness in the autumn and white, not grey, snow in the winter. It's such a cosy little house and yet has such heaps of room. I shall put in a third bathroom and hope for ye.'

Back in Venice, however, Nancy entered zestfully into the sociabilities of her hostess Contessa Cicogna until, as occasionally happened when she saw too many people or kept late hours, she lost her voice and had to retire. 'Here I am in what is still the most beautiful place in the world and, in spite of many horrors, the most unspoilt,' she wrote Sir Hugh Jackson in July. 'One rages against shop windows going slap through Byzantine arches and such things, which would be unthinkable in France, and against the ever-increasing motor traffic and against plastic bottles bobbing in the canals (and one has the awful feeling that they are indestructible, unlike glass ones, and will still be bobbing in a thousand years) but all the same there

176

9. The Garden at Rue Monsieur

10. At Rue Monsieur

are acres of marvels. One or two signs that the Italians are beginning to realize what Venice is. Since last year San Sebastiano has been marvellously restored by a rich woman from Milan. It is Veronese's church and one of the very most lovely and fascinating . . .

'I'm reading a life of William III—struggling with it rather as it is almost unreadable. The American author doesn't bother to explain two things I have never fully understood—the title of Orange and the exact position of the House of Nassau in the Republic. I'm also reading an excellent life of Voltaire by Jean Orieux . . . The other book is £3, imagine, and not specially well produced. Mine is going to be 3 guineas but then it has got masses of pictures and a beautiful binding—huge print and lovely paper. I've got an advance copy and am delighted with it.'

To her sister Debo she wrote in more frivolous vein: 'Two English beatniks in trousers and long hair made a scene on the beach, bagged somebody's cabin and the bagninos first told them to go and then manhandled them and the beatniks knocked out two and a policeman. When they were finally arrested they were found to be girls. That's the stuff. I saw one elderly man, balding, with long grey hair to the shoulders and a wreath of gardenias. Eet was deesgosting . . .'

'I sat next to Charlie Wrightsman four meals running . . . I asked him what had changed him from a polo playing tycoon into an art collector and it was seeing a Louis XV commode. He said, I've spent eight million dollars on objects of art.' (In parentheses, Mr. Wrightsman was one of the few male Americans whose company she relished. He amazed and amused her, and she admired his taste in French furniture.)

'I'm still here for another week,' she told Sir Hugh Jackson on 4th August, 'my enjoyment distinctly modified by a total extinction de voix. Having struggled away for several days of huge luncheon and dinner parties I have now collapsed into my bed—a bore for everybody. The funny thing is, however chatty people are by nature, if you can't put in a word here and there they dry up. The town is full of amusing people, a French general called Stehlin who was intimate with Goering before the war and who sent home accounts of the full extent of Nazi armament which of course nobody read—Mary McCarthy— Isaiah Berlin—John Sparrow—as well as all my delightful Italian friends, it's really annoying to miss it all . . . I'm reading a life of Goethe, roughly translated from German into American. I see that after Tolstoy he was the nastiest living person—I wonder why geniuses have to be so horrible. I expect the writer of this very poor book misses a good deal of the point—one could make Voltaire unrelievedly horrible I suppose by not understanding him. As I don't know German I daresay I shall never get under the skin of Goethe and must take his genius for granted.

'Fifty-two years now from the outbreak of war which I well remember. I really think that the world today is worse not better? and getting worse all the time? If on top of all, there is to be black ruin the outlook is poor. A Frenchman said to me there is much to be said for living in a country which has had its revolution. Yes, but we are always told we have had ours, bloodlessly and painlessly—perhaps in fact the tumbrils are ahead! Certainly Mr Wilson seems more powerful every day in England and more slavish in America . . . I shall bury my head like an ostrich at Versailles.' [Referring to proofs of *The Sun King* she had sent Sir Hugh] 'Misprints not my fault, mistakes which are, so that I quite dread what the critics will say. You must be truthful.'

Launched under favourable auspices, *The Sun King* met with a reception beyond Nancy's most sanguine expectations. 'The coffee tables seem to be loaded,' she told Robin McDouall, 'and my grateful European publishers are giving me a banquet at the Frankfurt book fair which will be a rare lark, their names sound like a team of footballers. My agent says 100,000 have been sold in England and Europe—not yet out in America . . .' The banquet disagreed with her: 'Try being polite to 200 German booksellers at 10 a.m. in an ogre's castle feeling sick!'

The success of *The Sun King* was well earned and well deserved: edition followed edition while Nancy concentrated on the little house she had bought at Versailles, 4 rue d'Artois.

Nancy was more of a novelist in life than in literature. She superimposed her own image on what she was seeing, yet she wished to be seen in the role she had assumed, a Muse of Comedy—and to appear more worldly than she was. For all her pseudo-Parisian sophistication and the growth of her fame she retained her pristine naïvety. A virginally romantic sensibility coloured her outlook. Great wealth and historic genealogies cast a glamour on their possessors even when these were dowdy and

178

plain. Her next abode was much prettier in her mind's eye than in reality. Its façade on the street was unassuming but its interior was adaptable, and she proceeded to arrange the rooms with discriminating taste. The street itself was quiet and suburban, with a solid grey parish church round the corner. For Nancy the garden behind the house was its cynosure. With her cult of fresh air she could read and write in it when the weather was fine. The garden was her 'necessary luxury'.

Her Parisian apartment was more elegant and she had improved it over the years, but having decided to leave it she did so without apparent regret, though most of her friends were sorry, not for selfish reasons but because 'Mr Street' and its environment fitted her like a glove. Whenever I pass it I stop at number seven and it does not strain my imagination to picture her smiling hatless in the courtyard. Her halcyon years were spent there. Alas, the same could not be said of rue d'Artois—a name associated with a monarch she detested.

Already in October she made frequent if not daily excursions to the new house to supervise its transformation: 'such fun and I'm in love with all the workmen. It looks as if my move will be at about Christmas,' she told Alvilde Lees-Milne. 'All goes swimmingly so far—my neighbours are perfect, sensible and kind, the sort of neighbours one dreams of and the femme de ménage lives opposite and acts as a concierge and is one of those fixers. I only pray she and Marie will get on.' And to her sister Debo she wrote enthusiastically: 'Everything to do with the house is made easy and delightful on account of the great sweetness of all concerned. Immediately after buying it I had nightmares about what I supposed would be a stroggle [sic] but you see all goes on wheels.' She wanted 'a lot of weed seeds' for the garden—'poppies, valerian, irises, orchids, butter-cups, marsh marrows, daisies and hare bells. Can one buy them? You'll have to tell me how to sow grass. Isn't it exciting . . .

'Oh dear, last night I sat next to an American at dinner and I said, talking of Paris, "there was a book, not very good, about Paris in the Terror." "*I wrote it*". Sleepless night and I doubt if I shall ever sleep again. What's more he said gloomily that it had taken seven years of research. It has aged me by 20 years, oi am now *auld* [sic].'

The new house was half-way (about seven minutes walk)

between the two stations to St. Lazare and les Invalides. As Nancy did not own a motor she would go up and down in the train 'which is now much quicker and far more peaceful.'

On 18th December: 'I went yesterday and made a huge bonfire in the garden (oh how enjoyable) and, in spite of being Saturday afternoon the sweet deaf and dumb painter was there and of course joined in. Nobody ever can resist, can they? Marvellous sunset and rooks flying home and a moon coming up—goodness, I long to move. The old servant of the next door chemist was shutting the shutters. I never saw such a dear old face, like olden times . . . The first thing any Versailles person says to you is you'll see how much you'll *love* being here. It's really most striking—last week the telephone man and the removals man both said it, quite unsolicited.'

On 4th January, 1967, still from rue Monsieur: 'Men are in the drawing room taking away my curtains and carpet—I feel like a criminal who hears the guillotine being put in the prison yard. In fact I feel exactly as if I were going to die next week: a plunge into the unknown. How odd . . . Keep writing to make me feel I'm still alive'. And to Mark she wrote at the same time: 'I move next week, a week today. Feel as if I were dying'.

In spite of Nancy's habitual tendency to verbal exaggeration I suspect that a genuine premonition dictated these words. All her friends received a postcard-size photograph of her lifting the lid of her drawing-room stove with a demure smile—slender and neat in a tartan skirt, she seemed a young woman of thirty. 'Farewell rue Monsieur' was inscribed above and 'Hail 4 rue d'Artois, Versailles, on 12 January, 1967' below. At the back she wrote to me: 'I'm engulfed in my move and greatly enjoying it though I suppose the actual day will be like the death of Damien'. The fatal note recurred.

On 29th January she wrote to her sister Pam [the Hon. Mrs. Derek Jackson]: 'We are still in a tremendous muddle here and nothing seems to make much progress but I suppose it does, invisibly! But I like the house very much in fact I love it—so warm and sunny and cheerful. The move was quite harmless—absolutely nothing either lost or even chipped and the weather was both warm and dry, so rare at this time of year! The local charwoman is a marvel; don't know what we should have done without her, she is one of those get a move oners and so nice.

Then I've got a dear little boy who works in the garden one day a week. Yesterday we planted about ten rose trees, two wistaria, two jasmine and other climbers. The walls are old and real, which is by no means always the case at Versailles, and covered with plants growing out of them.

'Marie is loving it here. We've got a grand new gas cooker—very complicated so that now I can't even boil an egg if left alone because I can't light it—an oil heater which does the house and the baths—boiling water in floods—I'm getting a plate washer and a new frigidaire and washing machine, so we ought to be comfortable I hope. People are so rich that not only nobody wants the old machines as a present which work perfectly well, but you have to pay to get them removed!'

'I'm recovering from the move but it was tiring,' she told Mark. 'At the height I had a feeling of *total* exhaustion, which reminded me of the war—working in bookshop and fire-watching twice a week . . . I shall never regret coming here I'm sure: at present I'm in a state of wild happiness and if one feels like that in January, what will April bring?'

'*Sun King* is still top of the pops am I pleased! Generally Xmas kills a book like that. It was *the* top of the whole of 1966.'

As usual she was deluged with fan mail. A communication from a descendant of François Francine, who designed the fountains at Versailles, was among the more interesting. As Nancy informed M. Jacques Brousse, her French translator: 'I've got a letter from an American Mr Jacques-Louis Francine, complaining that on page 43 of my book I have killed off the whole of his large family at one blow. It seems his ancestor was not guillotined at all: he emigrated. I answered most politely saying I'm too sorry but pointing out that in my view the New World and the Next World count the same.

'However I'd be glad if you would change the passage . . . Francine is evidently an educated man and sent a good deal of chapter and verse for his claim although the French genealogist of the family says it perished in the revolution. Probably both versions are true as there were most likely several Françines by then.'

'The French movers are extraordinary,' she told Sir Hugh Jackson. 'They even kept the little heap of pennies under my big clock, to balance it, and put them back in the same place and started it again. The system is, *everything* is wrapped up, however small, and every book separately, and all the furniture from top to toe. Then they lead the things at street level on to a platform which rises to the level of the rooms, and the things float in through the windows—none of that wrestling on the stairs. It took three whole days and I haven't got so very much furniture. They even make your beds and would probably cook your dinner if you asked them. They were so adorable—we parted in silence and tears and *enormous* tips. The high spot was when old Marie said must I give my valise to the men? Well, Marie, I'm giving mine. Frantic whispers: "There's a thousand pounds in it." So we took a taxi. Isn't that France all over! I said I suppose it's in a stocking? and she said yes it is. I wish you could see this vast heiress! . . . I'm wanted here every minute by the workmen or by the arrival of hundreds of roses to plant . . .

'I wonder if you ever read the letters of the Stanley of Alderley family which I edited before the war. Hamish Hamilton is going to republish them so I've been reading them—goodness they are amusing, I'd quite forgotten. Such a picture of a naughty Victorian husband and his neglected huge family (12 children, 8 survivors). As so often seems to happen, I believe, there is now only one male heir. My grandfather Redesdale had 5 sons and there is no heir at all.'

Since her removal to Versailles, Nancy chose to become a semi-recluse, abstemious but never austere. Her garden—a cultivated wilderness—drew her gently back into the world of children's fairy tales. A young gardener called Dominique helped her to cultivate it in the style, or lack of style, she favoured, rustic and informal, like a canvas by Monet in which cottage flowers predominated. 'I've sent for more climbing roses,' she told Mark Ogilvie-Grant. 'Dominique has torn down all the horrid vigne vierge so I've got a mass of South wall waiting—and also wistaria and jasmine. Princess Sixte de Bourbon popped in and telling about her sister Duchess (Geranium) Mouchy, she said *elle est assommante avec son jardin ma chère, selon elle les poirots s'appellent pommes de terre et les épinards sont vraiment des laitues. C'est à ne rien comprendre.* How I agree—my ducal sister is just the same.'

Mark was an amateur botanist, and several years previously Nancy had sent him a Christmas card illuminated with the motto:

The kiss of the wind for lumbago,
The stab of a thorn for mirth,
One is nearer to Death in a garden
Than anywhere else on earth

Beside which she commented: 'This is the French idea of a Christmas card, also their view, correct I think, of gardens. Oh do come and be Lady Di's gardeness—one reply said "why I turned an Indian jungle into a perfect English garden".' Of course she was joking.

Later—again she wrote to Mark: 'My garden looks as if 1000 Edwardian hats (roses) had fallen into it. It's really waste for me to have a garden where things do so well. A hollyhock I sowed last year is taller than me and huge like a tree and all is on those lines—but all I really want is a weedy meadow. But I love the roses . . .' A typical instance of her gratuitous kindness: 'Fancy I got Dominique into the gardens at Versailles. I feel it's a good deed of a lifetime—he was utterly dreading the factory—in despair, poor little boy. Now he works at the Orangery and proudly tells the great age of the trees, and he goes twice a week to Paris to learn botany. He's so happy you can't think—I only hope it'll last. Things one arranges so seldom succeed do they?

'What must I do to keep my tortoise alive all the winter? Do you know? She's a frightful fool and I don't trust her to make her own arrangements and then our winter is so long . . .

'A man I met in Bayreuth had been to Chatsworth and chummed up with a gardener who said, "if you hide in that bush you will soon see the Duchess go by". Don't you love the idea of all the bushes being full of Duchess-watchers? Quite creepy.'

Nancy would lie in a deck chair among her flowers and birds and tortoises, basking in the sheer joy of existence. 'I can't tell you how much I like living here,' she told Alvilde Lees-Milne (1st April, 1967), 'it suits me perfectly in every way. I did have doubts soon after buying it, but in fact I like it 100 times more than I would ever have expected to. It's a dear little house and I long to show it to you. Christopher Sykes opened, or launched, the spare room and found it quite comfortable, or so he kindly said. I suppose I can't lure you?

'The garden amuses me and is just the right size, nothing but

183

roses and lilies is my idea and I've managed to find my favourite Dorothy Perkins to drape everywhere. Can you tell me what a bird is, a bit bigger than a sparrow, with slate-blue head and body and an orange tail? I've never seen another—it honours me all the time and is so pretty. I wonder if it may have escaped from an aviary . . . There's a new rule in Paris, you pay a huge extra amount of rent for a garden now. I think I was very wise to skip off and buy something of my very own . . . Wherever I look I see nothing but pear blossom—oh the Spring, isn't it heavenly?

' . . . I say, the English are loving that oil aren't they, dashing about washing birds and so on, as good as the good old Blitz . . . Lesley [Blanch] and Auntie Vi [Trefusis] are still as thick as thieves—Lesley believes every single word she says, including that she is the 30th in the succession for the throne. The télé gave out the death, at 93, of Mme Marie-Louise Bousquet—we were all very sad. But it was another Marie-Louise Bousquet and our old duck is alive and kicking, rather put out by people telephoning in dozens to ask about the funeral.' And on 5th May: 'The cold here beats all but my weed seeds are whizzing up and the feral grass is full of buttercups. The bird is called, here, *rossignol de murail*. I find a garden leads to the most appalling waste of time but no doubt you know that . . . Marie complains of the dawn chorus here, it certainly wakes one up (she loves it really). But no cuckoo or nightingale until one gets to the park, just sweet suburban birds of all varieties.'

In September she wrote in the same strain to Sir Hugh Jackson: 'Yes I'm totally happy here—I've found a heap of sand and have buried my head in it. The Versailles people are so gentle and polite—utterly unlike the Parisians, whom I love but who are tiring no doubt. Then the town is so pretty and the traffic not at all too bad until you come to the Château.

'I can't get English television here, I wish I could. But when I'm writing I have to keep off it as it's an extra strain on the eyes . . . Such lovely boiling weather, even at night. I sit out of doors all day and feel so well.'

The devoted Marie had piloted Nancy through the exhausting process of removal and for the time being she postponed the retirement which Nancy dreaded. Nancy could turn again with relief to the eighteenth century. An essay on

Carlyle and Frederick the Great led her gradually towards a revaluation of the latter, shorn of his Carlylean trappings, and she decided to write his biography. She had been toying with the idea since 1963. Her study of Voltaire encouraged her to scrutinize his Francophile patron, to whom the French language was more familiar than his own, and she became increasingly fascinated by the complexity of his strange character. She always had a partiality for military leaders, dead or alive, and she followed their campaigns nostalgically, wishing she had been on the spot.

'I'm frantically busy,' she informed Alvilde Lees-Milne in September 1967, 'having taken on a long essay on Carlyle and Frederick the Great which of course amuses me to death—one screams out loud as with P. G. Wodehouse—but now Rainbird is to re-issue *Pompadour* as a companion volume to *Sun King*. Painless childbirth, yes, but I want to do a lot of revision and have only got until end of November. So I feel that drowning in work which always upsets me. I'm too stupid to do two things at once and Frederick goes slowly because the eight volumes are like a huge plum cake; one can't digest much at a time.

'My garden has been taken over by a fragile white morning glory very different from the ghastly Eton and Harrow sort. Through it smile the roses—the whole effect is ravishing.'

Apropos of her revision of 'Pomp' Nancy had told Sir Hugh Jackson that for eighteenth-century information the costly new edition of Voltaire's letters proved invaluable. 'I find for instance that it was *entirely* Louis XV who, informed of course by Voltaire, got the Calas judgement quashed. Then Voltaire, though a great friend of Choiseul's, was on the King's side over his dismissal when everybody else was making such a song and dance. Nobody ever mentions these things owing to stupid prejudice . . . but the letters speak for themselves. Choiseul's dismissal of course is after Pomp's death but I have done a bit about Calas over which she was most helpful . . . Yes, nobody has heard of Tam but I am taking the line that Tom was always pronounced Tam in Scotland because I can't resist calling my essay Tam and Fritz! There is one small piece of evidence in the text. Carlyle mentions Thomson's *Seasons* and then in his mad way he adds, "Jamie Tamson, Jamie Tamson, oh!" '

'Can't remember if I told you,' she confided to Sir Hugh in

March 1968, 'but I have definitely embarked on Frederick the Great. It is difficult because of the length of his life—I'm greatly enjoying it however. All new to me—I know very little German history . . . In August I go to Germany to see the places relevant to the new book.'

With macabre humour—somewhat sinister in retrospect—Nancy wrote to her sister Debo about her tomb and burial (1st March, 1968): 'Colonel and I were in the local marble shop—they've got a spiffing urn there. I said I think I'll buy that for my tomb. He said you can't have satyrs all over your tomb. I said, but as I'm sure to be killed by the satyr? (There is somebody called Le Satyr de la Banlieue who *does* young ladies and strangles old ones.) And so the world wags on . . .

'As for plantage—just wherever I drop, with unforgettable tomb and a great deal of Pompes Funèbres which Marie will enjoy. There seems to be an English church here where a few hurried prayers and Holy Holy Holy (to make Honks cry) can be muttered. Rope in the Colonel or the Duchess-loving van der Kemp or Mogens—people like to be asked.

'My neighbours are so nice. I went to tea yesterday (two English sisters very young with thousands of children). They had seen Woman [her sister Pam, the Hon. Mrs. Derek Jackson] and asked if she was my only sister which I found most refreshing. The elder neighbour bought this (my) house about 14 years ago for £2000—sold it for £18,000 and I paid £40,000. Makes you think. And now I would get, I am told, £60,000. It was clever of the eldest neighbour because the French regard this district as frightfully dowdy and the house, then, was a laundry.'

Her jealous friend Violet Trefusis was itching to verify the least flattering reports about Nancy's new abode but Nancy was firm with her. To Alvilde (22nd April, 1968): 'Following exchange with Aunty. She telephones: Can she come to tea?
N. Violet, I shan't be here.
V. Can I come tomorrow?
N. I say, it's now two years since you wrote to say how vile I am and how everybody hates me. What is all this telephoning all of a sudden?
V. I'm sorry if I gave offence.
N. You didn't give offence but you did give me an excuse. Goodbye.

'I didn't add that everybody . . . says that Violet is déchainée against me . . . My anti-garden is a dream of beauty and my hedgehogs have had children. But I *die* for Germany. I get letters from old Grafs saying they will tell all about their ancestors and Fritz if I'll go and see them, which I can't wait to do. I'll be shown a lock of the "fair and smooth" hair of Lieutenant Katte. Alphy [Prince Clary] of course is hopping with excitement and loathing of my dear Frederick and says six weeks in Venice won't be long enough for all he wants to tell me . . .'

Violet Trefusis was nothing if not persistent and she was accustomed to having her way. In November, 'Oh the old creature got people to tell me she was dying, then rang up in a dying voice to say could she come down. I can't really keep things up, I mean hates, so I said yes and she arrived one and a half hours late so that the afternoon was wasted. She was rather thin but just as horrid. However that's that and I shan't have to see her again. Geoffrey [Gilmour] said she couldn't bear it when people talked (why do they talk?) about rue d'Artois and she hadn't seen it. She told L. who passed it on at once that she thought it all very *moche*. Then she tried to draw me into a row with the Brandos [Conte and Contessa Brandolini] and you can imagine how far that went!'

Of the Communist and student riots in Paris which did not affect Versailles, Nancy wrote an account in the *Spectator*. 'As I telephoned the copy to them (it took one and a half hours each time and nearly killed me) I know it will be full of boring misprints . . . all the same I think it gives an idea of what life was like down here. I would have loved to have seen the riots but couldn't move from here as all transport was at a standstill and I haven't got a motor. There seems to have been much more shouting than fighting and the police were simply wonderful, so patient and good. Luckily we have got a first class préfet de police. I can tell you, it's very alarming to live through an attempted Communist take-over. The workers were terrorized by faceless Communist agents THEY. The whole thing had been organised down to the smallest detail and when THEY decreed the strike, the workers, who knew that whereas, if they obeyed, the General would do nothing to them if he won, THEY, if they did not obey, would have some horrid revenge, so felt they had no choice. "Some men from St Cyr came and told me I must stop work." The General's timing was perfect; he had the courage to let the thing go from bad to worse until everybody could see for themselves the truth of the situation and then, at exactly the right moment he put a stop to it. If he had acted sooner, we should have been told there never was any plot, all invented by him. Now I think everything will be all right except that the economy has had a nasty jolt. They say it will take eighteen months to recover but I've noticed that French economy is resilient . . .

'I'm off for my summer travels, Greece, Venice, and Potsdam. It seems that the Germans were much better informed than our own police here and had sent two warnings to the Government which they simply did not believe.' (26th June, 1968, to Sir Hugh Jackson).

To Alvilde Lees-Milne she wrote in a more euphoric strain on 3rd July: for the time being General de Gaulle had eclipsed Frederick the Great in her imagination. 'The revolution was thrilling except that I never got to a riot on account of the train strike. But one could listen to them on the wireless all night, and as there was much more shouting than fighting that was the best of it, and then in the morning people rang up and told. The telephone and electricity worked throughout so there was no discomfort . . . Versailles is very *bien-pensant* and my neighbours were all perfect, popping in from time to time and telling what they had gleaned. Oh how I love it when things happen. The General as per simply too brilliant, and when everybody had seen for themselves Mendés-France marching with the Commies and Mitterrand egging them all on, he packed up his archives and went off to Colombey whereupon they started illegally to seize the pouvoir whereupon he came back and said stop like a red traffic light and it stopped . . .

'Masses more has been done at Versailles this summer—the Dauphin's rooms are furnished and so on—it's a marvel now . . .

'My poppies are in full fig I can't stop gazing at them, but next year I think I must have a *potager*. It's really too silly to buy faded old veges when one has got a big garden.'

Only last year she had written to Mark Ogilvie-Grant: 'I've always wanted to have poppies and cornflowers since seeing them at Fontaines and also in my favourite Impressionist picture "le chemin des coquelicots". But these ideas are in the air. Vilmorin's (the French Sutton's) sell a packet of seeds called le champ fleuri—as I also discovered the other day, and a famous garden in Portugal has had poppies under lemon trees for many years. The Duc d'Harcourt also goes in for weeds in a big way . . . I've now got another very successful wheeze: huge sunflowers round my *perron*, also taken from a picture I saw years ago.'

Ever since the 'angel called Contessa Cicogna' had taken Nancy in charge, Venice had been a second home. She no longer went to Fontaines, since Mme Costa had followed dear Mrs. Ham to the grave and the château was occupied by a louder and less pious generation. In Venice she could work as well as bake blithely on the Lido with a group of laughter-loving Italians though she greatly missed Victor Cunard. From there she wrote to Sir Hugh Jackson, 20th July, 1968: 'I think the English are so spiteful about the French who, blessed with a huge feeling of superiority, never seem to notice the fact. Thank goodness for me, since I live in France. I enclose the General's beautiful speech, on the Marne battlefield where he lunched with 400 poilus—I should have been in tears throughout!

'I sat next to an American at dinner last night who thinks Venice ought to be bulldozed, the pictures torn from the churches and put in a museum in New York; a few monuments, he kindly said, can be left to show what Venice used to be. I'm very glad not to be young and hope I won't live to see these abominations. Meanwhile Venice seems very solid and very prosperous—it stood up to quite a severe earth tremor the other day (which incidentally rattled me about in my bed in Greece). I always tell the Venetians that Lord Byron used to urge his friends to come, saying in another ten years it will be in the sea.

'I've now got to answer about 100 letters from animal lovers. I was unwise enough to utter some rather mild strictures on the horrible cruelty that goes on. The article was reprinted in the *Vancouver Sun* and every animal lover in Canada seems to have sent me her views with revolting descriptions which of course I skip. There's no more boring category in the world than the animal and especially the *cat* lover, unfortunately.'

Peter Rodd, from whom she had been separated for the last ten years, had died recently, and while she expressed regret and

189

even remorse to her sister Debo (though she had no cause whatever for the latter) she added candidly: 'But I couldn't live with him. I don't believe a saint could have without going mad.' As for her first fiancé Hamish Erskine, whom she saw occasionally for old sake's sake, she was intensely relieved that she had not married him. He had aged without any evidence of intellectual development, a faded butterfly flapping feeble wings on the periphery of café society—when they were not folded in heavy slumber. Of café society in general Nancy remarked, 'What will they be like in twenty years' time, I worry rather. Old cold coffee with skin on the milk and no sugar is so horrid.'

Her greatest and enduring love remained in Paris, and if she was wounded by his eventual marriage, she accepted it philosophically, realizing that she valued his friendship above all else. Even with close friends she maintained a strict reserve about her deepest emotions. Her most intimate and amusing letters were written to her sister Debo, and during the previous February she wrote to her: 'Mrs G., of the *Observer* telephones. Will I write an article on Love? No. Can Mrs. G. of the *Observer* come and interview me about Love? All right. Mrs G. came yesterday, apparently aged 14 . . . incredibly sweet. Well it seems all the young people in England are *in despair* about Love and Mrs G. described this despair so vividly and with such a wealth of detail that I soon saw she too was in despair. She says they all talk non-stop about *what went wrong*? For hours and hours about W W W—I said, but how do they have time—I thought they all had jobs? It seems jobs don't take one's mind off W W W one scrap. She said when you're old do you stop falling in love? I said certainly not and pointed to Emerald [Cunard], Princess Mathilde, Mme du Deffand, all rising 90 and suffering martyrdoms. At this she literally welled. Oh dear. She was so nice. I don't believe French people go in for all this weltering emotion but I may be wrong. Mme du Deffand never fell in love at all until over 60 and blind—Princess Mathilde certainly had a steady most of her life but the fuss began when she was past 70. We talked for hours—what will the result be! . . . I greatly recommend Mrs. G. though I fear suicide may claim her before one's friendship can ripen.'

For the present Nancy was chiefly absorbed by Frederick and everything that concerned him, including that rare disease about which she had procured a pamphlet entitled *Porphyria, a Royal Malady*, published by the Royal Medical Society. 'I love Frederick,' she told Sir Hugh Jackson, 'he is everything I like, brave, funny, no nonsense, marvellous taste, common sense, interested in everything. He had a sad life because by the time he was fifty all the people he loved had died and also he knew quite well that his nephew was no good. Have you heard of a disease oddly named porphyria? Mary Queen of Scots had it and transmitted it to many of her descendants, among others Frederick. The symptoms are unbearable and unexplainable pains. His father had it even worse than he did . . .' The pamphlet, she noted, failed to mention any cure. 'The pain comes and goes . . . when it has gone the person's real nature reappears until the next attack.' Alas, Nancy herself was soon to experience pains as unbearable and inexplicable.

Inevitably the problem of how to interpret Frederick's passionate friendships perturbed her and she appealed for enlightenment to Peter Quennell, who had published some of her writings in *History Today*. 'I don't want to bore you,' she wrote (30th December, 1968), 'but there is nobody who takes the faintest interest in Fritz's sex life. It is such a puzzle to me. The story of the young officer after breakfast comes from Voltaire after the quarrel when nothing was bad enough for F so it may or may not be true. But when you remember that homosexuality in those days was considered such a sin that it was punishable by the stake (in France) it seems unlikely that someone so careful as F would have put himself in the power of any pretty young officer? I don't mean that he could have been had up but public opinion—

'Katte, I suppose, is pretty certainly a love, but they were public school age so that means nothing (Katte's great nephew I probably told you has written to beg me not to perpetrate this monstrous libel).

'Keyserling was his great and greatest friend for years—they used to be shut up together for hours on end—Keyserling not allowed to go near the window for fear of being seen. Yet at the height of what you'd think was an affair, it was Keyserling who wrote to Algarotti saying come as quickly as you can (when F's father died). When Keyserling fell in love with a woman and married F wrote "he is not the first person who has had his head turned by love"—he gave fêtes and parties for the wedding and liked the lady very much. When Keyserling died two years later F was utterly heartbroken and cast down for months; did all he could to help the widow and orphan. I may be naïve but none of this seems to add up.

'Algarotti lasted a very short time as a love, if he ever was one, though F liked his company and conversation. He had nothing to do with him for five years after Algarotti had written a cheeky letter—quite at the beginning of their friendship. This hardly looks like passion.

'No women at the Court. But pederasts love women as a rule. I think it was because he couldn't stick the Queen and if there had been women it would have been too rude not to include her. At Rheinsberg, where there were women, he used to say that there could be no good conversation without them.

'I think perhaps I fail to understand the nature of homosexuality—I am excessively normal myself and have never had the slightest leanings in that direction even as a child. My own feeling about F is that he was almost or quite sexless. I suppose Monty is—Napoleon was as sexless as a Corsican could be—these people are interested in power.

'The thing is, shall I weigh the pros and cons as I see them or simply tell the story and let the reader deduce what he likes from it? . . .

'The interest of a love affair lies in the changing nature of the relationship and if there is no evidence available how can one describe it? Allez-oop with young officers is really very dull.

'Don't bother to answer. Dr Halsband says he'll know more about Algarotti presently and impart.'

Peter Quennell's reply must have been pertinent if not instructive: I regret I could not find it among Nancy's papers at Chatsworth. The word 'pansy', so often employed by Nancy with a tolerant twinkle, was certainly inept in connection with the Great Frederick, though I have heard it applied to Michelangelo by a woman who should have known better. Nancy had the naïvety of the pure of heart. I doubt if she realized how many of her friends had what the French call 'special tastes'. As she admitted to Mark Ogilvie-Grant (whom she begged not to become a monk with long black hair when he went to Mount Athos): 'Nobody has ever been so ferociously normal as me, and the idea of Gomorrah gives me the jim-jams. In fact I prefer not to think about it.' A thoroughly lady-like attitude.

Valentine Lawford, whose book *Bound for Diplomacy* had delighted Nancy, now stepped forward, as a student of German history, to help her with sources for *Frederick the Great* since, as she confessed, nearly all her sources were in French and she knew no German. 'I think if I could bring off this book and if it had the same enormous public as the *Sun King*, it might do a little good from a European point of view,' she told him. 'English people regard Frederick the Great as a sort of Hitler I believe.' With Mr. Lawford Nancy could frankly discuss the complexities of Frederick's personal relationships. He sent her learned notes on various German works, historical and psycho-analytical, dealing with Frederick's peculiarities, and offered to translate important letters for her. He even procured photographs of Katte, family-portraits from one of Katte's descendants and provided her with such curious information as that 'the bow tying Katte's hair, preserved in his coffin at Wust, had been stolen from his tomb in the 1920s, and that an English tourist had removed Katte's severed spinal cord as a souvenir at about the same time, as a result of which the family had walled up the vault in 1926 to prevent further depredations.'

'I worship the bow and the spinal cord bagged by an English tourist,' she replied gleefully. 'They do make life difficult. By pulling all the strings in the world to get into the Scotch chapel here where all James II's bogus Dukes are buried I have never succeeded because it was desecrated in some way by an English tourist. (A bit hard, with Ogilvy and Dillon Jacobite ancestors both of whom owned regiments at Versailles.)'

All the same she was 'suffering from slight doubt over this book. How to interest an enormous public without any love at all to sugar the pill?' She thirsted for a long gossip about him with Valentine Lawford, for 'nobody in Paris knows the first beginnings about Frederick.' Having taken time off to read Michael Holroyd's *Lytton Strachey*, she remarked it was 'rather wonderful and terrible how *all* could now be said.' The question remained: 'Shall I ever be able to put across the fascination—if not I shall have totally failed.'

Nancy wrote that she was 'encouraged, to my surprise, by my German publisher. I suppose there are no light-weight biographers in Germany now.' As her old Austrian friend Prince Clary detested Frederick, Valentine Lawford's assistance was a boon. If only he did not live in America! Nancy could not understand 'how a real European like yourself can go and live among savages. Oh do explain. It's so terribly unnatural.'

So many questions cropped up that needed answering. Was she right in thinking Frederick didn't care for Bach's music? Should she enter into his fiscal, agrarian and military reforms? Perhaps she could indicate his absorption in those things 'without boring myself and therefore the reader . . .' What was his attitude towards the Jews? Nancy continued to consult Mr. Lawford and send him 'progress reports' until her book was finished.

An article on the new vernacular in the *Listener* was a momentary distraction from Frederick. To her sister Debo she explained: 'Roughly my song is this: the BBC ought to be for England what the Académie is for France, a guardian of the lingo. Now I must go at it with slightly kid gloves on account of silly old U and non U. I say on the whole the *announcers* are good and when you turn on you know at once you are in England, not the voice of America. I then go for the *guest* speakers (are they called that?) I say I don't think pronunciation matters much, it changes every fifty years or so, but I do mention changes I have noticed (without saying they make me sick) and so far I've got INcrease, WestMINster, Cabinut, Ufrica, countree, HostESS goes in, thanks, any more?

'Then I absolutely go for the talkers—how they begin elaborate sentences which they can't finish and flounder about ums and ers, but I say the chief horror is over-emphasis. Instead of saying "people aren't very nice about him" he has to be "undergoing character assassination". *This* is always used to emphasize: "I think so" becomes "This I believe to be true". "Nowadays" is "this day and age". People don't *say*, they *claim*. They don't *meet* or *think*, they *meet up* and *think up*. G. M. Young used to say, let the English language take care of itself—meaning don't fuss—and that's what they won't do.'

The visit to Potsdam Nancy longed for had to be postponed. From Versailles she wrote to Sir Hugh Jackson in September: 'I had rather an agitating time when I left Venice, trying to get to East Germany. I got as far as Bayreuth, then heard that the hotels were not honouring their vouchers (the rooms full of Russian officers probably). The young people who were to take me in their motor not at all anxious to have a try and in the end

194

I abandoned the idea. I saw Wilhelmina's pretty little palace at Bayreuth and called on Frau Winifred Wagner who is an old friend of my family's (Siegfried Wagner an intimate friend of my Redesdale grandfather's). She is not very old because she married at sixteen when her husband was in his fifties but she seems a sort of historical monument and is now the Queen of Bayreuth. I loved her.

'Then I went to my sister [Pam] near Zürich and rather fell in love with that part of Switzerland. It is so very clean and unspoilt (not Zürich itself but the country), the little villages looking like Victorian coloured engravings of Switzerland all in points.

'Now I've begun my book. An excellent little book on Frederick has just appeared by a German, Ritter, now dead. I've been reading a book about Maria Theresa by an American professor Pick (?) full of interesting things but the English so appalling one often has to read a sentence two or three times to see what he's getting at. Isn't it funny that they can't seem to master the language . . . All quiet here and the students are behaving themselves again and the workers busy doing over-time to make up for May. Thank goodness.'

'There's a fascinating Exposition Hoche at our town hall here,' she told Sir Hugh Jackson. 'He is the local boy who made good. It seems he tried to land an army at Bantry Bay in conjunction with Wolf Tone. Well, in 1920 (note the date) the Irish sent a bronze laurel leaf to the town of Versailles saying Ireland thanks Hoche, and our Embassy made such a song and dance about it that it has been hidden ever since. But it's the first thing you see at the exhibition! Hoche must have been an enormous man, they've got his coat. Next year of course is the bicentenary of Napoleon and great junketings are planned.

'I must get back to my work, it is very difficult but I begin to see daylight. I think I shall take nearly everything out of his own letters, which are so funny, and let him explain himself. P.S. How do you translate the word *esprit*? I think it's impossible. A reviewer once said Miss M. clearly doesn't know French, she translates *esprit* (un homme d'esprit) as a clever, amusing person. *Honnête homme* do you think "gentleman"?'

In compensation for Potsdam Nancy was able to visit Prague in October as a guest of the French Ambassador. From the Palais Buquoy she wrote enthusiastically to her sister Debo on

6th November: 'I'm terribly glad I came. You never saw such a marvellous town—I put it after Paris and Venice and only after Paris because I happen to prefer French architecture. Miles before Leningrad. There are acres and acres of marvels and every now and then you turn a corner and there is a forest, a real one, not a public park.

'The Russians are pathetic and vile. Dreadful stupid-looking very young dwarfs. The shop windows which would be a joke if not so sad—tasteful displays of paper clips or plastic waste paper baskets—simply fascinate the Conquerors, they stand glued. It seems they are told "see how the Czechs live, on *your* money—Russia has been subsidizing them for twenty years." As nobody can speak Russian or would speak to them if they could, everything is believed.

'I've seen an incredible lot of people as well as things. Went to call on a professor in Alphy's mother's house (Kinsky). "I've got all the Clary archives in that cupboard." "Oh indeed!" All the foreigners here love the Czechs, at least the ones I've seen do. Our English Ambassador is a nice clever man who speaks Czech so of course is being replaced at Xmas by one who doesn't.

'The general level of drabness tells the tale of twenty years of Socialism. I suppose Mr Wilson hopes to make England like that how strange. Everywhere *Liberté* (in French) is painted on the walls and photographs of Dubcek among the paper clips. The embassies all have little lorries which go to a German market town for food—here there is nothing but red cabbages like in my garden. Smashing food in this house of course. The Ambassador goes out shooting a lot which it seems is marvellous—black with pheasants—and is an invisible export. You can shoot a bear for 4000 dollars. My plane was full of people with guns. Coming?'

To Alvilde Lees-Milne she described her visit to Prague as 'a huge success'. 'THE FOREST—real, not Hyde Park, creeping in everywhere,' delighted her even more than the great Baroque palaces of Italian inspiration which had survived the Seven Years' War and Russian conquest. 'I had a lovely time altogether and being the only new face for weeks was made a fuss of! And I feel, for my book, I've had a taste of Central Europe.'

Next year she planned to go to Potsdam and Dresden with

196

her sister Pam, 'then on to see l'Abbé-Prince Lubomirski who lives in a little country town in the middle of the brave boy's battlefields . . . Home via Prague which I long to see in the spring sunshine.'

CHAPTER THIRTEEN

ALTHOUGH SHE COMPLAINED of low stamina and 'a mass of allergics' Nancy had seldom been seriously ill. Having kept her youthful features and figure, she produced an impression of glowing health.

Since childhood her mother had inculcated in her a confidence in the recuperative powers of the Good Body and she had steered clear of the medical profession. Commiserating with Sir Hugh Jackson's arthritis, she had written: 'Those wretched doctors always go on as if they had conquered pain and illness but really all they can do is to give plastic kidneys to business men or whatever it is. Everybody else has the same diseases as our grandparents—no cure possible.' When I asked her to recommend a Parisian doctor she replied with a faint air of disgust that she had never needed one. It was as if I had asked her for something improper. Of the renowned American Hospital at Neuilly she spoke as of a charnel-house. One could not suspect that her sparkling eyes had given her trouble, but this was probably due to prolonged sessions of reading and small print.

Reading was Nancy's sole excess; in everything else she was moderate. Thanking Valentine Lawford for the treat he had given her with his *Bound for Diplomacy*, she remarked: 'I am obliged to ration myself for fear of finishing too soon and you don't know how unusual that is—I generally finish off a book by turning 3 pages at a time and into the poubelle (whence these wretched time-wasters are retrieved by a young student who lives chez Monseigneur à côté and who gives my concierge a box of chocs at Christmas in return). Yours will go straight into the book case I need hardly add.'

While she had a fastidious palate she ate and drank sparingly. Even in her twenties Evelyn Waugh had remarked to Maurice Bowra that she was a 'nice cheap girl to take out for the evening. Costs you only eighteen and six for an orangeade at a night club.' She used to quote with approval Eddy Sackville's dictum that rich food does nobody any harm: it is poor food that kills people. Generally she tried to avoid late nights. After ten o'clock, as she said, she dropped off her perch, yet she relished the accounts of her friends' nocturnal outings, of their fancy dress parties and frolics. 'People come with widely differing accounts of balls and what they must have cost,' she told Robin Mc Douall. 'The giver really ought to chalk it up somewhere as it's the only feature of the entertainment which really interests the convives. How awful the next day must be, with hangover, filthy house, furious neighbours and the Bill.'

In spite of low stamina an inner flame of vitality sustained her, whereas most of her friends required some additional stimulant.

Twenty years previously, on 16th February, 1948, Nancy had written to her mother: 'I've been awfully unwell, better now and up, for the first time for a week, today. I had such ghastly pains all over, specially in my back, that I had to be completely doped for three whole days and nothing makes one feel worse than that . . . Couldn't read or write or even turn on the wireless it was such torture to move an inch.

'I think Evelyn [Waugh] did it—his dedication of his new book [The Loved One] is an urn with N.M. on it—he sent it to me to see and *at once* I was laid low. The book is a yell . . . I don't think I've ever screamed more with laughter—can't imagine what the public will make of it. He has been warned it will ruin him in America.'

Since then the pains had vanished completely, and all of us who had seen Nancy during the last twenty years were struck by her apparent immunity to disease. In the meantime *The Loved One* had become a minor classic.

Now towards the end of January 1969 she began to suffer from excruciating pain. The cause was mysterious and there were many conjectures—sciatica, rheumatism, spinal arthritis— but the pain was lancinating, ghoulish. During rare intervals of relief she unburdened herself in letters to her sisters and closest friends. Her work on Frederick was suspended. That it ever came to fruition was a triumph of her will power and a proof that Clio, the muse of history, was a guardian angel who never failed her in sickness as in health. Gleams of stoical humour broke through the dense clouds of her suffering. Hope was often deferred yet 'against hope she believed in hope'. All her friends conspired to persuade her that a cure would soon be found. The death of her old friend Mark Ogilvie-Grant at this time was a cruel blow. He died of cancer but at least he was spared the prolonged agony to which Nancy was condemned. In Mark she had lost a confidant who for his sympathy and instinctive understanding almost replaced her beloved brother Tom. His influence on her early life cannot be overestimated.

Nancy's letters from now on are a chronicle of suffering endured with a determination to see the funny side of even the most harrowing experiences. Were it not for the flashes of her gallant spirit I would forbear to quote them. Perhaps having known her I hear her laugh through her misery. She still took pleasure in so many of life's hors d'oeuvre, and this makes her letters all the more poignant. Those to women friends are the most vivid and revealing: she thought aloud in them—they are letters of flesh and blood. To Alvilde Lees-Milne for instance, 24th March, 1969:

'Yes I've been on my back for a month with a colonne vertébrale dégradée in such pain that I only longed to SPEAK. Stop stop I'll tell you everything. However, I managed not to be lugged off to a hospital but to stay in my own pretty room. Then just as I was (am) much better they have discovered a lump on my liver and lights which has got to be investigated (THE END of course) this week in circumstances of barbaric torture including 24 hours without drinking. So for about a week I prepared to meet my God and then THEY seemed very much surprised that I harboured such gloomy thoughts (screaming with laughter actually of course) and said nobody who looks as well as I do could be on the way out. They might have said so in the first place. But they want to know exactly what it is. Anyway I adore the doctor who is young and charming and the whole neighbourhood here has been so angelic sending fresh eggs and things. I think the Versailles people are the very nicest in the world. Then I've had Diana [her sister] daily and of course old Marie and Colonel the regulars—I haven't felt up to anybody else. But have managed to work a bit.

'So—all very dull I fear, it's awful what a bore one becomes. I bore poor Diana to death. I mean hot news is whether I have or have not taken a drug.

'Excuse writing I'm upside down. I must say nobody could mind a month in bed less than me, it's the pain I object to.

'I do hear lovely things on the English wireless viz. England is now the abortion centre of the world and we can earn millions, more than Fords, in foreign currency from it.

'Oh Mark. I mind terribly—it was cancer. He was taken to England where the doctors killed him in about a fortnight. Anna Maria says why can't we all go together, how I agree.'

To Geoffrey Gilmour, with whom she usually spent Christmas in the rue du Bac after Marie's retirement, she wrote on 29th March: 'I did the tests yesterday. The comic relief was so great I hardly minded them it was like a horror film of the worst variety. One was constantly left, naked, in the dark while they developed the films, like children with a Brownie, in a sort of kitchen sink next door. Everybody divine like they are here at Versailles. Of course now we have *les fêtes* so I shan't know my fate I suppose for another age but the lump remains mysterious, nothing to do with kidney (said to be très joli) and the radiologist wouldn't hazard a guess. I wonder if it's my twin brother one has heard of that: a little old man with a white beard. Little Lord Redesdale, shrieking away, might be an addition to rue d'Artois and Diana's dinner parties—*la coqueluche de Paris*. Anything for a new face.'

To Sir Hugh Jackson, who had become her literary arbiter, she wrote: 'As a matter of fact what I've got is painful but not dangerous. I've had it since Christmas and when finally last week I went to the doctor the following dialogue took place. "Why didn't you come sooner?" "Because everybody told me it would go away." "Who is everybody?" "Oh, the *femme de ménage* and so on." "Funny sort of professors you have."

'Frederick was excessively odd but not bad. Of course he was Voltairean though I think he believed in God more than

201

Voltaire did—probably in predestination. He became a Free-mason early in life to annoy his father and soon dropped it saying that it was great rubbish. He loved his friends deeply, it is quite untrue that he behaved badly to them—they nearly all died young, to his despair. In the end he was left with the old Earl Marischal and he too died before Frederick who then became a real hermit.

'I can't imagine that he would have wanted a revolution anywhere—he was all for order and quite clever enough to see that one revolution leads to another. The odd thing is that, although he lived until the Affaire du Collier he never seems to have realized that things were so dicky in France. But then, did anybody? We should have loved him, if only for the jokes.

'I've just finished with the Seven Years War and am au bout de souffle not quite knowing how to deal with the last years—23 of them. Carlyle drops him like a hot potato at this point and so, I see, do most biographers. The Partition of Poland daunts me. I must confess the Seven Years War is completely fascinating.

'I'm supposed, in May, to go to Dresden, Potsdam and the battlefields. I've got an old friend Lubomirski, a Jesuit (I call him l'Abbé Prince) who lives at Kalisz and will escort me to the Silesian points of interest. If I can't go owing to health it will kill me with disappointment mais n'anticipons pas.'

On 1st April: 'My health drags on the same. I did all the tests and am now waiting to hear what is thought of them. If I can't go to Germany, where Pam and I and Joy Law are to be the guests of the Communist government!!! (screams, as all will be so furious) I shall die of disappointment that's all. It's now five weeks I've been in bed being a nuisance to every-body—though apart from that fact none could mind less than I do. It's the pain that I object to. The doctors never loom, they are far too busy injecting blood into the lunatics who kill and maim thousands every day on the roads. I said to Marie this morning how nice it was in the old days when doctors used to look in to see how you were and she says even in her village, where things were far from perfect, the doctor would come along in his gig and see what was up. Oh gig oh isn't the world vile. Now you telephone and some horrid secretary says she will *faire la commission*. No doubt they

202

think at one's age it's hardly worth bothering—but then they ought to finish you off. I'm told they do in England.

23rd April: 'I'm in a perfectly heavenly clinic—view on trees—dead quiet—huge old-fashioned room—nuns and three-star food. I'm to be cut up tomorrow. The surgeon is a very cold man of few words. He said, *Madame vous êtes un mystère. Si vous permettez je vous opérerai jeudi matin.* They haven't the faintest idea what IT is, won't they be surprised when little Lord Redesdale makes his bow! The bore is it probably won't cure my back, though it possibly may.

'Oh servants—X has got a very grand expensive couple, the woman says my husband's in the toilet and he says the puppy has had a motion in the hall. It transpires that they are debtors how sinister. I can't understand why those thousands of unemployed we hear about don't queue up for a spot of gracious living . . . instead of hanging about the empty mines . . . Diana comes tomorrow to hear Famous Last Words.'

May Day, from Clinique Georges Bizet: 'They literally sawed me in half . . . and the appalling pain in my back has gone and it was nothing to do with rheumatism (I was dreading a rheumy old age) but caused by a large lump exactly in my waist. How odd! The pain was bottom of my back and one leg, so much time was wasted on X-raying, etc., all that . . . Debo and Diana sat and listened to my ravings after the operation all day—if that's not faithful!'

6th June, home in Versailles: 'I'm very miserable. The pain has come back worse than ever and I have the choice between the drugs they give me which make me stupid and give me a headache—make me feel as if I'd been in a night-club, or literally bellowing with anguish. In neither case can I work. The doctors look at me sadly because there is nothing wrong with my back whatever, it is pristine. They swim in a sea of total ignorance in fact and fall back on that meaningless word rheumatism.

'Poor Marie is so affected seeing me like this that it makes her ill, so I'm sending her home to *prendre sa retraite.* I've got a very nice person (I think and hope) to replace her, a doctor's daughter who is fed up with working in offices. She perhaps won't mind the moans and groans of a stranger. Marie literally suffers herself she minds so much. I must say it's an appalling pain . . . I've had to chuck Venice.'

14th June: 'Yesterday I had to have an injection of morphia which properly laid me out—today I'm managing with a pill . . . My tortoises married yesterday. I could hear the noise from up here. They butt each other with clash of steel for ages and do incredibly dirty things. Marie was shocked.

'Great excitement at Jouy where aboriginal beavers (quite different from American ones) have been found in the Bièvre. A French beaver is called a Bièvre it seems, the word derives from that. Wild appeals on the télé etc. to preserve them. Diana thinks she has got them in her lake. In Blighty colonels would surge with dogs and do them in no doubt (great fun probably one must admit). They look (on télé) too sweet . . .

'Colonel has just telephoned to say Kay [Clark] is a lord. I thought lords were over but I'm awfully pleased, he *does* deserve it.'

In July there was a sudden magical improvement. 'The replacer of Marie, seeing me writhing about, said she could cure me. I said all right but *don't touch my back*. She seized my back and practically jumped on it and in three days I had given up the drugs and in three weeks (last week) was completely cured. It turned out that she was a trained masseuse but, being a Belgian, not allowed to practise here. She took this situation to be near a married sister—is a first-class cook. The backache was caused by a twisted muscle which didn't show in the X-rays. So you see God was on my side—made me put an advert. in the local paper for a cook and I got this marvellous person. As Mme Botkin (aged 95 who lives in Venice) always says, dans la vie tout s'arrange.

'So now I'm back with Frederick. All this time I've read tremendously as you may imagine, and nothing else but his own works and those of his contemporaries, so now my book is writing itself, it's all so much in my head. I can't go to Venice—I'm still weak and thin—but hope for Silesia and Potsdam in October. Meanwhile the lovely weather and my garden are compensating for being stuck here.

'Carlyle. That is an idea. But is there not too much about him? I must find a new subject when I've done with Fritz.'

On the 20th she wrote: 'I'm better every day—no more bed at all in fact, it is *made*, with its cover . . . There's nothing like being out of pain for the first time for seven months I can tell you. Went to the hairdresser and walked there and back (only 100 yards, but still).' And on 24th July: 'I'm working like mad again. The weather is a help too . . . I know it's awful but the moon bores me. The men are so vile and always having to have a rest. I thought of Captain Scott. But Clem and Alph (Sir Alfred and Lady Beit—Clem was her cousin) got up in their pyjamas at the Meurice ("I set my alarm watch." Only Clem would have one) like an air raid to see these sewers. Now Braun I suppose is an interesting man (he tried to kill us all never mind that) but they don't show him.'

Nancy's resilience was remarkable. In spite of her physical anguish she told Raymond Mortimer on 25th July: 'Frederick has really benefited. I have read tremendously. All Besterman's 100 volumes, all Frederick's own works and so on, and then thought about him non-stop. What an extraordinary creature. The porphyria *y était pour beaucoup.*

'I wonder if you've got Besterman's life of Voltaire. As I always observe, only those with no sense of humour write about him—there is not one single joke. But of course, I was riveted. He is grossly unfair to Frederick. I knew he would be by the way the letters were edited—say, he engendered Hitler. Oh *honestly*! I wrote (to Theodore) saying I suppose you go on like that because you are frightened of what the old scamp (Voltaire I mean) will say when you see him in the Elysian Fields. He replied that Voltaire had anyway put a curse on whoever would edit his letters!

'Yesterday I received a book the size of a house, picture book on the 18th century. There are some heavenly things— the text is by dear Dr Cobban therefore perfect—and yet and yet—some gruesome mistakes: Frederick the Great with his son and grandson; Louis XV arriving at Versailles, which had been empty since the death of Louis XIV, in 1772. I read Antonia's [Fraser's] book but seemed to know it all already. I envy the professional work and deplore the way it is written— she falls into the modern clichés, "her personal clothes", you know. The government is always called "the central government". I note you didn't review it. Peter Quennell says its success is due to prayer—the whole Pakenham family on its knees for weeks according to him. It conjures up a vision of Weidenfeld, with Spring and Autumn lists at the Wailing Wall and Jamie [Hamilton] at the Kirk.'

To Sir Hugh Jackson she wrote on 10th August: 'I'm really cured though I get sort of growing pains which are nasty but bearable. The lump which they carved out (benign like Bossuet) had nothing to do with the back, it was just an extra treat discovered by some busybody while examining me. Alas Marie has gone to her retraite—the whole thing upset her terribly and I was afraid she would fall ill. I miss her more than I can say after 22 years of her solid peasant wisdom and goodness. But I've got the nice person who cured me so I'm really lucky. The sad thing is that Marie lives so far away that it's a separation like death. We write love letters almost daily.

'Frederick whizzes. I sit in the garden scribbling, without specs on account of the brilliant light—have done about a quarter . . .

'I've discovered something so amusing. You know Mme de Maintenon used to say there is a highly placed spy at Versailles and at Blenheim I think they've got some of his reports. Well Eugene told Frederick it was the *maître des postes* and that he, Eugene, used to get the orders before the French generals! The spy was never caught. I must now find out who the *maître des postes* was and another historical mystery will have been solved, too late alas for the *Sun King*.

'My book, the best I've ever written and next to *King Solomon's Mines* ever read, is very far advanced,' she told Raymond Mortimer. Though far from cured, for she suffered from 'deep cramp in back and leg' and was very weak and thin, Nancy wrote again in September: 'I go to Potsdam and Dresden on 16th October pain or no pain, but I've chucked Silesia. In a way I want to see that most. Frederick loved it much more than his old Mark—the people so much cleverer and the land so beautiful . . .'

Nancy mustered all her strength and courage for a journey particularly strenuous in her fragile condition, but she was accompanied by her sister Pam, so appropriately nicknamed 'Woman' for she had all the charm and sweetness of her sex with the gentle Mitford voice and azure eyes. Her enthusiastic accounts in letters show how cheerfully she could overcome her painful predicament.

To Alvilde Lees-Milne she wrote in November: 'The journey was simply amazing and I'm thankful I went. I took

Pam and the Laws and wormed a huge sum of foreign currency out of the Banque de France, every penny of which I brought back. We weren't allowed to pay for so much as a cup of coffee. They gave us two huge black Russian cars in which we bowled about in great comfort on empty roads—the speed limit is 50 m.p.h. Bliss, and the government agent who arranged the trip came everywhere with us. The curators all standing to attention at the door as we arrived and showed us everything—the one at the Zwinger in Dresden took two whole days so did the second in command at Potsdam, entirely devoted to us. I still don't quite understand it but so it was. Then they were all so *nice*. Mr Friedlander the agent is a shrieker so you may imagine the jokes! Not always in the best of taste . . . Friedlander speaks English but nobody else—they didn't know French let alone English, they all speak Russian and the notices in the hotels are in German and Russian.

'Of course we saw *marvels* and then there was the interest of it all. I had a lot of pain but no worse than when I'm here and they were so kind about bringing chairs and bringing the car to forbidden places and so on. The only thing was no baths, only showers, and I depend greatly on lying in a hot bath so that was rather a blow. Food delicious because they haven't got round to broilers and so on and the taste was what one has forgotten, but of course if you say so they are deeply offended and say by next year all the farms will be factories. Like in all Commy countries nothing works and the first evening I was stuck in a mad lift which whirled up and down for 35 minutes. I thought I was for it and Pam thought I'd been kidnapped. We had nine days in East Germany and two in West Berlin—staying at Potsdam, Dresden and East Berlin. I thought East Berlin vastly preferable to West, which is like one huge Oxford Street, the people are so much nicer. What Pam calls Check Point Charlie is too sinister—a gun in your tummy wherever you look. And we noticed that we were never left alone with anybody for a minute or allowed out alone, not that one minded.

'So that's the journey—I've seldom enjoyed myself more. I've finished the book which is now being typed and my health has taken a distinct turn for the better so everything seems rosy again.'

To Sir Hugh Jackson she confided that she still had a lot

of pain: 'I suppose I must make up my mind to that—specially in the morning.' But her obsession with Frederick was almost analgesic; 'The accounts of his personality all tally with each other so one can describe him much better than say, Louis XV, whose observers were more subjective. His sex life (as they say nowadays) is more mysterious but I suppose it consisted quite straightforwardly of footmen! He may have had two serious attachments, Keyserling and Rothenbourg, but there is no proof, no love letters as far as I know. In any case he had nothing like mignons and was uninfluenced by anybody . . . The Silesian journey I hope to make in the spring.

'East Germany fascinated me . . . and I saw all the things I wanted to though alas sometimes in a fog. Saxony is too beautiful: Dresden, *n'en parlons pas.* A heap of rubble with a few skyscrapers. But all the pictures were saved as well as the stunning treasure, by being buried under a prison for French generals! As for present living conditions, by our standards they are poor but of course that makes touring more agreeable. No motors on the roads and a very strict speed limit . . . East Berlin is shabby and badly lit but there are no advertisements, all the pretty old buildings are there more or less restored after the raids . . . Except for the tyranny and terror of which one got an occasional glimpse I would much rather live in the Eastern part . . .'

She was beginning to feel better: 'My masseuse says something has moved in my spine of its own accord and indeed I can see it has—about time too.' The future of Potsdam worried her and she wrote to Raymond Mortimer, who had become her chief literary mentor since the death of Evelyn Waugh: 'Will you join my Save Potsdam Campaign? They are going to pull down that exquisite town and put up workers' flats. Some Germans are putting up a bitter fight and one must try and help them . . . Mr Friedlander, the government agent whom I loved because he was in many little ways so kind to me and such a shrieker, is really only interested in turbines— I am the first pen pusher he has ever had there. So I imagine his outlook is typical. When the Conservateur (deputy) took me round the town (he gave up two days—first the palaces, then town and gardens) I said "This town is really unique."— "Yes, it's sad that it must go."—"*Go?*"—"Yes, people can't live in these houses any more, they must have heating, etc.

11. Mrs. Violet Trefusis, with her maid

12. Talking to schoolgirls at the Collège Féminin de Bouffémont

etc." "But" says I, "all that can be put in these houses very easily nowadays and people have far happier lives in them. In France as soon as they have a little money they ooze out of the skyscrapers into little houses. If you do this, Mr Friedlander, you will regret it in fifty years or less."—"Very possibly, but it's a question of money." Then I said to the Conservateur, "surely *you* can object, what's the good of a palace in the middle of an industrial complex? The conservateur of Versailles is very powerful in these ways."— "Alas, we are not."

'Then I saw a professor who came to give me a history lesson and she said she has got a friend on the Potsdam council who is putting up a bitter fight and any comment from abroad would be a help. The point partly is that the Germans don't admire the eighteenth century and Frederick is thought to have been far too Frenchified—Potsdam actually more Italian than French but still (and in parts Dutch). If they could be made to see that the eighteenth century is greatly prized now— that their things are regarded as treasures, I believe it would help. I believe I slightly shook Mr Friedlander. The first evening we arrived we went to the hotel, a ghastly skyscraper opposite Frederick's lovely stables and I said, "Mr Friedlander *pull that down!*"—"But we've only just put it up."— "Well, it's a mistake—pull it down again." He shook with laughter but I believe something sunk.

'You know when towns are demolished it just happens— comes the bulldozer and all is over in a trice. Hard to have any precise information, especially behind the darling curtain where people are very properly subject to discipline and seldom tell you their true thoughts!

'If you could sort of worm praise of the town of Potsdam into an article, I think it might be a great help if they were made to feel they are sacrificing something more than a lot of dirty old houses nobody wants. I saw that, at Dresden, the line is aren't we lucky to have this lovely new town so up to date (vertical slums). I'm afraid Friedlander has already forgotten me like nurses do the moment you've left the clinic . . . Do pass on what I've said to Sir John Summerson. I think words of praise *for what exists* would be of immense help.'

The German journey had given Nancy a salutary fillip, as we may deduce from her correspondence. Apparently she could not convert Raymond Mortimer to her infatuation for Frederick. 'Do you think Frederick so German?' she expostulated with him. 'I see him as a purely eighteenth-century character, in some ways so modern. It seems to me his reign, after Frederick William's, is into a Watteau out of a Rembrandt. *Battles*. It is the sorrow of my life never to have been in one. I suppose a cavalry charge must be the nearest thing to heaven on this earth. When I was little I was so jealous of my great-uncle for being killed in one (against the Boers—so wicked when I was a child and so wicked again now).

'Very hard on my old dad that he died too soon—if murder had been allowed when he was in his prime our home would have been like the last act of Othello almost daily—it's a shame. Various characters, like Lloyd George, would soon have been dealt with, at least one of my aunts, and innumerable neighbours. It *is* unfair.'

Everything seemed less and less rosy in 1970, and Nancy had to endure waves of shooting pain until she died. On 3rd January she wrote to Alvilde: 'I've had 'flu and can't get going and my leg though better now has been worse than ever before . . . This 'flu is the devil. Mme Guimont (char) is gravely ill with it. But far the worst on Xmas eve my little Marie was run over and lies in hospital over two hours drive from here with a broken leg and concussion. I can't go to her—I can't even go downstairs. When I ring up they hardly say anything but I've had a letter from her neighbours saying she's *dans un triste état*.

'I can't work, I can only read Simenon. I don't think I've ever been so low in my life.'

Pain killers were suggested but she argued stoically against them. 'If one has a perpetual pain this is what happens. They kill it. They also give you a headache, make you stupid and stop you going to the loo. Then after about four hours the pain comes back and as well you have got a headache and can't go to the loo and feel like death as well as having the pain. What they are good for is something like migraine which, when it is over, is over.

'If I weren't afraid of it not working and permanently ruining my brain what there is of it, I would have tried to take an overdose of something ages ago because I would much sooner be dead than have this awful pain all the time.'

On 30th January she engaged a Moroccan servant called Hassan who appeared to have admirable qualities, for her previous attendant had shown signs of fatigue and ill temper which added mental discomfort to physical distress. 'It would be so wonderful to have somebody who is never tired and a slave—I mean it will be wonderful until he murders me . . . I've got a new doctor and am having various tests nearly every day in Paris: it's a bore but I have faith in him for some reason . . . Mme Guimont's grandson went skiing as they all do now (free) and she went to the station to meet him. She says the yard was crammed with ambulances and you couldn't move for stretchers and it was like the trains coming back from Verdun! "*Mais Christian est indemne.*" I screamed at the account.

'Yes, dear little Tony [Gandarillas]. He fell down at a dinner chez Schiaparelli and they thought he had hurt his shoulder but I suppose really it was a stroke. Rather perfect as I don't think he knew much about it and died four or five days later. Marie-Laure [de Noailles] was marvellous, saw to everything and paid the hospital . . . He was much more like ninety—no age in the *Figaro.*'

The big-hearted and versatile Marie-Laure herself was to die soon after nursing our ancient Chilean friend.

After a whole week of gruelling tests Nancy's doctor decided that she had neither arthritis nor tuberculosis (which he had suspected because she was so emaciated) nor a slipped disc. But he could not diagnose the disease and insisted that she be examined further in a hospital. 'He cleverly said people who have a *métier* they like are never *malades imaginaires.*'

Hassan soon endeared himself to the rue d'Artois. 'He is a real cook, absolutely the top—I'm so thrilled. Then so smart and nice and kind; he found one of my hedgehogs and brought it in and so on—you know, the sort of person one can do with. Everybody loves him already—Mme Guimont (char) IN love and comes free! on her days off to give a hand if he seems to want her. I can't believe my luck . . . I'm only afraid he'll be bored down here but he says not . . .

'Will you come round the world next year in the *France* with me? . . . Oh do. I've got a letter from Gerry [Wellington] on a cruise saying he had never met middle-class people before, "they are quite different from us". Isn't he awful! . . . I've got a new pill which keeps the pain under control.'

In spite of the ache in her bones Nancy drove off to visit Marie a few days later: 'Pam took me to see old Marie—nearly a hundred miles—I wish to goodness she were nearer . . . I never saw such a nice hospital—she is in a huge sunny room with only two others and the prettiest view of old houses and fruit trees—she is amused by watching the people in them. She's still rather muddled and one eye is shut and she can't walk but they seem to say in time all will be well. She's had no pain whatever. Very good colour and simply delighted to see us. Hassan continues to be perfect . . .

Of Elizabeth Longford Nancy wrote with admiration: 'She was that rare bird when I was young an undergraduette at Oxford (now one would say student I suppose). She was as beautiful and merry as she was brilliant—everybody courted her and lucky Frank Pakenham got her. (I was frantically jealous of her.) They had eight children, now mostly grown up, and became R.C's. We never meet but the friendship endures—I love Pakenhams anyway. Frank is a goose but a great dear. He worries about the dull lives of those people who tortured little girls to death on moors—I can't say I do but it shows a Christian nature.'

Assuring Sir Hugh Jackson that he would enjoy Elizabeth Longford's book on Wellington, she wrote (23rd March 1970): 'One always likes reading about what one knows already, if well done . . . My only criticism would be that she doesn't see either the genius or the glamour of Napoleon so that, for instance, the hundred days, the return and all that become rather incomprehensible. During Waterloo there is not quite enough about what happened on the French side. The fog of war and the poor intelligence must have made battles chancy no doubt. Frederick used to say that *all* battles are a lottery.

'I suppose the death of Berthier was decisive. Elizabeth merely says he fell out of a window without relating the pathetic facts. One really hates Soult for the muddles.

'About the horses—she says the French cavalrymen slept *on* their horses during that night of terrible rain so of course the poor things were tired the next day. I loved the Brunswickers going into battle looking like a hearse (all in black for their duke killed at Jena). How fascinating what you say about the roads being blocked. Do you remember when, in '58, we expected the parachutists here from Algiers and

Malraux made the population block the road from Orly with their motors? Good idea.

'Frederick will appear in October. I do hope you will approve. I'm reading Martet's *Conversations with Clemenceau,* very highly enjoyable. In 1928 he *knew* what would happen in 1939 and never stopped warning people. He had an operation in the lovely clinic where I was last year—like me he was in love with the nuns, like me he handed out his last book to them. How unchanging Paris is, thank goodness.'

'Have you read *Wellington?*' she wrote again to Sir Hugh. 'It is masterly. I read Waterloo four times, what a lovely battle. Wellington and Frederick the Great have an amazing amount in common and of course there is so little time between them that the very campaigns have certain similarities. They are both the no-nonsense type of general, incapable of putting on charm, showing off and so on—the opposite of Monty and Nelson. The funny thing is that both sorts succeed about equally with the men. Of course Frederick's battles against fearful odds were far more *desperate* and he quite often lost them, as Wellington never did, but then Frederick didn't have dithering politicians to cope with, surely a huge advantage. I suppose almost any Parliament would have sued for peace long before the end of the Seven Years War as it seemed hopeless from the very start, for the Prussians . . .

'I think of writing about Clemenceau. What would you say to that?

'The publishers [of *Frederick the Great*] took it upon them to change many colloquialisms as I know they do in America and Russia—hadn't realized that the habit has taken on here. "They had a good gossip" became "they reminisced" and so on. La moutarde m'est montée au nez and I brought up big guns—made a fearful fuss and got my own way. All this, if you please, on the *proofs,* so changing back will I hope cost them a fortune! No wonder American books read so dull and flat—I'm told every publisher employs several re-writers. It was really super-cheek on the part of mine because Raymond Mortimer, a master of English, had been over the typescript and removed many horrors as I'm the first to admit—I naturally accepted all his changes but then the high school girls at Rainbird's took over. Oh No. Luckily I bring them in money and they don't really want to kill the goose.'

To Mr. Brian Pearce, whose translation of Professor A. D. Lublinskaya's *French Absolutism* had fascinated her—'it inspires total confidence which is the first necessary merit of a history book and rather rare!'—and who had had to revise another translation from scratch, though only paid on a 'revision' basis, Nancy wrote feelingly: 'Publishers are the limit and usually only saved by some bright girl in the office who, as soon as one gets used to her, immediately marries. Somebody said, when I was in Greece, this country is entirely run by boys of 14; when they are 15 they take to love and become useless. Like publishers' young ladies.'

Nancy dreaded the prospect of entering a hospital in March but in the meantime Hassan was a comfort. 'All is so easy with Hassan, thank Allah for him. Only, not a week-end as he rushes to the arms of his mistress and I live on porridge, all I know how to make. Saturday afternoon until Monday brekker which is now my favourite meal of the week, I am starving for it . . . I was examined by about twenty doctors this morning—the terror!' 'Hassan like all very young people thinks pain rather funny and that's good for me, stops me moaning and groaning. But he is truly kind and seems to like me and to like it here, thank Allah.'

From the Hôpital Rothschild Nancy wrote to her 'unique and indispensable' friend Raymond Mortimer (8th April, 1970): 'Have you ever been in a hospital? You can't conceive the horror, at least to somebody who, like me, is thoroughly spoilt. On this étage all the patients have got skin diseases and one queues up for the loo with people like that picture of Napoleon at Aleppo—male and female—who have not been trained in use of same by English nannies. I've got an old Romanian who is the double of Abdul Hamid—she has red things all over her poor face and is in agonies. Day and night she groans—all penetrate my *boules quies*. But she won't allow the window to be opened. The heat is like in Venice when the servants say it is *infernale*—if we were in summer I'm sure she would complain bitterly of it—it's not that I mind, but the stuffiness.

'By far the worst, they can't find anything wrong with me so I suppose I am condemned to this horrible pain for life—also to never again going for walks. I feel in deep despair. Don't know when they will let me out. I can't crawl out on all fours, my clothes in my teeth, as that would look so ungrateful. The people, of course, except Abdul Hamid, are completely heavenly one and all, as French people always are to me, from the great Panjandrum Himself who swaggers in with a quartier général of young men looking like Austrian officers, down to the smallest little housemaid.

'Abdul asks questions non-stop. "Where is your husband?" "Dead." "Never marry again." "You're telling me—once bitten twice shy." Rather disobliging of her as her poor old husband comes every day with little gifts . . . One thing about Abdul, she has neither wireless nor TV. I vastly prefer her groans. Well, you see, I suffer. Don't know for how long . . .'

Nancy's English friends suspected that the French doctors were mistakenly opposed to the use of pain killers. Nancy wrote again on the subject to Raymond Mortimer (18th April, 1970): 'You mustn't blame the French doctors anent (as Sir Hugh Jackson always says) pain killers. For months they have begged and implored me, sometimes in tears, to take them. My philosophy is this (A) If we are sent a pain in the leg it must be for some reason unknown to us—if we dodge it the result might be bad in other ways. (B) I have got a little spot of grey matter and I don't want to spoil it with drugs or drink or anything else. My horror of drugs is the greatest of all my many prejudices.

'The last week at the hospital (I came back yesterday in an ambulance) was the most devilish I have ever known. I was cast on my back, no pillow, unable to write and almost unable to read, with, as fellow, the wife of a vigneron from Champagne —and I don't mean Odette Pol-Roger! She refused a chink of window and indeed had to have heavy linoleum curtains drawn over it and DID, all night, into a pot between our beds, never emptied or covered . . . Then all the things they did to me, wheeling me on a stretcher to a torture *chambre dans le sous-sol*, hurt fearfully . . . Meanwhile I have collapsed as regards pain killers in spite of my brave words above.

'As I lay there I held over my head whenever I could Mauriac's *Vie Intérieure*. Never again will a group of intellectuals have so much fun as he, Jammes, du Bos, Maritain, Bernanos and the others had over Gide, Mme Gide and God. Say what you like, God is really more interesting than human beings are and Mauriac more interesting than Robbe-Grillet.

215

'My garden is a paradise. Having been mocked for long grass and weeds I am now praised by professional gardeners for the prettiness. Then Hassan has practically repainted the whole house while I was away—he is a good boy, the best thing that has happened for ages.'

Even out of the hospital she had to submit to more tests: 'a liver test (what for? my liver has always been pristine) and it has tickled me up properly and I'm in that state no pain killer can cope with . . . But it will all calm down,' she added optimistically.

In the meantime she told Sir Hugh: 'I've asked for two lots of page proofs [of *Frederick*]—I'm so anxious for your verdict. I only pray the printers will have attended to the work I did on the galleys. Isn't the misprinting horrible nowadays? The papers often read like a joke—nobody cares a bit. You never see a misprint in old books and we know Balzac wrote his novels on the proofs. Now they charge you pounds for the tiniest alteration and telephone from London begging you to think again on account of their wretched time table! Oh how I hope I shall go to a different kind of world next time—I would like to be a pretty young general and gallop over Europe with Frederick the Great and never have another ache or pain. All very well, Frederick himself was never without one and Maréchal de Belleisle had to give up soldiering because of his sciatica. One can't escape I suppose in any century.'

Though she confessed that she could hardly enjoy seeing people she decided to go to Venice in July: 'I put cards on the table to Anna Maria [Cicogna]—how often I have to stay in bed, etc., and asked if she really wanted me. She says all will turn themselves into nannies to look after me—she *is* a good friend. So I'll risk it . . . I've been looking at old letters. G.M. Young used to write "My Dearest Creature", how too funny—it all seems and indeed is another world.'

On 21st May: 'I'm off, full of hopes, to the doctor I've always wanted but who wouldn't take me on until I'd been to do all the tests. Now the other doctors have given him the green light. Meanwhile X has put my blood in a box which is going to cure me—so let's hope. I've had a perfectly horrible time of late . . .

'I've also seen Jamie [Hamilton] and A. D. Peters [Nancy's

agent] who both came between aeroplanes. I think they want to make sure that the goose who lays the golden eggs isn't on her way out. They are printing 50,000 more Pompadours, even I am impressed. I also had the good Joy [Law] and her hubby to work on the proofs of *Frederick*, so I've been pretty busy . . . I go to Venice 10th July if Italy is still on the map, it sounds very groggy.'

'Now send for a whacking brekker,' she wrote Sir Hugh (24th May): 'I am much better. I've got a new doctor who very gently, with a trembling motion, is putting my back into place—I'm so much better already that I believe he may cure me altogether. You ARE kind to be interested.

'I've been doing my proofs, my goodness the modern printer, I've never in a long life seen such a mess! I thought people were educated nowadays. However, the publisher assures me that all may yet be well.

'There's a new book on the Poisons (Louis XIV) which strictly between you and me because it sounds rather swanky to say so, is the *Sun King* very slightly rewritten. I hardly could believe my eyes as I read it. It's scissors and paste in style, a long quotation in almost every paragraph. I found this so irritating that I began to wonder if I've done the same thing too much in *Frederick*. I thought that the sound of his voice would help to bring him alive and I have continually quoted from his writings. Oh dear, now I have doubts. What do the great biographers do about that? (The greatest of all, Boswell, never stops of course). I began it in *Voltaire in Love* and am now wondering if it's not a boring technique. I think the fact is this book is awfully bad apart from the style.'

'The angelic Anna Maria won't mind if I can't always put in an appearance,' she told Raymond Mortimer at the same time. 'I've been asked to write about a forgotten masterpiece for an American mag (1000 dollars). The forgotten master-pieces already bagged are: *Wuthering Heights*; *À la Recherche*, etc, *Paradise Lost* and two others equally obscure . . . I've just read Elena Vlachov's book she sent me. Very evocative of Athens where I shall never go again now that Mark is dead—including a sort of pervading silliness which I fear is a trait of the no doubt noble Greeks. We used to see quite a lot of her—she is the Anna Maria of Athens with a lovely beach where we used to swim. I can't make out what has happened to her husband, it looks in the book as if he is quietly starving to death in her flat . . .

'David Pryce-Jones says . . . that the eight to fourteen-year-olds hate and despise the hippies, isn't it too funny to think of them already overtaken by the still younger generation. Liliane [de Rothschild] has had her porte cochère blown in by a bomb and has a police guard. Debo, in Ireland, had to have a policeman whenever she left the house. What a world! Andrew [Duke of Devonshire] was rung up and asked how the Sinn Feiners got into Lismore? "By the door I should imagine." They, the Devs, had left or one envisages Debo as Marie-Antoinette with the mob in her bedroom.'

Experience had attenuated and finally extinguished Nancy's Socialist sympathies. Under the Labour government she feared that 'the old land is running down like an old grandfather clock,' and to Raymond Mortimer she declared (31st May, 1970): 'I am an old fashioned Liberal and I strongly feel that if blacks want to play cricket (strikes me as odd but let that pass) they ought to be allowed to. But if people must demonstrate I suppose it is cheaper, and nicer, for the police to stop the 'ole thing. Since living—well, not actually *living*, co-existing—with Hassan, now known as the Beamish Boy, my view of *le tiers monde* is greatly modified. He is a dear soul but the thought of giving him a vote makes me shriek. My considered opinion is that the world has been wretched ever since the abolition of slavery. *À bas* Wilberforce. Beamish *is* a slave (he knelt to his former owner to thank for being given to me) and look how happy we both are. *Look* I mean come and look.

'It was Gold Cup day at the rue d'Artois yesterday, many new rooms have been opened at the Château so the invités more dead than alive came here to be refreshed. I had a steady stream from 12.30 onwards. Unfortunately I had an awful pain—it has begun again, oh *what* can it be? I'm keeping the only pill which holds it off without, so far as I can see, demolishing me in other ways, for Venice because it is only magic for about a fortnight at a time.'

Nancy's garden remained her greatest solace. To Alvilde Lees-Milne, who shared her love of nature, she wrote in early June: 'Fearful drama going on about the blackbirds' nest which has been half blown down while two vile cats sit gazing at it. Hassan being *so* good about it, he must think one is a bit mad. But he has tied it up as if it were the treasure of the Incas. Do send the name of the anti-cat stuff or better still to save time tell Harrods to send it here on my account. There are still only eggs so it will be a fortnight before the birdies fly . . . I wish you could see the garden now there is the annual explosion of roses, really wonderful because of the mixture of colours, one forgets how divine it is. No credit to me, I found these wonderful roses.

'I think I am better. The morning is horrid but the pain doesn't last so long and for several days has not come back after my bath. Touch wood. The doctor does a little more each time but won't see me more than once a week.' Ten days later, 'Hassan put his curly head among the roses and announced three half-fledged babies (blackbirds) but I dread the day when they fly.'

CHAPTER FOURTEEN

NANCY'S NEXT AND last visit to Venice, like the next and last years of her life, was a losing battle with bouts of agony. Venice itself, where Wagner and Diaghilev and the hero of Thomas Mann's famous story had died, always meant abundance of life and health to Nancy, and in her heart she may still have expected a miraculous cure there. Her life wish exceeded any death wish she felt in time of torment. Her hostess Anna Maria Cicogna provided her with the society she most enjoyed, and Prince Clary, whom she called 'Alph the Sacred River', a perambulating Almanac de Gotha, was an endless source of the recondite information she hankered after. Other Venetian friends led the same sort of existence as their ancestors in the eighteenth century, except that sea and sun-bathing on the Lido had replaced card-playing on the Brenta. The gossip was lively, frivolous, and sprinkled with salty jokes. And there was the vaudeville of the English, who behaved so oddly near the Adriatic, whether 'draped round Cipriani's pool' or 'undressing to stark in the cabin with curtains wide open—a wondrous sight'—in the case of a buxom duchess.

'Life ticks on most agreeably here,' she wrote. But for once her supreme effort to carry on normally was defeated. The zigzags of her 'upping and downing' were as acute as they were sudden. To Alvilde Lees-Milne she wrote on 23rd July: 'I've spent half my time on an electric blanket, fearfully lame and hardly able to hobble. However, yesterday Anna Maria anted up a doctor who rather frightened me with some rough stuff (manipulation) but who has considerably relieved me for the moment. Time will show. If it could be a cure my life would be transformed—I was beginning to have serious thoughts of suicide because how can one enjoy anything in such a state? Cecil [Beaton] says there is a £400 pill which kills at once. Who sells this lovely stuff?'

On 10th September: 'Posting letters here is rather like throwing them into the canal but anyway here goes . . . The doctor here saves me from the very worst by putting my back in when it pops out but he can't cure my leg and I have as usual varying degrees of pain. I now think of trying the man who indubitably cured Alphy [Clary] and at 83 has turned him into a two-year-old. He is English but one hasn't heard of him actually killing anybody, unlike most English doctors. The horror of going to London and seeing Knightsbridge barracks, which I had hoped for ever to avoid, might be compensated for if I could be cured of this grinding pain. I'd really go to Hell—anywhere except New York in fact.

'When not in extremis I've adored it here as usual. Anna Maria has shown a new side to her nature, she is extraordinary when one is ill and knows at once when I'm in anguish. The other day she got up at a huge dinner and sent for the motor boat and packed me into it—I thought nobody could have noticed. But that hasn't happened often and I've stood up to the life pretty well . . . Still hot and lovely and we go to the beach . . .

'It seems the Saving of Venice is at last getting under weigh . . . There's a government here now which can and does take certain vital decisions. The clever French have bagged the Salute and are doing it up with great placards everywhere Comité Français. The English are relegated to the Madonna dell'Orto and are anyway running out of money . . .

'Fanny Botkin's flat may be for sale, perhaps the nicest flat in Europe. But I couldn't live anywhere except France and never have much desire for two houses.'

That she even considered Mme Botkin's flat shows that Nancy could still look forward confidently to a cure. I saw her at this time as the guest of Contessa Cicogna and the change in her appearance gave me a shock I attempted to camouflage with a gush of gossip. Her emaciation, and the sharp, almost audible twinges of pain as she dragged one poor leg after the other were distressing to witness. Her charming features were tense with anxiety when she fell silent and when she moved one

221

pretended to look in another direction. But having received an advance copy of her *Frederick the Great* I could tell her honestly of my admiration for what was, after all, a triumph in the circumstances, a tour de force when much of her force had ebbed. Her choice of a hero seemed to me perverse though Nancy doted on military commanders. It was as if she were coming round full circle to her father's views. Because the corpse-crammed career of her hero was repugnant to my nature she too might brand me a 'sewer'. Sans Souci and Voltaire and the flute-playing could not obscure for me the reality of Spartan drills, manoeuvres, harsh discipline, carnage and destruction. I failed to warm towards such a martial monarch but I suppose Nancy's femininity was attracted to his resolute maleness. At times she nearly succeeded in making him sympathetic. Her book betrays no symptom of mental or physical fatigue.

My young German friend Alexander Zielcke also cheered her with his enthusiasm, and I was amazed when she decided to join us in Anna Maria's motor boat after luncheon for an excursion to the Madonna dell'Orto, which had recently been restored with the aid of English funds. Together we gazed at Giovanni Bellini's blithe Virgin and Cima's elegant Renaissance Saints, and the huge Tintorettos glowed dramatically in the afternoon light, but Nancy had to sit down on the steps of the altar in evident anguish and the desperate swarm of Tintoretto's *Last Judgement* alarmed me less than her forlorn figure, though she assured me in a whisper that she would soon be quite all right. Her face had become that of a martyr. Our return to Cà Cicogna through the flickering canals was overcast with sombre premonitions. The lithe Nancy I had known was reduced to a limping shadow yet her keenly observant spirit was still ready to laugh. Though we corresponded frequently I was never to see her again.

On 17th September she informed Sir Hugh: 'I am in considerable pain nearly all the time. I go home next week having been here since 10 July . . . I love this town more and more but haven't been able to see anything as the only relief comes from lying in the hot sun on the beach. Luckily my room has got a most heavenly view over the Zattere and I can see the huge ships, some even bigger than the churches, going up to the port. It's very amusing.

'Don't you think all these men in aeroplanes who let themselves be captured are too feeble for words? I can't see any of my relations putting up with it for a minute and I despise them from the bottom of my heart. I hope you'll enjoy *Frederick*. P.S. A Pakistani went into a wine merchant's. "Can you recommend a good port?" "Yes, Southampton and now b— off."

'I suppose though I greatly fear it will be the usual story: one thinks one is cured for a bit then all begins again,' Nancy confessed to Alvilde Lees-Milne. However, she made an appointment with a London specialist recommended by Prince Clary. 'Perhaps he will cure me at once. Alphy swears he will,' she told Princess Loewenstein, who had invited her to stay during the ordeal. 'If he doesn't cure me I think I will *mettre fin à mes jours* but how? ' she asked Raymond Mortimer. 'It's so difficult, because I can't see the point of its being a punishment. I think I've been punished enough. Après rack very soon ended in a nice little hanging after all . . . English doctors have killed three quarters of my friends and the joke is the remaining quarter go on recommending them, so odd is human nature. We have seen the same thing with Louis XIV and Fagon. You may say I long for death, well yes, but I long even more to be cured. Dr. S. hasn't killed anybody known to me and has cured three, so I don't mind trying him . . . My good doctor here says *"il faut frapper à toutes les portes."* I shall get to know Europe. I haven't been to England for three years and had hoped never to go again . . .'

'If I hadn't been so unwell I would have enjoyed my visit to you more than any for years—even with the racking pain thrown in I absolutely loved it,' she wrote to Prince Rupert Loewenstein on 8th November. 'Now I am *far* worse—can hardly crawl and the pain is horrible. But oddly enough I still have confidence in S. and a speedy cure . . . I've seen nobody. I'm too bad to and have no desire to bestir myself: Sister Pam is here thank goodness.'

'Useless to pretend that I am any better,' she wrote again on the 13th. 'I only hope Dig [Mrs. Henry Yorke, whom she had invited to stay] won't have too dull a time but of course the awful truth is she *will*. I had the romantic idea that I should be leaping about and able to go sightseeing with her but all I can do is limp round the garden looking for my tortoise who, like Captain Oates, has gone out into the cold and disappeared . . . Lesley Blanch came just now. She is writing a book on Pavilions of the Heart and wants to turn the Monster of Glamis into a Demon Lover. I said, but Lesley he was a poor old thing with an elephant's head who lived on worms. She is the archetype of the Lady Writer and I love teasing her.'

During Dig Yorke's visit Nancy felt that 'on the whole there is progress. Dig is being too lovely. We sit all day chatting and I'm being put in the picture about my contemporaries: N. Then what about So and so? D. Haven't you *heard*? And what I haven't heard is never that they have won the Irish Sweep.'

After Dig left, Nancy had a fearful relapse, 'mostly in tears of pain mixed with rage and despair . . . Oh the world! how much better off we shall all be in the next one. And yet one's pretty house, the sunshine, the bird's moving in for the winter, Hassan and his niceness and all one's friends can't but attach one to it. If only somebody would invent a pain killer which killed pain, everything would be so delightful.' But her doctor would only allow brandy for the time being. 'I never expected to be an old lady with a tell-tale bottle in the bathroom. The worst of it is that while I'm drunk I'm all right but I've got a very strong head, it takes a huge amount and the effect doesn't last very long and then I feel of course liverish as well . . .'

'No words to describe what I'm enduring now,' she told Raymond Mortimer. 'I don't ask anybody here unless they suggest coming as I'm so dull. The Brandos and various regulars appear, but it worries them and tires me though I expect it's a good thing sometimes . . . My consolation these awful days has been Goethe's Italian journey (Penguin). Written in 1786, it describes Italy as you and I have known it. Oh dear that earnest, noble young German, how different from Voltaire and the Great King and how much one prefers really those two old sinners! His great hope in Italy is that he may find the Primal Plant, whatever that may be! But his descriptions of landscapes and buildings and Vesuvius erupting are masterly. Then, what's so funny, he keeps describing his own works and makes them sound utterly unreadable.'

Brief periods of hope alternated with black despair. It was a distraction and a relief to write letters and she wrote a great many to her friends in a script always clear even when tremulous. Those to Raymond Mortimer and myself prove that books were the most effective adjutants to pain killers: 'I read about a book a day.' And she envisaged writing her memoirs:

'My souvenirs will have the piquant originality of starting poor. They nearly always start rich, don't they!'

She tried to count her blessings: 'I can't go downstairs but the garden is divine to look at from my room and my servants so infinitely good and kind (Hassan and the daily), and I've found a dear little Portuguese for Sundays. All that is a great great comfort.

'Don't speak of birds' nests. From where I sit I've actually seen three gobbled by crows and one father blackbird eaten by the neighbours' vile hateful cat. I'm getting a water pistol for Hassan, would gladly give him a real gun.

'... I'm going to plant masses more roses as I see they are perfectly happy in my long grass. Do tell the names of those you mentioned which begin later. Mine will be over next week. I can hardly bear it . . . Roses again. Do you know one called Queen Victoria? It's a very pretty little thing, like the one Pompadour was always painted with, lovely smell. But prettiest of all is out of Marie's garden—it's beginning to take in mine. Like a Redouté, pale and delicate. It seems a lady driving by stopped and begged old Marie for a cutting, saying impossible to get it any more. I rather love this lady for noticing. Perhaps Marie's ancestor the Grognard*—she has got his medal— planted it. I read somewhere that in Louis XIV's reign there were only ten varieties of roses but by the time of Josephine hundreds. Marie's is only at one remove from the wild rose— double, heavenly smell which fills the room.'

Nancy kept rotten apples for the blackbirds: 'They like them better than anything.' 'Do you know of a good but extremely simple bird book?' she asked Alvilde. 'I get a bird's eye view of birds from my window, what mysterious little things they are. Thank goodness baby time is over so I am less agitated—they don't seem to try again and I'm really worried about the blackbird population so sadly diminished.'

She was to experience the whole gamut of treatments medical, spiritual and spurious: a major operation with cobalt rays and cortisone: acupuncture, osteopathy, a faith healer, and all sorts of drugs. After the failure of the operation in February 1971 the pain was more intense. 'I have to take a strong drug which makes me idiotic,' she wrote to Princess Loewenstein from Versailles; 'If I've got to have my neck cut I'll have it done

* Veteran of the first French Empire.

here, they are much more used to doing it (their old guillotine) and I've lost all faith in English doctors dressed as for White's. The bills! And I keep reading that English doctors are underpaid. All I can say is Coo!'

And to James Lees-Milne (29th May, 1971): 'Doctors! Don't make me laugh. I got two letters by one post from London medicos. (1) If you are feeling better it is because of the cobalt rays—the result will last several more weeks. (2) The agony you are in at present is due to the cobalt rays and unfortunately the result will last several more weeks. As the Americans say, peeriod.

'Lewes (G. H. Lewes's *Life of Goethe*). Well I lived in it—perhaps the contrast between Goethe and Voltaire tickled me and then the jokes! When he fingered the metre of his verses on his wife's body in bed! You know it must be rather good still to be in print. Voltaire used to say a book that is out of print is a rotten book. As for the greatness I suppose if one doesn't know German one must take it on trust. I was listening to *Werther* on the French wireless the other day when I heard Gladwyn's unmistakable laugh breaking in—I too gladly twiddled the knob and switched from the wild complaints of Werther to an urbane description of Ernie Bevin. That Duke of Weimar was Frederick's favourite great-nephew—he said (when Weimar was 14) that he was the cleverest of his generation. Those possibly innocent homosexual relationships were so strange in those days (I mean Goethe and the Duke) . . . Here comes Sister Woman for a few days oh the joy—nobody knows what she is when one is ill, complete perfection . . .'

Eventually she was informed that there was no cure for her disease, diagnosed as fibromyositis, 'awfully rare in our countries, much more prevalent and equally incurable in America . . . As for the intense pain, there is nothing but an injection of morphia which must be given by the doctor, who of course when one rings up—I tried it once—is out until six.'

'I think the worst feature of this horrible disease is that one is no longer a pleasure to one's friends but a worry and a bore,' she told Alvilde (27th July, 1971). 'I know I ought to retire like Captain Oates, but the mechanics are so difficult—poor Hassan, really I think fond of me, would hate to find me stiff in the morning. As I said in one of my books, it's bad enough finding a white mouse dead in its cage. But I am a fearful burden, to Diana notably and my saintly femme de ménage. I won't let anybody come to see me, except Colonel, I can't count on not bursting into tears . . .' Yet the second flowering of her roses was almost lovelier than the first: 'I gaze and gaze and the smell comes into my bedroom. Oh dear, the world is so agreeable . . .'

'If I hadn't lost all sense of humour I should think it funny,' she remarked when an inspired friend sent her a faith healer. Others sent Lourdes water and had masses said for her recovery. Fortunately her sense of humour never deserted her: 'Tom Driberg's Mass, owing to a deaf priest taking my name, was offered for Pansy Todd.' 'I don't quite know how I'm expected to earn my living,' she told Raymond Mortimer, 'but for the moment I am kept, like many another lady, by the Sun King (350,000 copies. Can you tell me why?)'

'The faith healer!' she exclaimed to Alvilde. 'You see I had envisaged a motherly soul who would sing a few hymns. Not at all. A sort of poor man's Liz Taylor loomed, accompanied by French husband. I loathed them on sight. Then, instead of hymns, she fell upon my ill nerve and teased it just as Alphy's London quack did, so that I've had three days of martyrdom, no drug the very slightest use. Like all quacks (I'm beginning to know the breed) she says I won't feel results for a week or two. Today I'm vaguely back to normal, viz. not crying all the time, drugs functioning more or less. What a joke it will be if she cures me! I can't help a sneaking hope—she said she would get my digestion working and I'm bound to admit she has . . . Oh what a dull letter but what can I tell? I see nobody. I'm fascinated by the idea of X running away with a man over seventy. I don't think running is the right word after one is forty and absolutely not at seventy. Y proposes "to go and live either in Ireland or in Morocco". She never reads the papers so is not aware of the barbarities which are perpetrated in those lands—she thinks they are quiet, cheap and full of highly trained servants. To my mind the worst barbarity in Ireland is the climate.'

Wasting away to under six stone, unable to move, fed with little squares of cheese by Hassan, Nancy's condition became so desperate in August that she 'came off her high horse', as she put it, and implored the London doctor she despised for something to stop the agony 'or suicide would be the note'. 'Well, he posted me a magic pill and after three days I could sit up and after six days I was in the garden planting wallflowers. For three weeks never a twinge but you see one gets used to these medicines and now twinges have rebegun, quite a lot of pain but nothing to what it was . . . Hassan, having offered to forgo his holiday, went off to Morocco and writes *votre fidèle serviteur*, at least the scribe does. So Zara, a Portuguese with small baby, came to cook—she's the nearest thing to Marie only a much better cook. Diana says I rang her up to say Hassan has gone, what shall I do? and the other day she said, only a week now before Hassan comes back and I said don't remind me, what *shall* I do without Zara? When one's so ill it's comfortable to have a woman but I really love the old swashbuckler . . . The Bismarcks have offered material if I want to write about the Pilot, do say a good joke . . . I think I shall write my memoirs beginning in 1945 when I first lived in France. That cuts out Uncle Matthew and so on, already overdone. But I must get well first.'

This was dated October 1971: in November she 'slid back a little' and it was 'wriggle wriggle and cry cry'. She found a sympathetic new doctor: 'he is serious, good, kind, and takes a wild interest in what I've got. I really loathe those young money grubbers dressed for White's. New doctor said what did the English surgeon operate for? I said £200. He said you mustn't talk about doctors like that. I said you don't know English doctors.'

*

The saga of her sufferings meandered on with relatively calm intervals until she died but even the increasingly potent pain killers—and she clutched at every available straw—failed to dull her wits. Her sympathies and antipathies, often violent and unfair, were, like her indomitable sense of fun, tokens of her youthful spirit. Intellectually she was never detached. Her curiosity about life was too vibrant to succumb to accidie or melancholia. She was certainly preoccupied with the anticipation of her *Souvenirs*, 'under which *sweet* title my memoirs will appear,' as she told Princess Loewenstein, and I imagined that their composition might become a more solid and engrossing distraction.

In January 1972 her first fiancé Hamish Erskine came to stay with Nancy for two nights: 'very bitter about having been penniless until over sixty. He said, "we would have been married now for thirty years." Help!! He is very dull and might have been more difficult to get rid of than poor Prod was. I don't like being married. I suppose too selfish. Anyway it would have been far worse for me, this illness, with some wretched old husband hanging about and either telling one one hasn't got anything or forcing one into ever more hospitals.' Written to her sister Debo, this shows that Nancy had ceased to contemplate marriage even, as many surmised, to her adored Colonel. She remained in love with him to the end; he had been the principal go-between in her long liaison with France; and his visits and telephone calls were still her chief sustenance.

Mindful of the annoyance caused by Jessica's *Hons and Rebels*, she wrote to her sister Debo (29th October, 1971): 'I repeat and can't repeat too often that all sisters will receive copies of the book and will have the right of veto. If one writes an autobiography it's not enough, as so many people seem to suppose, to tell how many housemaids one's father employed—one must *unmask* oneself. Roughly speaking I shall say what an unsatisfactory relationship I had with Muv to explain my love for old ladies: Aunt Vi (Peter's), Mrs Ham, Mme Costa, and others. I would like vaguely to try and find out if this relationship, shared with Decca and Honks [Diana] but not with you and Tom, was one's fault or hers. The others loved her in old age. I deeply respected her and liked her company and jokes but never loved her. Owing to your right of veto I shan't mind asking questions—shan't leave things out for fear of annoying which might not annoy at all. That was Decca's great mistake in my view. I might make each of you write a review of Decca's book. Incidentally my book will begin in 1945 when I came here with flashbacks at the death of Bowd [Unity], Muv and Farve. I won't bore the public again with our childhood to the extent of more than a few pages. Never thought of Muv as bossy, far too vague.'

Nancy's reticence was too deeply ingrained to enable her to unmask herself. She could skate on the thinnest of ice but that is a different matter. We may be sure that she would have skated most gracefully in her memoirs. While she avoided probing surfaces and considered that religion, for instance, was a private concern, she respected Roman Catholicism. As Mme Costa's guest at Fontaines she was surrounded by conservative Catholics whose company she enjoyed, but she smiled sceptically at some of the dogmas professed by Evelyn Waugh. In a letter to Raymond Mortimer (27th March, 1972) she stated candidly: 'The longer I live the more Christian I become—Christian civilisation with all its faults has been by far the best in historical times, do admit.' And again: 'Given the evil of human nature and the horrors of the Ancient World it seems to me there was a slow, very slow improvement—chivalry, Sir Philip Sydney, St Louis (don't tease about the Crusades please), some humble little saints like Sainte-Beuve who was just like Marie . . .'

Presumably Mortimer was an agnostic, for she expostulated with him: 'How can you say we know literally nothing of somebody among whose works we live? And certainly He has always been an interesting *topic*—you can't deny that. Do you know Fulco's [Duke of Verdura's] story—St Peter to the assembled throng: "You are about to see God and there are one or two things I want to tell you—in the first place She's black."'

'Oh the jazzy Mass I saw on the télé! The Catholics here say the true religion will come back to us from the East . . .'

Nearest to religion, almost confused with it, was Nancy's attachment to her sisters. What she considered her mother's vagueness was probably the veneer of a reticence stronger than her own, which prevented her from communicating the real warmth of her affection. And Nancy longed for this warmth. Mme Costa was French, Mrs. Hammersley half French; they and her Italian friends could express their love in so many ways without that embarrassing self-consciousness which is peculiarly English. The constant muzzling of emotion tends to freeze the heart. With her sisters she could share her most intimate feelings; they were united by their extraordinary childhood under Lord Redesdale's patriarchal domination.

In September 1968 Nancy had told Mark Ogilvie-Grant: 'Debo came for two days, and she and Diana and I have got a great craving for Farve so we're going to get a medium and call up the old boy. Diana says they won't be able to pull the wool over our heads over Farve.' And later: 'Don Antonio [our Chilean

230

friend Gandarillas] says he is a first-class medium and will get Farve for us in no time. Woman writes to say she'll come as she's sure he would be easy "to contact". I fear he might start using bad language at Tony who is not the kind of person he really likes. There might be references to nuts—better a stranger . . .'

Though Nancy might not have 'unmasked' herself in memoirs it is probable that she held many a rich surprise in store. We may be certain of a passionate tribute to France. As she told Raymond Mortimer (12th July 1972): 'There's at last a literary agent here who seems clever and has forced Pompadour down the throats of the Yugoslavs. He's called Ulmann. Came to see me and began wailing (*c'est de sa race*) about Paris. I said "you ought to see London". One must never compare anything French with other countries, only with perfection. Exactly what I feel.'

When I begged her to persevere and make notes Nancy replied (8th December, 1971): 'It's sometimes difficult for me to write owing to the muzziness induced by very strong pain killers—then of course when I can write it has to be to the bank and so on. What will happen to my Souvenirs?

'Mrs Law, who gets the pictures for my books, thought she'd make a spot of cash by bringing out a book called *The Making of a Book* which would be her and my letters on the subject. So she had mine typed at great expense and found there was at least one major libel suit in each as well as one or two suicides. I'm glad to say it is doctors and publishers who come under fire, not one's friends. Well, they are pathetic, so bad at their work. In my Souvenirs the people are nearly always dead. Diana went to a concert for Sauguet—somebody remarked there are very few gens de connaissance here. Diana said All dead and the word went round all dead all dead.'

Six months later she wrote to Raymond Mortimer: 'If I could get better and write my memoirs I promise they would amuse and not embarrass you, but I feel I never will. I can't help slightly wishing to be dead, my life has become such a bore.'

If she could get better . . . She had been told that she was suffering from an inflammation of a nerve root for which there was no remedy; that it generally lasted a few years when the nerve would wear itself out. It had lasted three years when she wrote to Raymond Mortimer: 'That is a huge relief as everything so far has made me worse. He (the soi-disant best neurologist in Europe) gave me an injectable pain killer to be used if I feel I must . . . My great mistake was going to London, allowing all those treatments which lowered my general health and left me £3000 poorer—quite serious as I can't work. However, I got that for my beautiful Chinese screens which have gone, not to some hateful museum but to a young man who adores them and has arranged a special room for them.

'I have joined you as a Legionary of Honour. I'm most excessively pleased. But nobody will ever know as the *Figaro* didn't say a word—only mentioned a historian of intense vulgarity called Decaux (television programmes about, for instance, *les amours de Fersen*).'

The Légion d'Honneur was, she said, the only honour she had ever wanted and she looked forward to sewing the red ribbon on her dresses, but she was glued to her bed 'crunching pain killers which really and truly don't do much.' She could only see her garden, 'incredibly pretty in a Beatrix Potterish way', from the bedroom window.

There was a repetition of blackbird drama: 'two huge cats fell on my half tame hen blackbird. Hassan heard her screams and rescued her but she has got a wing down and can't fly. I put her loose in my bathroom but she wouldn't eat so I had the choice between seeing her die of starvation every time I went to the loo or putting her out again to almost certain death in the garden. I've done the latter . . . The birdie had a good rest, nearly two days, and that's all one can do for her. Forcible feeding? I didn't want to upset her any more. I've got a wing down myself and know what it's like.'

She read so rapidly that she clamoured for more books, most of which were sent to her by Handy Buchanan, her former partner at Heywood Hill's. 'Evelyn and the book-shop are greatly missed by me as you guessed,' she told him (25th April, 1972). 'In the case of Evelyn it's the teasing one misses, as with Osbert, Victor, Mark Ogilvie-Grant and others . . .' [Sentence unfinished.] Next day. 'I leave this to show the kind of dottiness that overcomes me owing to the dope I must take. It is the answer to those who say I ought to make an effort and write a book! Your kind letter. A neighbour has counted up about seven books which I ought to have read and will enjoy so I'm no longer desperate. I wake up at six and lie waiting for the pain to begin which it does at about nine, so you see it is essential to have something to read . . . Trollope. Yes, I know all the Ducal novels. I had thought the clergymen would bore me but I note that *Barchester Towers* is his very best, or at least the first two thirds of it . . . I think please I had better have the Gibbon as an insurance—I love Oxford Classics and Penguins because I can read them flat on my back. But now those silly Penguins are bringing out Frederick large, floppy and unreadable, having asked and then not taken my advice! All the same Handy try to sell it because I can't work at present as you see—I utterly depend on my old books for a spot of nourishment. P.S. About Trollope. Don't feel drawn to the one before Barch: but would like the next two chosen by you. Have read *The Small House.*'

To me Nancy wrote at the same time: 'Thrillers fail to thrill me except Simenon. But I did absolutely love that book about trying to kill the Général: *The Day of the Jackal*. So did the Colonel, who found few mistakes which must be a good sign. I've just been reading a book by the Hayters' daughter called *Hayter of the Bourgeoisie*. It's about the coming revolution (How I hate being called a Bourgeois, don't you?). The book is incredibly naif and one simply longs to argue. For instance she says millionaires—all fairly well off people are called millionaires—will have to give up holidays on the Mediterranean. But they *have*, ages ago, driven away by the workers. The great comfort is how much the workers are going to loathe the rules laid down by Miss H. No cosmetics to be allowed—all motor cars to be pooled and only used for an emergency—holidays to be taken in turns. Then we've got to be good and give up our possessions. But why should a black man have my Longhi rather than me? The blacks are the only people good and disinterested enough to govern us. It's a very funny book if it were not so terrifying. Of course I know all the stuff from Sister Decca. Both ladies seem to think we are in mid-nineteenth century.

'I'm now reading *The Miserables*—one is struck on every page by the amazing improvements there have been in 150 years.

'What a dull letter. I'll try and do better in a few days. I wanted to make a sign of life.'

Again; 'Gladwyn's memoirs are dazzling, the best political memoirs I've read for years. What a terrifying world we do live in!'

After receiving the Légion d'Honneur Nancy was awarded the C.B.E. 'I'd never heard of the C.B.E. but of course I'm delighted to have it now that I know Raymond [Mortimer] and Rose Macaulay have,' she told Roger Machell. 'I hear it ranks above a knight's widow, oh good. There is no more B.E. so at first I thought it was a joke until I remembered there was no real Golden Fleece or Holy Ghost, all have been shadowy knightly dreams. I think it was so brilliant of Napoleon to have the same order for everybody.' To Robin Mc Douall she wrote (12th May, 1972): 'I don't live in the world of honours and had to look up to see what C.B.E. is. I suppose it's what Evelyn [Waugh] said was an insult and refused. But I accepted with pleasure as a mark that it is not thought unpatriotic for me to live abroad . . . About being called Mitford, a man came from the Embassy with all the forms etc and I had to decide. I asked his advice, which was for M. on the grounds that I am being rewarded for what I have signed M. Had I not already written some (very poor) books before marriage I would have certainly called myself Mrs Rodd but as I didn't I think it is more sensible to be M. for the medal. Anyway it's done now.'

Enclosing a printed card in a letter to me: 'Miss Nancy Mitford is unable to do as you ask', she added, 'This is what you need. You'll find it serves every purpose in an amazing way. I only use it on Americans as one doesn't want to hurt people's feelings and they haven't got any.' Reminding her that I was half American and interspersing my letters with Mark Twainish Americanisms was one of my teases, but she insisted that I was a European pukka sahib *malgré moi*. I treated her 'Angry-Saxon' attitude as just another tease.

On 21st July she wrote to Raymond Mortimer: 'I have nothing but misfortunes to recount . . . Leaning slightly to pick up a book I had a pain like the end of the world . . . Everything is torment . . . Perhaps I'll get better but it's now ten days since the worst occurred and I can't put my hand out for a glass of water without pain all over my body . . . Evangeline [Bruce] is very kind to me—she rings up for a little chat, having found out the hour when I am most human, and sends Bath Oliver biscuits for which I have a craving as of a pregnant woman . . . A nice man from the BBC télé came to see me. He plans a sort of Forsyte Saga from my books. At present he is doing *Clochemerle*. I became quite excited until I heard it will take four years . . .' (In parenthesis Evangeline Bruce was the American wife of the American Ambassador.)

Hitherto Nancy had found temporary relief in books, but in August she wrote to me (and one marvelled that she could still write so neatly and clearly): 'I literally can't read, it's a new horror because until now I've been saved by reading. I can't concentrate, it's the pain killers I'm obliged to take . . . When I feel that I can read something I take half a page of Gibbon, so interesting and so marvellously written it gives one a taste for life.'

Nancy's rare disease continued to baffle the physicians though they could not fail to realize its gravity. Her general condition deteriorated. So intense was the pain that she was prevailed upon to return to the Nuffield Hospital in London, whence she wrote to me on 17th December that according to the doctors she had been 'within inches of an agonizing death (and *with* the agony so that I begged to die) . . . I still see nobody but quiet women friends who bring soup. I am completely exhausted after four years of torment—well, think of it, a cancer inside a vertebra bursting its way out. The crack is mending now that my truly wonderful young doctors have got to work on me. I daresay the fatigue is actually worse than when I was iller. I feel quite done up . . .'

29th December: 'I suppose the truth is that I shall have to lead a sort of half life in my nice little house with pain killers at hand. Can't complain. Dr Powell Brett says I would have been dead in three weeks when Cynthia [Lady Gladwyn] gathered me up and brought me here. I suppose I'm pleased that she did but the struggle up the slope is tedious. P-B asked me yesterday if I thought it worth while and I said 50/50 but luckily these things are not arranged by us. He is a very go-ahead young man and thinks as I do that the doctors who let thalidomide babies live were literal criminals.'

On 26th January, 1973, Nancy believed she was cured: 'I go home on Tuesday by night ferry . . . I've had five months here (and a nasty letter from the Treasury)—such a dull way of spending one's pathetic savings. However, I'm released from my pain which was terrible at worst and never otherwise than vile.'

The magical release did not last long after her return to Versailles. She endured another six months of agony and weakness, and she continued to write poignant letters to her friends. 'I've got a nurse,' she told me on 30th March, 'a real *infirmière de luxe* who toddles about on high heels and waters my flowers while a good French peasant washes ME. Nursey not very kind. She says she found me crying with pain in my sleep—when I woke up the tears turned to screams but she didn't seem to mind very much! I said can't I have an injection but she administered a huge pill which I must say did the trick. Now I'm all right for a while. I like writing letters you know.' 'I like your letters the best, do keep on—at present I can't,' she wrote again on 7th April.

My problem was to know what to say, but I wrote whatever I imagined might amuse her and sent her light holiday novels, such as *Vestal Fires*.

The squalid excerpts from Evelyn Waugh's diary recently published, so difficult to associate with the author we both admired, disconcerted her but as she remarked to Christopher Sykes, who was engaged on his biography: 'Your task becomes more interesting than it seemed at first.'

I suspected that Evelyn's diary was no more than an aide-mémoire not intended for publication. With Evelyn (as occasionally with Nancy) one was impressed by the truth of Logan Pearsall Smith's aphorism: 'Hearts that are delicate and kind and tongues that are neither—these make the finest company in the world.'

What posthumous teases and shocks were still in store for Evelyn's friends? His marginal notes to Cyril Connolly's *Unquiet Grave* had caused Nancy to exclaim: 'Wasn't Evelyn a monster—oh how I miss him!' At the time of the anti-death penalty bill he had written to Nancy saying: 'Smartyboots [his nickname for Connolly] is in a fearful state over this bill—like all Irishmen he has a healthy terror of the gallows.'

Cyril Connolly had attended the last luncheon party given by Nancy in the rue d'Artois, which she described to Raymond Mortimer. 'Cyril did that thing I call rude of, as if one's entrée were sure to be uneatable, bringing plover's eggs from

Hédiard. They were raw. So the first ones went over everybody's clothes and the second lot were hot . . . I am told that plover's eggs are sold raw here and in Holland because they are thought to be better when freshly cooked. Another joke (black) of that awful meal was that P. had never heard of eating them so he wasn't a bit impressed by *le don Connolly* . . . His [Cyril's] wife was quite amiable but how I pitied her. Diana thinks those eggs are £3 each and I dare say they are not very rich . . .'

To faithful Alvilde Lees-Milne who offered to visit her she replied: 'No, don't come, it's five to one I shouldn't be able to see you, much as I'd love it . . . I ought to kill myself but truly don't know how. One doesn't want to wake up with a damaged brain and odd as it may seem I get a lot of happiness, notably when the pain stops! The garden is already very nice.

'Then there is Gibbon, not a great English classic for nothing, simply not to be put down . . . Then there are the jokes of Mme Guimont and the goodness of Hassan (and of Hassan's food). So you see, but when the pain is awful nothing seems worth it. It's been so long my nerves are no longer very good but this, shut up with Mother Gamp, is far the worst.'

And to her sister Debo she confided on 15th April: 'The awful thing about my situation is I can't live or, as I long to, die. What is to kill and what is to cure me?'

To her lifelong friend James Lees-Milne, alias 'Grumpy', 'Old Furious', or 'Grumpikins', she sent one of her last long letters (8th May, 1973): 'When not asleep (morphia) I like writing letters. Oh dear . . . I am one of the few people on whom morphia has a very limited effect, so like *one's* luck. When I complained to the doctor he said any doctor on earth would tell you you are under morphia now. Then why does it not take the pain away? I don't believe doctors mind about pain a bit, only life and death. Curious race . . . About books. They are for reading in the night so must be either Penguins or Oxford or World . . . Gibbon kept me going until they got to Constantinople when I bogged down as I got weaker and sadder and in much more pain. I now require nursery food— it's the morphia I suppose and one of the reasons why they quite rightly refuse to let one have it. Indeed they say so.

'They say my garden is dazzling, indeed if the flowers they bring are anything to go by it must be, so the torment of being unable to see it is very great. I can't move further than my arm can reach because I'm all swollen up like Louis XVIII, oh what a fate. Then there is some sort of *crise* not understood by me among the servants. Let's hope it won't *faire tache d'huile*, that side has hitherto been so perfect. Mme Costa used to say, when *mes serviteurs* fall out I never listen, I just sack them all. Yes, but then she used to send her old coachman Charles into Meaux to come back with the required substitutes. I doubt if that would work in these days.

'Many thanks for your good offer of books. You do see that the sort I write are not really wanted, could not in fact be faced, but something far more humble—How sad Kurtz (Harold Kurtz, author of *The Empress Eugénie* and *The Trial of Marshal Ney*, had just died) couldn't finish his Kaiser Bill. I was longing for that.'

Nancy's will to survive—what philosophers would call her Life-Force—was evidently powerful, while she must have realized that she was condemned and no doctors could save her. All they could do was to try and alleviate her suffering. For the final diagnosis was Hodgkin's disease, the same which was to kill President Pompidou.

'Keep in touch'—how many of Nancy's letters ended with these poignant words. When she had not the strength or the desire to see friends for fear of harrowing them by the spectacle of her agony, she wrote more and more letters in progressively weaker calligraphy, petitions for news, pathetic substitutes for conversation.

In spite of the strong sedatives her mind remained lucid. So long as she could work she needed periods of seclusion, but when it was forced upon her she missed the pleasures of social intercourse, of intelligent and amusing conversation. Her only real happiness was with her sisters and 'the Colonel', but she was afraid of depressing and boring them. Much as they loved her they had their own lives to lead. No sisters could have been more tenderly devoted: they gave her all the time they could spare. Her sister Diana lived within convenient distance by motor at Orsay in the Chevreuse valley, some 20 kilometres from Paris, and it was her misfortune as Nancy's chief link with the outside world to witness almost day by day the desolating stages of Nancy's decline. Her other sisters Pam and Debo also took turns to tend her when the professional nurse was unavailable. Jessica made the long journey from California for a final glimpse. Nancy had floated so lightly on the crest of the wave that it was terrible for them to watch her sink by such slow degrees.

Nancy, who had loved life so intensely and communicated her joy to a myriad readers besides her coterie of friends, left it peacefully on 30th June, 1973, worn out by her cruel illness. At least she was granted one consolation. 'How I hate hospitals and hope to be allowed to die here,' she had written. She had always dreaded becoming an incubus to her sisters and friends.

Her faithful friend the Colonel was the last person to see her alive. Passing through Versailles and propelled by a strong presentiment, he had called at 4 rue d'Artois that very morning. Though Nancy appeared to be unconscious he could observe the shadow of a smile on her features, as if she were aware of his presence.

Her sister Diana wrote: 'She would have been such a marvellous sharp old lady, dealing out snubs and jokes to new generations. Her life seems almost too sad to contemplate, despite great successes with the books. And the end of it this cruel illness.'

Perhaps deep down below the surface her life was sad, but she had the courage to banish melancholy and all that was life-diminishing. Had Falstaff known her he would have said: she was not only gay in herself, but the cause that gaiety was in other men. As Anne Thackeray Ritchie wrote of the author of *Our Village*: 'Certainly few human beings were ever created more fit for this present world, and more capable of admiring and enjoying its beauties, than Miss Mitford,' and unlike her estimable namesake, Nancy was beautiful herself.

A LIST OF
NANCY MITFORD'S BOOKS

Highland Fling		1931
	new edition	1975
Christmas Pudding		1932
	new edition	1975
Wigs on the Green		1935
Pigeon Pie		1940
The Pursuit of Love		1945
Love in a Cold Climate		1949
The Blessing		1951
Madame de Pompadour		1953
	new edition	1968
Voltaire In Love		1957
Don't Tell Alfred		1960
The Water Beetle		1962
The Sun King		1966
Frederick the Great		1970

Edited

The Ladies of Alderley		1938
	new edition	1967
The Stanleys of Alderley		1939
	new edition	1968
Noblesse Oblige		1956

INDEX